TESTED

ALPESH H. PATEL

TESTED

THE DREAM IS FREE, BUT THE
HU$TLE
COMES AT A COST

A TRUE STORY

Bulk enquiries: alpesh@peshmode.com

Cover Layout and Photography:
Annabel Brandon and Rozzyn Boy

AUTHOR DISCLAIMER

All views and opinions are my own and I am speaking from my
perspective only. My words have not been fact checked and I have
omitted and / or abbreviated names of people and companies.

WWW.PESHMODE.COM

WHEN PEOPLE CROSS YOUR PATH

some stop for a while and some stop for a few seconds. There are thousands and thousands of people I have met on my journey. Whether the experience was good or bad or whether you inspired me or perspired me, I am forever grateful for your teachings.

For my angels above who have always watched over me.

For my angels on Earth who are forever by my side,
Rene, Shanti, Omala, Pramila, Hasmukh and Nikesh.

CONTENTS

FOREWORD

O ver the past 17 years I've spent my life travelling the globe working with some of the largest and most successful companies in the world. I have worked across industry sectors, primarily working with their senior management, middle management, hungry sales teams and service-orientated account managers. This has given me the opportunity to meet and work with some incredibly gifted individuals and see how the fruits of entrepreneurship and intrapreneurship have catapulted a small percentage of those people, their careers, companies and start-ups to incredible heights.

Conversely, a larger percentage of those I've had the pleasure of working with have entertained the idea of pursuing entrepreneurial and intrapreneurial dreams and have then taken the easier option. Similarly, they have tried to pursue such ambitions, but when the going got tough, they dumbed down and settled for comfortable mediocrity or, to quote Pink Floyd, settled for being 'comfortably numb'. I personally have no problem with this, as it is a very personal choice.

That said, every company, every country and every continent needs the indomitable spirit of the lone entrepreneur who will go where others fear to tread; they will dare to dream and pursue their vision regardless of impending danger. They talk the talk, walk the walk and do it with zeal and a smile on their face, powered by a belief in the good of what they're doing, with the potential rewards and the desire to leave something of real value to the world. Alpesh H Patel is one of these people and that is why writing this foreword was a no-brainer. As a peripheral witness and close friend, I have seen his fascinating journey unfold and the lessons we can all learn are immeasurable.

Maverick entrepreneur, visionary, marketing guru, fashionista, super-salesman and innovator, Alpesh H Patel, one of Africa's best-kept secrets, is the personification of persistence and the adage 'if at first you don't succeed try, try, try again' (and when all else fails change the f…..g game!).

Since disembarking a plane at Heathrow as a refugee from Uganda, his life has been one of forced reinvention, personal transformation and audacious game changing in the pursuit of business success as a university student, super-salesman, intrapreneur and entrepreneur, culminating as the founder of a multimillion-dollar pan-African brand.

Tested is as unconventional as its author and his rollercoaster journey of highs and lows, including, but not limited to:

- Selling replica leatherwear to rich students at university
- Making his first million aged 23 trading mobile phones as a suitcase trader between London and Hong Kong – and then losing it all!
- Generating US$500m+ in sales for Motorola in Africa
- Creating the *first* African mobile device brand
- Creating the *first* black emoticons in the world, way before Apple did
- Collapsed business deal with hip-hop mogul 50 Cent
- Securing major investment from a multibillion-dollar publicly listed firm

And much, much more in between.

The rhythm of *Tested* is as palpable as a hard-hitting, hip-hop classic from Jay Z, as humorous as a Russell Howard or SNL skit and as emotional as an R&B ballad From Marvin Gaye or Beyoncé. All of this is underpinned by a cheeky, cocky west London attitude with an Afro-Indian edge! Incidentally, this could easily represent a soundtrack and a commentary to Alpesh's fascinating career to date.

Tested is a summation of Alpesh's journey so far and reveals two roads; one to follow and one not to follow. The beauty of the journey is determining which is which; sometimes it's not easy to distinguish but one thing is for sure; whether you're running a start-up, you're a CEO of a FTSE/Fortune 500 company, a sales or marketing director, a hungry salesperson/ client manager, venturing into new markets, or on your own unique personal journey, this book will help you.

Alpesh is a dear friend whom I've known for the best part of 30 years. You may not have known him for long, but I'm sure you'll share the same sentiments at the end of *Tested*. It's one hell of a journey!

BUKI MOSAKU

Founder of Inquire Management, International Corporate Development & Sales Training Consultancy

PROLOGUE

This book is not a step-by-step guide on how to do things, but more so on how *not* to do things. It's about the immense number of experiences I have been through that have tested my spirit to breaking point and beyond. I have been tested in the art of the hustle and how to keep going no matter what.

This is not a rule book, but it's a pretty good read about life lessons of joy, pleasure, pain and suffering. It is a journey based on how life unfolds because of decisions made at specific moments. It's a journey based on what happens to you whilst you are busy discovering your purpose.

Did I reach the Promised Land?
No! But no one promised me anything in the first place!

Hopefully, if anything, this memoir will reinforce the importance of making the right decisions and emphasise how vital it is to have your vision executed *well*. I have made so many mistakes and failed so many times I have lost count. I could have been in a much better place, but if it wasn't for the angels watching over me, I could have ended up in a far worse one.

I needed to put pen to paper. The only way I could express myself fully was to share my thoughts and experiences with you. I am not a professional writer and I did not want to use a ghost writer. The voice in this book is as if I am having a long dinner conversation with you, the reader. It's raw, it's informal and it's straight from the heart.

This book is aptly titled *TESTED* because that's what life is all about, from the day we are born to the day we die – what happens in between is a series of tests. Some tests we pass and some we fail. My story is a collection of real life tests that I have been through.

So, strap up while I take you on an action-packed trip down memory lane from the early 1970s to 2017. I think you will find this global rollercoaster ride full of exhilarating twists and turns, highs and lows that will resonate in parts with your own life, both business and personal. Hopefully, learning from both my mistakes and successes can assist in fast-tracking you to your chosen destination.

Let's do this!

CHAPTER 1

THE ORIGINAL REFUGEE

I was *born rich*.

I want to get that straight from the start. This is not a rags to riches story. I was born in Uganda 1966 in the midst of poverty but my family was by no means poor. In 1895 my grandfather decided to board a boat that travelled from India to East Africa. We are known as the Gujaratis.

The state of Gujarat is in western India. The people of that land are known as Gujaratis. Our people are famed for being India's greatest merchants, industrialists and entrepreneurs and, consequently, have migrated all over the world, particularly to regions that were part of the British Empire. Ever since European travellers began visiting Gujarat in the 15th century, the people have been observed as kind, considerate, caring of the environment and virtuous. Quite true I must say. We are some of the nicest people you will ever meet.

In the 1890s, 32,000 Gujarati labourers from British India were brought to the, then, British East African colonies under indentured labour contracts to work on the construction of the Uganda railway. It started in the Kenyan port city of Mombasa and ended in Kisumu on the Kenyan side of Lake Victoria, with consequent rail extensions into the Ugandan interior. Most of the surviving Indians returned home, but 6,724 individuals decided to remain in the African Great Lakes region after the railway line was completed. My grandfather was one of these individuals. He was the original hustler and a real pioneer in a new land full of opportunities. I guess there was nothing back in India waiting for him.

After working on the railroads, he very soon found some trading opportunities and started accumulating his cash pile. Around the early 1950s he ventured into the cinema business by opening the first Odeon cinema franchise. Within a decade or so he had Odeon cinemas in Kampala, Jinja, Nairobi and Dar es Salaam. He had created his presence throughout East Africa.

His eldest son, my father, started working in the family business. In those days there were no videos, DVDs or movie streaming. Cinemas were the only places for entertainment. On some days cinemas would screen Western films and on others the old Bollywood movies. The cinema became the main talk of the town and a central gathering place for the community. The business was a money-spinner for my family. As they say, 'there's no business like show business'.

At the age of 18, my mum gave birth to my older brother Nikesh and I was born two years later. When she was eight months pregnant with me my father decided to take her away for a few days into the rural parts of Uganda just outside the main capital city Kampala for some 'time out'. She started feeling pains and without any indication of timings she went into labour. She did not expect this to happen and due to the circumstances at that time she had no option but to give birth to me outside a hospital. I came out early and was born in the very early morning of 30th September 1966.

Within a few hours I was transferred to Nsambya Hospital in Kampala, where I was officially recorded. Born rich, but born in the bush. How this combination of two extremes would stay with me for the rest of my life. Little did I know that what lay ahead of me would be a path strewn with riches, but a path that would be as rough as the African bush where I was born.

Our life was good. We were blessed. The few years after I was born, from 1966 to 1972, were the most joyous years of my parents' lives. We had a great business and a strong network of extended family members and friends. Both my parents had been born in East Africa, so the African continent had always been our home. Yes, we did have cultural links back to India via our language, our food, our religion and our bloodlines, but our hearts were African. I have always said, "My blood may be Indian, but my heart is African."

In 1972 the Asian community of Uganda received some shocking news. Our lives were about to be ripped apart. Some Ugandan politicians in the early 1960s believed that the Indians were responsible for economic exploitation. Work permits and trade licences were introduced and Indians were segregated and discriminated against in all walks of life. Indians were labelled greedy, conniving and *dukawallas* (an occupational term that degenerated into an anti-Indian slur during Amin's time). Furthermore, the Indians were considered to always be cheating, conspiring and plotting to subvert Uganda. As a result of this growing animosity towards them, some of the Asians started moving either to the UK or India; however, restrictive British immigration policies made this difficult. In 1971 General Idi Amin Dada ordered all Asians out of Uganda within a 90-day period.

We had to get out. Fast!

From a nationalistic point of view, I do understand why someone would want to protect their country and eliminate foreigners in order to create more opportunities for the native people of the land. If I were an indigenous person I, too, would be pissed off if foreigners owned the majority of the wealth – but not to the extent that Idi Amin was. Amin went on a rampage of brutality, murder, rape and reported cannibalism. The guy was crazy and in a matter of weeks he had transformed Uganda, the pearl of Africa, into a hellhole nightmare.

This was a tumultuous time for my parents – they were young and had two small boys. Even thinking about it now, I dread to imagine what they were going through at that time. All of a sudden everything we had lived for was about to be confiscated. We could not keep anything and were allowed to leave with only the clothes on our backs and a few hundred dollars per family.

Amin declared that the responsibility of the Indians would rest on the British. As we were British subjects, the only place we could go was the UK. The Gujaratis in Uganda were Hindus and there was also a small community of Gujarati Ismailis. They had a central figure in the Aga Khan, the imam of the Ismaili community. Apparently, he had cut his own deal for his people with his friend Pierre Trudeau, the Canadian prime minister, and had arranged for all the Ismailis to move to Canada.

No one made a plan for us. We had no one representing us. There were 50,000 Gujarati Hindus who were British subjects. Before the expulsion, the Asians owned many large businesses in Uganda. As part of the expulsion, many firms, ranches, farms and agricultural estates were reallocated to the government and state organisations, along with cars, homes and all kinds of household goods. The Ugandan economy suffered as a result of the Asian exodus. By 1987, President Yoweri Museveni had inherited an economy that was suffering the poorest growth rate in Africa.

It was Her Majesty's UK government that took us from Uganda to the UK. Both Kenya and Tanzania had closed their borders to the Ugandan Asians. Even our ancestral homeland of India refused to take us. They said we were the UK's problem – I just could not believe that when I read it somewhere. Our own original country refused to take us back! Nobody wanted us, so the UK was the only place to go. We were, after all, British subjects carrying valid British passports, so it was impossible for the UK not to take us in.

I was six years old and don't remember how we got to Uganda's international airport, known as Entebbe, nor do I recall boarding the plane to the UK. I do remember, however, disembarking the plane and seeing some cameras; a very hazy memory, but one that was refreshed fully 20 years later when we found a video from a news archive showing me and my brother in the airport walkway with our pillows in our hands.

We were the original refugees.

We were then transferred to a holding facility near Heathrow Airport in west London where we were to spend our next 30 days until someone had figured out the plan. Now I see why my mum always used to say, "What happened to all of us was a shock. A clear message from God that we should never take anything for granted."

Life can change in a blink of an eye

If it hadn't been for the UK taking us in, I don't know what would have happened. The UK government did not have a choice, but they faced a massive backlash from the local British residents who did not want us in their country. Karma works in funny ways because, for many years, the British had been in India and parts of Africa without really having asked permission from any of the locals. The UK was our default new abode. There was nowhere else to go and we had to get used to that fact.

There was certainly no 'red carpet' warm welcome from the locals upon our arrival and, to make things worse, it was November 1972, the beginning of the British winter. Coming from the tropics, we had never experienced cold like this and I don't even know where we managed to find warm clothes. After the holding camp we ended up in northwest London. Most of our extended family was with us and we only really had each other, with the result we had no choice but to stick together, considering the environment we were in. One of my uncles announced that he had managed to secure a property in northwest London for £30 per week rent and all the adults had to pay their share. Around 10 of us moved into that three-bedroom semi-detached house in London NW9. My uncle eventually bought that place and, after all this time, he still lives there. That house was special for many of us.

My dad didn't leave Uganda with us. He held a Kenyan passport and therefore was not allowed into the UK. Consequently, I didn't see him for a few years. It was all down to my mum to raise my brother and me until my dad had figured out a way to get over to the UK. A true warrior and the rock of my family, my mum worked three jobs a day. She had been one of Uganda's top socialites, but she now had no choice other than to work. She somehow managed to put us into government schooling immediately, while also toiling away making pennies. I know that we never experienced the pain of hunger. My mum always had a plan to put food on the table and clothes on our backs.

We moved around quite a bit in the UK, from one extended family member to the next. My mum, brother and I were like gypsies. Every other family was complete, but for us, it was just my brother, Mum and me, with no Dad. We were the odd ones out. I think this episode made my mum much stronger. She is actually a real hustler. She figured out the UK system pretty quickly and discovered she was eligible to apply for a free government-issued council house. While we were on the long waiting list for a house, we were given temporary six to 12-month housing in various parts of west London.

Finally, in 1980, my dad managed to get his passport and he was then able to join us in London. By this time we also received the good news that we were to be allocated a permanent council house. We could not choose the area and had to take what was offered, so it was a 'take it or leave it' kind of situation. You can guess the choice we made. My mum promptly signed up and we were allocated our new house in Acton, west London. My mum was so proud, because not only had she secured housing for us, she had also managed to get us a place in a brand-new housing project. In our mind we were moving into a luxury five-star apartment complex.

It was the early 1980s and I had started growing up on the streets of west London. By no means was I a street urchin, but right from the early days, I had some kind of affiliation with the street culture and fell in love with it. What made it more enticing was the introduction into the UK of the phenomenon known as hip-hop. I witnessed and participated in the beginnings of the hip-hop culture that had originated in the USA in the 1970s and had very quickly transferred itself into the UK. I have always been a true hip-hop head from way back and my love for hip-hop has stayed with me ever since. It has defined key elements in my persona.

All the families in my housing estate were from the low-income working classes. The majority were white, but there were also a few families of Caribbean origin. In fact, we were the only Indians living there. You could see youth groups everywhere – the skinheads, punk rockers and the Caribbean crowd. Everyone I saw belonged to something, whereas I was the odd one out. My natural inclination and love for hip-hop music drew me into the black community in my neighbourhood and I started hanging out with Caribbean kids of my age. They took me in and I felt a sense of belonging. There was always good music, lots of chatter and, funnily enough, a feeling of protection. The neighbourhood was pretty rough terrain and the skinheads were always roaming about but for some reason they never messed with the blacks on my housing estate and in that way they also didn't mess with me.

I recall my first paid job as a newspaper boy delivering papers at 6 a.m. to the rest of the local housing estates. It was pretty scary going up and down large buildings with cranky elevators, not knowing what surprises lay in the cold corridors. I also did a stint working in Bejam, a famous frozen-food supermarket chain store. I clearly remember the times I had to clean the floors as a result of babies pissing and vomiting all over the place. What choice did I have? I was just happy making spare cash as, for sure, my mum was not giving me anything.

Our education was freely provided for by the state and at school my closest friends were the Caribbeans. Every day I would catch the bus from Acton to Brentside High in Greenford. I was always the first to get on the bus because I lived the furthest away, so I would always capture the back seats and over the bus journey my mates would get on at the stops near where they lived. The back of the bus upstairs is where we had the most laughs and some of the guys would carry small stereos in their bags so we could listen to the latest hip-hop tracks.

My mum didn't approve of my love for hip-hop and the black street culture. She barred me from going out at night and house parties were a no go. She wasn't a racist but she felt that we should not hang out with other communities. She was an African but she had never mixed with the Uganda local African community – there was always some kind of distance. After the history with Idi Amin and the whole Africanisation episode, I guess she just became more self-protective.

I also started to rebel against some of my parents' ways of thinking and acting. I know they wanted the best for my brother and me, but my heart was not in academics. My eyes were looking elsewhere – the lifestyle. Between school classes, my mates and I would gather in the playground and have body popping dance battles. I would practise the moves every night at home in my room. Very soon I became known for my body popping abilities and I would regularly battle with others at school and at daytime events. I was mesmerised and in love with this street culture, but at the back of my mind I was always fearful of my parents. Thankfully, I never did get drawn into the dark side of street life where drugs and alcohol were in rampant use. I was rebellious to a point, but I was also grounded and never found myself in bad situations.

I did my best at school, but I didn't really know what I wanted to do besides having a confidence that I wanted to be *someone*. I started to imagine some of the possibilities of what I could do, but facing the daily distractions was not easy. All my friends had their own girlfriends and when we planned days out together I would always be the one without a girl. I didn't want think about having a girlfriend then – my mum would have killed me for sure. You see my mum was a tough, conservative Indian woman – Indian kids out there will relate to what I'm saying when it comes to Indian mothers. They are very protective over their sons and dating at an early age was a cultural no-go. I couldn't even imagine a girl calling my home telephone number, so I started pulling away from my friends, not because I didn't want to hang out with them, but I didn't want to be the odd one out all the time. It was not 'cool' at that age.

I started focusing on my studies a bit more. At 16 I achieved some very good O level grades and I decided to stay on at the same school to do my A levels in economics, sociology and accounting. The sixth form was a more mature crowd and I fitted in quite quickly. By this time, the male hormones had kicked in and I began friendships with some of the girls. I still kept a distance and when I was invited to go out I would politely decline, not because I did not want to go; I did not want to face the hassle of dealing with the wrath of my mum.

I also had to think about what I was going to do after my A levels. Should I get a job or should I go to university? My mum insisted that she wouldn't accept anything less than a proper university education and I followed her orders. She was OK with me having part-time jobs here and there, but a full-time job at 18 was not going to cut it for her and, in any case, I did actually *want* to go to university. Besides the prestige of going to university, the main reason was that I wanted to be independent. I wanted to leave home to be able to do what *I* wanted to do. I wanted to be on my own. I wanted to be free and back then, there was only one way to get this done – study hard, get good grades and be accepted by a university. There were no ifs, no buts, no excuses. If I wanted to go to university I had to achieve top marks. Period.

For my family, it was not a case of who we knew or how much money we had, because neither applied to us. Studying hard to get the required grades was the only way I could leave home with the respect of my parents. I locked myself away for three months to study my A levels. I hustled the teachers and classmates to give me all the schoolwork. I asked teachers in advance what the syllabus was for the term ahead and every few days, I would ask classmates to give me the notes for the classes I had missed, which I then studied from home. I did not want to be distracted in any way.

I applied to three universities, as was the standard practice, and all of them were pretty far away from home. My brother went to the University of London and he was home every weekend – there was no way in hell I was going home every Friday – the weekends were what I was waiting for. Two universities accepted me conditionally, but when I got my

A level results I could only qualify to get into one place, the University of Hull in Yorkshire.

This was actually my first hustle. I hustled my way into university and it was purely down to understanding the system and putting in the work. I wasn't the most academic guy, but I knew that the education would be free. I would be going to a prestigious university and the government would *give* me money to study. What a deal! Every term I would have £700 going straight into my bank account to pay for my upkeep. My mum did not have any money for me but she was proud that I was going to university. In her eyes, I had achieved something. In my eyes, I was just happy to be leaving home.

In 1985 my whole world opened up. I was leaving home for the first time. I was on my own and didn't know anyone.

My life adventure had just started.

DON'T BE TOO COMFORTABLE IN YOUR SURROUNDINGS

Be prepared to reinvent yourself, your company and/or your product to reach your goals

CHAPTER 2

THE UNDERGRADUATE

Moving to Hull was a big deal. It was about a six-hour train ride from central London and I was raring to go. The day I got to Hull University, I was put into a sharing room with a guy I would never have hung out with back home. He was a tall, lanky white guy called Stephen. He was a bit nerdish with definite shortcomings in his sense of fashion. Roommates were paired randomly, so we all had to make the most of it. Funnily enough, we never had any issues and managed to get along pretty well from the outset. I settled in quickly and my confidence grew day by day as I kept meeting more and more fellow students. We were all in the same predicament; we would be together for the next three years and we had all arrived alone. The only thing we could do was to get along.

I joined a few of the university society clubs. There were various clubs catering for all kinds of interests; a chess club, the French club, the cooking club and so on … but what caught my eye was the soul music club. This was something that I *had* to be part of, a club dedicated to nights out on the town listening to the best soul, hip-hop and RnB music out there. I knew that by joining this club I would meet some very cool folks – and I did.

The very first people I met were the Nigerians!

I was in awe of these Africans. Where did they come from? Their way of speaking, their manner of dress, the bravado, the intelligence and impeccable manners they had. I was an African too, but for the previous 12 years I'd had contact with not one single person from that continent whatsoever. I was simply amazed at how cool these Nigerians were. I made an instant connection with them. Was it my African roots or was it because I had associated so closely with black culture? The Nigerians seemed a natural replacement for the Caribbean friends I had left back in London. Whatever it was, my bond with them has grown from that day and is still strong today. They are my second family.

Studies started in the first term, I had assembled my clique and we started to socialise. I noticed how flashy the Nigerians were. I mean back then, the naira (Nigerian currency) was much stronger than it is today and all the Nigerian university students had *paid* to come to England to study. Yes, these were kids of high-income Nigerian parents and none of them were on government grants like I was. Hull University had a prestigious law faculty and most of the Nigerians were there to study law. They all came from wealthy families and one of them was the son of a highly distinguished ambassador. This guy even spoke Spanish. I had never heard a black guy speak Spanish before. Nor were the Nigerians a shy bunch. They were the ultimate show-offs and loved to flaunt their style. I wanted to be like them.

I met my first Indian friend at university and, come to think of it, he was my first Indian friend ever; a guy by the name of Shoey, who was from Blackburn. We shared the same surname 'Patel', but he was Muslim and I was a Hindu. We clicked naturally because we both spoke the same Gujarati language. It was nice to have someone at university with whom I shared the same language and we remain brothers to this day.

One day, midway through our first term, we started talking about travelling and getting away. We made a plan to go somewhere that Christmas holiday, partly because I did not feel like hanging out at home for four weeks. We wanted to go somewhere warm; Hull was a terrible place when it came to the cold.

We also wanted to make some money. But how?

"Let's go somewhere where we can buy stuff, bring it back to Hull and sell it to the folks here," I said to Shoey.

What could we honestly buy that we could make money from at university where the majority of the students were just like us, living off grants? We decided that we would go to Morocco. I had started to become fascinated by Morocco – maybe it's because at university I also started dabbling in hashish – Moroccan hashish. I was never into this, but as my circle of friends grew, I became ever more curious and found myself wanting to try new things.

"We ain't going to Morocco to buy hash though," I recall Shoey saying. "That's not for us, man."

"Yes, I know, but let's at least go there as I hear they have some wicked leathers. Maybe we can buy some leather goods and bring them back here?"

We agreed and looked at a map of Morocco.

"It's a fucking big country," I said.

"Pick a spot," Shoey replied.

I went to the university library and looked at the books on Morocco that had pictures. Rabat looked like a government town, Casablanca was just too big and Marrakech seemed to be in the middle of nowhere. None of those places appealed to me. As I was closing the book I saw images of a place called Tangier.

'That's it!' I said to myself. 'That's the place to go to. It's nearest to Europe and looks like the most cosmopolitan.'

I saw Shoey later that afternoon and he seemed cool with my chosen destination. Shoey was like that; he was just cool with everything. I had to do some research on Tangier first, though. How could we get there? What would we do once we got there? There was no internet back then so it was a case of hardcore reading and visiting the student travel agent offices. We also worked out the costs for our two-week trip – air, cheap hotel, food and money to buy things.

"We will use our government grant money," I told Shoey. "We use this to get there, buy goods and bring them back. We can double-up for sure." Double-up is slang for doubling your money, so if we bought something for $100 and sold for $200, we would have doubled our money. We had no clue as to how we could or would double-up, but we both agreed that for the next few weeks we would eat only canned food and bread to save the money for our trip.

December 1985 came and off we went to Tangier. We got the cheapest tickets and booked a flight to Gibraltar. From Gibraltar we took a ferry to Ceuta and from there we took a taxi to Tangier. When we arrived we were just gobsmacked. Never had I seen a place with so much hustle and bustle. Traders everywhere. Noise everywhere. Car horns tooting everywhere. We got into a very cheap backpacker type hotel on Boulevard Pasteur, the main strip in Tangier. I wanted us to be in the middle of the action. We dropped our bags and took a quick nap. We were tired as hell, but the excitement of being in a new city got the better of us. We had to hit the streets and soak it all in.

We walked and walked and saw one shop after another selling souvenirs, Moroccan rugs, lamps and leather goods. We didn't know anyone and didn't speak a word of Arabic or French. This was not going to be an easy task but we were slick – coming from the UK, we were wearing nice clothes and everywhere people would stare at us. Both Shoey and I could certainly have passed for Moroccans but our dress style gave it all away. We stuck out like sore thumbs and quite quickly the street hustlers were upon us. I guess we looked rich even though we didn't have much. The hustlers came up to us every few minutes asking if we wanted to buy leather jackets, rugs and even hash. I had seen the movie *Midnight Express,* so buying hash, let alone smoking it, was *not* going to happen! All we could hear was endless Arabic chatter.

"Engreesh?" They asked us.

"Yes, Engreesh," we replied.

We didn't know how to react and we certainly did not want to piss anyone off. This place was something that we had never seen before and we wanted to be on our guard. One guy persuaded us to enter his shop but the leather-wear was just not going to cut it with us. It was nice, but the designs were not to my taste. I couldn't buy something that I wouldn't have felt comfortable wearing myself. All we saw were red Michael Jackson *Thriller* style jackets everywhere. We already stood out; wearing red Michael Jackson jackets would not go down well. We left the shop and continued walking. By now, a couple of street vendors were following us – not in a bad way, just trying to strike up a conversation with us.

"Hey, Engreesh, you want design bags?" I stopped in my tracks.

"What design bags?" I replied.

"*Habibi,* we have many nice Louis Vuitton here. Good price. Good quality."

I looked at the vendor.

"Louis Vuitton? From where? How? Louis Vuitton is made in Paris not here!"

Louis Vuitton was a brand that I had never heard of before I got to university. I was never a luxury brand guy. I was from the streets of London. My style was Fred Perry, Diadora and Tacchini, *but* what made me stop, think and my eyes sparkle was the fact that I had seen some people at university carrying Louis Vuitton bags.

The Nigerians!

We asked the locals where we could buy Louis Vuitton bags and they told us they would meet us later to take us around. We agreed and met them a couple of hours later. They then led us into the deepest part of the *souk* market, where they kept stopping at shops to show us different items, trying their luck to sell us something along the way.

"We want Louis Vuitton and nothing else," I kept saying to them.

It was obvious that these guys were taking the piss. They wanted to tire us and get us to buy something that was clearly not Louis Vuitton. We had to walk away, but not in the *souk,* because we would never have been able to find our way out!

"We go back to the hotel, have coffee and discuss again," I told them.

They walked us back to the hotel, but I simply did not like

these guys. You know the feeling when you are with someone, or some people, and you simply don't want to be around them, but you have no choice other than to grin and bear it? They started asking us for money because in their eyes they had spent the last few hours with us as so-called tour guides. We were in a strange country and upset that we had not found what we wanted. We were also not in any mood to start fighting. We had no choice but to pay these guys so they would simply leave us alone. I was pissed off but there was nothing we could do. We decided to relax and enjoy Tangier. Over the next couple of days, all we did was hang out in sidewalk cafes drinking *café au lait* and eating croissants. We felt a bit jaded from being hustled by the locals.

"What we gonna do?"

"If we can't find the Louis Vuitton I really don't see what else we can buy. Maybe we should call it a day and go back home?" I said to Shoey.

I then noticed that there were a couple of guys on the next table staring at us.

"What are you guys looking for?" One of them asked.

I went silent for a bit.

"Where are you from?" They both asked one after another.

"London," I replied.

Their eyes lit up and they immediately started talking to us about English football. Next thing we knew, the guy asked us again, "What are you looking for?"

"We want to buy quality leather goods but they must be a famous brand name. We hear there are some good bargains here in Tangier?" I replied to his question with a sense of eagerness and desperation.

I guess it was our lucky day. One of the guys (his name was Abdul Aziz) told us to follow them to their shop, where we could have a chat. Once we got into his shop, he quickly announced that one of his cousins worked at a factory that made *all* the Louis Vuitton leather goods, which were then supplied to some select shops in the *souk*. I told him we were interested but we wanted to see the place first before committing to anything as we knew what we wanted and when we saw it, we would know. We also did not fancy being ripped off like we had been a couple of days earlier. Abdul Aziz told us all was well and that we should follow him to see his cousin. He advised us that we should make a quick stop at our hotel to get some of our cash if we were ready to make a purchase. After collecting our cash from the hotel, we followed Abdul Aziz into the back alleys that led to the heart of the *souk*. Our hearts were beating – very fast!

Shoey and I kept looking at each other as if to say, "is this for real?" It was like a scene from a movie. Two of us following two large Moroccan dudes in black leather jackets, going deep into the *souk* like a gangster drug deal was about to go down. After some serious walking, we seemed to be in the deepest part of the *souk* where there were no shops, just plain old buildings with hardly any sunlight coming through the roofs. We stopped at one door and Abdul Aziz gave a couple of hefty knocks. A small window in the top part of the door slid open and all we could see were some large bloodshot red eyes looking at us. A few seconds later, we heard what seemed like 20 chains and door locks being unshackled.

The Moroccan guys greeted each other, hugged and started talking in Arabic but the guy with the red eyes just kept on eyeing me and Shoey up and down. We were ushered inside and led into a room that had just a rug on the floor and some large Moroccan lamps at each corner. We followed our two guys and Mr Redeyes and sat on the floor with them. The place was musky and there was a scent of incense, cigarettes and hashish in the air. Mint tea was promptly served and the guys lit cigarette after cigarette. Abdul Aziz was a real smoker. Since the time we had met him in the café I'm sure he must have smoked two packets of Marlboros. The Arabic banter between the guys was in full flow. Shoey and I just sat there in silence looking at everyone, trying to smile and maintain our innocent naïve composure. Seemed to me that Mr Redeyes was checking us out by asking questions about us.

About 30 minutes later, the whole atmosphere changed. Mr Redeyes clapped his hands and shouted loudly in Arabic and suddenly it all started popping off. Like a theatrical circus show, the curtains at the back of the room came apart and, one by one, we saw young kids coming out of the woodwork with bags – lots of them. They quickly emptied the bags to reveal even smaller bags, belts, wallets and purses.

All of them were *Louis Vuitton!*

My eyes popped out of my head. I went crazy with excitement and couldn't keep my hands off the goods. The craftsmanship, the logos, the designs, the zips, the stitching were all *exactly* like the Louis Vuittons I had seen before. It goes without saying that we knew we were dealing in fakes and I'm not shy to admit that. Yes, we went to Tangier to buy leather goods but, fuck that, we were going to leave with fake *Louis Vuitton* leather goods!

The smile on our faces was unreal. We had found what

we were looking for. We now had to seal the deal and the haggling started. Coming from the UK we were not used to haggling like this, but that was when our Gujarati genes may have kicked in. We asked the price of each item and set aside what we wanted. Shoey was busy writing down the prices as they came out of Mr Redeye's mouth. Funnily enough, all of a sudden Mr Redeye's English also became much better. Once we had chosen all the items, we had to think about two things; how much money had we got and how the fuck were we going to carry all this stuff back to Hull?

My first experience of hardcore bargaining had started. I showed the Arab guys the money that we had on us. I knew if we showed our money it would be very hard for them not to sell us something. I also felt that as we had been introduced to them by other locals that maybe we could get a better bargain. They started high and we started low. The aim was to meet somewhere in the middle. We must have spent two hours in that joint and we must have drunk 20 gallons of mint tea, but the excitement was all around. Eventually, we settled on a price and a quantity that we could afford. To make the case stronger for better pricing, I started bullshitting and promised them tons of repeat orders. I told them we had a massive market back in the UK. The truth was we didn't have any market whatsoever. This was all just one big gamble with our government grant money.

We spent two weeks in Tangier and soon became best friends with Abdul Aziz. We hung out every day in his shop and every night we would eat together. By the time we left, we had our Moroccan brothers in place. After buying as much as we could for what money we had, we packed our bags and made our way back home. We even used some of the bags to carry our own clothes. There was a fear of getting stopped at customs, but there was no alternative. There was no DHL courier service back then. We had to take our chances.

It was January 1986 and the start of our second term at Hull. We were pumped, not because of the syllabus but more so on how we planned to move these leather goods. I told Shoey that we just needed to focus on one group of customers – our target market.

The Nigerians!

Dealing with the Nigerians I knew was not going to be easy. Many of them were already rich and pretty savvy; some were also intimidating. I had to muscle up the courage to start engaging with them one by one. I simply did not want to talk with them in a group setting. I had seen what happens when you have a group discussion with Nigerian people.

It was a whole new ball game haggling with the Nigerians. What made it fun was the fact that they all spoke with the funniest accent I had ever heard. I found out later that this was known as pidgin English, a mix between English and traditional Nigerian languages.

"This is fake ohhh. Where you dey get am?"

"I beg don't show me this nonsense, joh !"

"Na wa oh... LVeeeeeeeeee!"

Question after question. Comment after comment.

I wasn't going to give up that easily. You see status was a big thing with Nigerians– and it still is in a way. At the weekend, they would travel to London and to various universities where other Nigerians studied. Looking good was a prerequisite and I knew my Louis Vuitton stuff would make them look even better. That was my key selling point. We also made sure we bought a mixed range of products so that not everyone would have the same thing. Dealing with the Nigerians was like playing a mind game. I recall showing the bags to a young Nigerian female student, attractive but boisterous with a massive ego. I had to massage that ego; I kept showing her bags, insisting she looked at one *special* bag (the most expensive and the one that I was *desperate* to sell in order to get our money back plus our profit).

"You know that I am coming to you first, right? You are the most stylish woman in the university, so I had to come to you first and offer you this very special bag. The others have seen it and I know they want it; this one has your name on it, but I can't hold on to it for too long as others have seen it and are coming back to me. What do you wanna do?"

I knew she wanted to be different and have something that no one else had. We haggled like crazy that morning and she eventually bought the bag. I even walked with her to the university bank so she could pay me in cash. She knew it was fake but, with her style, it looked very genuine. We both knew that she could get away with it.

Over the following few weeks all our Moroccan goods sold out pretty quickly and we managed to double our investment. We started seeing some of the Nigerians walking around university wearing our Louis Vuitton belts and the women carrying our Louis Vuitton bags. I couldn't stop smiling.

I guess the term 'fake it 'til you make it' does make sense

By Easter 1986 we found ourselves back in Tangier – back to our guys and this time with much more confidence. We knew the place now, we had our sources and we knew what we wanted. We went to Tangier about four times that year – back and forth buying and selling. We continued selling to the Nigerians and by now some of them had started onward selling to Nigerians they knew in other universities. It was a nice setup and the money was good. It paid for our lifestyle as we couldn't rely on just our grant money to survive. We were out every night spending money. We caught the attention of the local Hull crowd and that's when we started to get girls. Lots of them.

In all this mayhem, I started to forget the reason why I was at Hull in the first place. I always found myself playing catch up with my studies. By the summer of 1986 I wanted to take a break with our trips to Morocco. With some money in my pocket by now, I was looking at travelling elsewhere. I was dying to see the USA, so I joined BUNAC, a transfer scheme between USA and UK universities through which students could travel and work in summer jobs in their respective guest countries. I immediately decided on New York. I had to experience the city, the birthplace of hip-hop. That summer in New York was just awesome.

Another mate from university called Riaz had joined me and we decided to go to Miami. We wanted the true 'American experience', so we decided to hitchhike. Yes, we crazy fools hitchhiked all the way from New York to Miami, stopping in Washington DC, Ocean Beach Maryland, South Carolina, Fort Lauderdale and Miami. Many a time we slept on the freeways and washed in the restrooms of roadside diners. As you might expect, we met quite a few strange characters, but also some good people, and we truly experienced American road life. I don't think anyone would have decided to do what we did, but I have always wanted to do things differently. Yes, it was tough, but what an experience it was. A couple of brown-skinned Indian boys dressed up, with their bags on their backs, walking along Interstate 95. What a sight that must have been.

Between 1985 and 1988 while still at Hull, I had travelled to Morocco a few more times and to the USA twice. I also spent the summer of 1987 in India to get some clothes to sell back to the university crowd. Between all of this, I had managed to squeeze in time for my studies at the last minute and I finally passed my degree and received a 2:2 in economics with honours. A 2:2 in UK university language was a 'medium-average-well-done kind' of score. I know I could have done better but my focus was simply not there. I was happy, but happier that I could make my parents proud. My mum had known all along about my frequent trips abroad and had kept warning me to keep my studies a priority. I had made her proud, but afterwards I could not even be bothered to go to my graduation ceremony or attend any recruitment fairs or interviews. I felt that it was not for me. I was way too caught up in myself and my lifestyle. I had seen how one could make money and live a different kind of life to the norm. I didn't want to be like everyone else. I wanted the 'good life' and a nine-to-five job was simply not going to cut it for me.

Thirty years ago, everyone around me wanted to be a doctor or a lawyer, but I wanted something different. Maybe I should have listened to my mum; she wanted me to study hard, get a job and be set for life. Not me. I left university in 1988 with a hustler's mentality. I felt that there was something bigger and better out there for me.

I had managed to get through university. I had turned my government grant money into something that had kept me going nicely over three years. I had been able to buy myself nice clothes, travel and party. I had seen places I would never have dreamt of.

The hustler bug had bitten me at a very early age.

But I wanted *more*.

A PESSIMIST SEES THE DIFFICULTY

in every opportunity;
the optimist sees the opportunity in every difficulty

Winston Churchill

BE BOLD AND TAKE CALCULATED RISKS

to fuel your engine of entrepreneurial success

CHAPTER 3

DOOR TO DOOR

By the time my three-year stint at Hull University was drawing to a close I had developed some very strong relationships, especially with the Nigerians. One such friend of mine called EO was actually like the sister I never had. I would frequently turn up at her student house and we became close. She was the first person to introduce me to the finest cuisine of Nigeria. She would regularly make me some of the most delicious mouth-watering dishes you could ever think of. She was very open with me, to the extent of telling me how much in love she was with a guy called LF. I saw this guy now and then as he used to visit her every few weeks – each time with a different luxury car. He was an older Nigerian guy and I was easily impressed by his flashy style, his rides and his cool demeanour. As he got to know me better he started opening up as to how he made his money. He told me there was big money to be made in selling designer kitchens.

"Kitchens?"

He told me I should call him when I was ready.

After I left university I moved back to my parents' house. They had by now decided to leave the hustle and bustle of London and had moved to Hampshire. Fortunately for me, LF's office was in Reading, Berkshire, and a 30-minute drive from my parents' house. He told me he would 'hook me up' and next thing I knew, in September 1986, he had secured me a position at Farouche Kitchens. This was not your everyday type of job. There was no salary; it was pure, hardcore cold calling by a team of telemarketers in one room, similar to one of those 'boiler room' trading floors. Sales leads were generated and given to the top management, who would then pass them down to their subordinates. There was a clear pecking order as the main guys wanted to keep the highly probable sales leads for themselves so that they did not have to share any of their sales commissions. If the lead was lukewarm it would get passed further down the line and if that lead converted to a sale, then the commission was split among the line managers. I reported to LF, so whatever I made he received a cut. Clever guy. He took me on to hustle on his behalf at no cost to him. He showed me some of his numbers, so I easily bought into the potential earnings I could make.

On one particular day a few weeks later, I found myself given a lead to visit a couple in Reading. This was my fourth time out and I still hadn't closed any deals. LF had started to doubt me.

"Come on, man, you told me you could do this. You need to come through pretty soon. I put my neck out for you," he told me.

I remember that night so well, driving to my evening appointment in Reading. It was cold and the place I was visiting didn't seem the most desirable of neighbourhoods. I got out of the car with my briefcase, walked up to the front door and rang the bell. I heard voices inside.

"Who is it, love?" (Obviously, the woman of the house asking the man of the house.)

I then saw the curtains on the side of the door open up and a guy staring at me.

"Some Paki kid outside," he shouted back.

There was silence, but I was thinking, "Shit. Why is he calling me a Paki?"

I had grown up with this term; a very derogatory term aimed at people from the Subcontinent. It was short for Pakistani, but had its own identity as a racial slur. I realised that I had ended up at the doorstep of a racist. In the past, I had been called Paki a few times by the skinheads on my housing estate, but here I was on a cold autumn evening, standing outside someone's house and hearing that term again.

'What the fuck?' I said to myself.

Should I just walk away or wait for the door to open? I knew the guy had seen me so I could not exactly walk back to my car. Also how could I tell LF and the kitchen bosses that I did not turn up for the appointment? They were the ones who had made the appointment. I was in a dilemma but within 30 seconds the door opened and I saw a big – and I mean a big – bald-headed white guy staring at me.

"What do you want?"

There was no politeness in his tone.

"Good evening, sir. I am from Farouche Kitchens. We made an appointment with you for tonight to have a look at your kitchen?"

"Oh yeah? So bloody what?" came the reply.

"Well, sir, I was asked to come and visit to see what we can do for you."

At the back of my mind I was cursing my manager and the lead generation team. The fuckers had set me up to fail by giving me this bullshit assignment. A woman then popped her head behind his at the door. I assumed that this was the guy's wife.

"Who is it?" she asked.

"Some guy about kitchens," he replied.

"Oh yes, let him in. I did them tell them to come around tonight."

Then she saw me, a skinny Indian guy shivering on her doorstep.

"Come in then," she told me, with her head nodding in approval.

The husband didn't seem to be of the same opinion and grunted as he opened the door further so I could step inside

"Let's get this over and done with," he barked at me. "We ain't got all bloody night."

I was really hoping he would tell me to fuck off and then I could just leave, but now I was in his house and the door had closed behind me. Now what? I'd never been in a house in which I was clearly not welcome. He had openly called me a Paki (that's like a white guy in the USA answering his door to a black guy and calling him a nigger). I was led straight into the kitchen, where I just stood looking around. I also smelt the place. There was a distinctive aroma of Indian food and then I saw the Indian takeaway cartons on the kitchen table.

"I see you like your curries."

I had to get some kind of conversation going.

The woman nodded, "Oh yeah, we love our curries."

"Best food for a cold winter's night, a good spicy chicken tikka masala," I cheekily replied, whilst getting out the stuff from my bag.

"How long have you lived here?" I said.

"Way too bloody long. That's why we want to sort out our house, starting with the kitchen," the guy blurted out.

I think the woman had started to feel a bit embarrassed about the cold attitude her husband was giving me.

"Would you like a cup of tea?" she asked.

"Yes please," I promptly replied. "Nothing like a nice cup of tea on a cold winter's night."

Half an hour had passed and the tea was well-received. I started showing them images of what the kitchen could look like; the colours of the doors, the materials they could have and the wife kept asking me for reassurance as to what I thought was the best one for them.

The conversation was flowing by now. I had just returned from Hull, a hard place and, remembering that there I had managed to make friends with some locals who had never seen a dark person before, I started feeling more at ease.

"You know what? You are the first Paki that has come into our house," said the husband.

I was not in a position to show my opposition to his comment.

"Yes, so you see we're not all that bad, are we?" I replied half-heartedly.

"I don't know what is it is about you lot, coming into our country ... ?"

I then went on to explain what had happened with us in Uganda, how Idi Amin had kicked us out and that we had always been British subjects. He listened carefully and started nodding his head more.

"We had no choice but the UK. God save the Queen! I can imagine how you feel but also let's not forget how many years the British were in India as colonial powers. You also came to our country as well."

There was silence. The man smiled slightly.

"Let's also not forget who makes those curries that you like so much." I kept pointing towards the empty takeaway cartons.

He turned around to his wife. "Never bloody thought of looking at it that way."

I ended up staying in that house for three hours being offered more tea and more biscuits. I priced up the fee for the kitchen and it came to around £3,000. It wasn't cheap but along the way we had customised the design according to their choice of materials. I knew they were both interested. We ended up signing the deal that night. We said our goodbyes and I assured them they were in good hands and all would be well. I assured them that if they had any problems they could always call me at the office and I would be able to fix anything for them.

"I really appreciate you coming out to see us," the man finished off. "It's been great chatting with you and I wish you luck on this new job."

This was the moment when I realised that anyone can be broken down; I realised I had a certain sales skill.

I can sell ice to the Eskimos and I can sell sand to the Arabs

My managers were very happy the next day even though I complained that they had sent me into the lion's den. I sold quite a few kitchens after that. I loved the feeling of closing a deal. In those six months working at Farouche I sold a number of kitchens and earned some good commission to play with. It helped me up my lifestyle and, in turn, I started spending weekends in London, usually staying at one of my Nigerian friends' luxury central London apartment.

One day in London I was introduced to the guy who was to be my first mentor – Chester. Another friend, Ian, had introduced us. Ian was going on about some real smooth guy that I needed to meet and together maybe there would be something we could all do. We met over a classic English breakfast at some greasy café in west London. I was immediately impressed by Chester. He was twice our age and had white hair, as well as a massive pot belly – I'm sure he hadn't seen his feet in a while. He immediately came across as a father figure. I don't know where he is today or even if he is still alive, but Chester was what I would call the 'true original gangster hustler'.

He did a variety of things. He was a second-hand car salesman and a stockbroker but his main gig was as a horse trader. He was definitely switched on. In that meeting he told Ian and me that he was planning to enter the mobile phone business. He had recently set up his company and had some good ideas on how to sell a lot of mobile phones and make some big money. He was looking to put together a team of co-partners to work on this with him and in particular he was keen to take on a sales manager. I felt a sense of immediate empowerment when I met him. I had never had a role model before, a hero, or a mentor. My dad should have been that guy, but I never looked at him that way. To me, he was just my dad.

This Chester guy could be the one to learn from.

I didn't have a clue about mobile phones but I knew that it was a far sexier and glamorous game than selling kitchens. I was excited and immediately agreed that I would join Chester. I was all in. This was when my first mobile phone hustle started – one that would eventually turn into a 30-year journey.

Chester's proposed hustle went as follows. Back in the late 1980s the mobile phone business was in its infancy stage and not many people had them. Many were still sceptical on whether this technology was going to take off.

Chester was also a brute with his use of the English language.

"We ain't fucking buying phones to make pennies. That's not why we are here. We're gonna buy phones and make a fucking killing!"

Apparently he had it all figured out. He just needed soldiers like me to execute his vision. He arranged for his company to become an authorised dealer and reseller for International Communications Ltd (ICL), a mobile network operator (MNO).

"We're gonna make big fucking cash from the sale of the handsets and the commission fees we get paid from the fucking operator."

Chester basically used the word 'fuck' all the time. Swearing and chain smoking just added to his demeanour. A gangster don.

Back in those days, every mobile phone came with an electronic serial number (an ESN) and once this was connected to a network operator we would receive a one-time commission fee. Chester soon figured out that we could connect the same ESN to two different networks (hence two phone numbers per phone) to receive two sets of commissions. The cost of us buying the phone was about £700 in those days and we got a commission from two networks, one of them being ICL. Using these two commissions we could then subsidise the price of the phone to sell below our cost and make our money via the commission fees. The maths worked out well. We sold our £700 phones at a 50% discount, collecting £350 in cash *plus* we got £300 from each network as our commission, so £350 + £600 = £950. Subtracting the cost of the phone at £700, we would end up with a massive £250 profit on each phone! All we had to do was to sell hundreds of these phone contracts. My work was clearly cut out for me. Just go and sell, sell ... *sell*!

At those prices, our aim was to do volume connections as we also had a rebate structure, whereby if we beat certain thresholds we would get even more commissions from the MNOs. Chester told me to leave everything to him, so while he focused on striking the deals with the MNOs and phone suppliers, I should focus on the sales side. He even told me how I could make some extra cash on my own with this setup. I took his advice and my own side hustle went as follows.

I was allowed to sell a phone for £700 at a maximum discount of 50% (£350). I did not have to go down to 50% as that was the floor that Chester wanted. I would normally go in at a 30% discount (£490) and pocket the difference between £490 and £350 (what I had to give to Chester). All I had to ensure was that all my customers knew that they would be receiving two bills for the same phone – that's why we were able to offer very low prices. Most of them were OK with this because they just wanted the phone; it was like a status symbol. I realised back then the power that mobile phones would have over people.

I had to start looking around for customers. I knew that the money was in London but I had been away for quite a while and needed to widen my network of relationships in the city. At that stage, the only people I knew with money were the friends from university who had moved back to London.

The Nigerians!

By late 1989 I had sold quite a few phones to the Nigerians and others as well. One of my first customers was a guy called Deji, who would end up being one of my best friends today. I met him in a smoky pool room on Finchley Road when I took him to my car and showed him the phone. He immediately handed over his cash.

The income streams from the carriers were coming in, but as we grew there was pressure from all sides on how to manage the business. Chester was getting more worked up as the MNOs kept taking longer and longer to pay us. Some customers started complaining about receiving high phone bills every month, which had the operators diving more into our business practices; they soon realised what we had been up to. Chester had found a legal loophole that had allowed us to work as we had done without breaking the law. I didn't really care about how Chester structured the deals. I trusted him. All I cared about was how to bring in the hard cash. There was a time he even asked me to slow down on the sales due to drop in supply from the operators. I didn't slow down, though, I just raised my prices. There was just so much demand.

I was still living at home in Hampshire but driving up and down to London every single day to sell the phones and collect the cash. I decided to tell my mum that I needed to leave home and set up in London.

Chester's phone hustle led me to get my first apartment in London. By late 1989, I owned my first property. It was a two-bedroom flat in Gilbert Street in Mayfair right on top of Bond Street tube station. None of my friends could comprehend how I had managed to swing this, but I had. It was one of the best locations to be in for central London. The place cost me £120,000 and I paid part cash and part mortgage. Now I had my spot, my flashy convertible car and I was a frequent visitor to some of London's top clubs and bars.

I was 23.

I was rocking and I was rolling.

THERE IS A SILVER LINING TO EVERY CLOUD
if you just look for it

SOME ROLE MODELS WILL REACH THEIR SELL-BY DATE
*Keep them as allies but always look for new role
models as times and your objectives change*

CHAPTER 4

THE HONG KONG HUSTLE

By early 1990 I was well settled into the London scene but my expenses had risen because of my lifestyle. Commission payments from Chester were also not flowing as smoothly; it was becoming harder for him to collect the money from the MNOs. I had a mortgage to pay, but I had no discipline when it came to managing my finances. I started to neglect my responsibilities, my apartment, my car – and my bills.

I had also started reading about Southeast Asia. One of my key subjects at university was Southeast Asian economies – the 'tiger economies'. How and why was this region growing so fast? I was fascinated by Eastern culture and wondered what the East was like. I had become restless again and the daily grind of selling phones and waiting for Chester to pay me had started to take its toll. One day, out of the blue, I had a thought. I felt an urge to see what kind of trading business I could start in Asia. So, in the early months of 1990, I decided to visit the Hong Kong Trade Development Council (HKTDC) in London. I walked into the reception office and spoke with the lady behind the desk. I was very straight with her in that I wanted to do business with Hong Kong. At that time Hong Kong was probably the most famous of all the Eastern cities, maybe because it was still a British colony. There was an automatic bond between the UK and Hong Kong and the rule of law was also British.

The person at the HKTDC asked me about my line of

interest and I blurted out, "I have mobile phones that I can supply. I am looking to start my export business. Can you please introduce me to some buyers in Hong Kong?"

I think they were a bit surprised to be asked this, as their main role was to promote the exports coming out of Hong Kong and not vice versa. I didn't want to *buy* anything from Hong Kong – I wanted to *sell* to them! They hesitantly took my details and advised me that if anyone was interested, I would be contacted. In no uncertain terms, I had the feeling that I should not be holding my breath for something to happen. I left it at that. I had tried and after that kind of reaction, I believed nothing would really come out of my visit to the HKTDC.

Spring of 1990 came along and I was still selling phones with Chester, but by this time it had become a drip-by-drip kind of business. To my pleasant surprise, in May of 1990, I received a letter from the HKTDC. When I saw the envelope by my letterbox with the HKTDC logo, I immediately ripped it open to check the contents. The letter was to advise me that the HKTDC had received an enquiry from someone in Hong Kong in reply to my 'noticeboard' posting in their trade bulletin of what I could supply. The HKTDC also attached the buyer's enquiry, which was a very specific request. The interested party wanted to purchase 183 Motorola 8500x mobile phones. I raised both my eyebrows in surprise and excitement. Wow!

The first question I asked myself was, why 183? This had me all worked up. I immediately wrote a letter back to the HKTDC.

"Yes! No problem, I can supply."

Never did it cross my mind where I might get my hands on 183 Motorola phones. I was used to selling single phone units – or at the most in the low double digits– every week and that supply was controlled by Chester, who was getting them from the MNOs. Also by now, the MNOs had cut down their supplies to Chester drastically as everyone had started feeling the heat over the amount of money that was being paid out to Chester. Other than this source, I had no idea where I could get the phones from.

In the letter from the HKTDC were also laid out the details of the proposed interested buyer in Hong Kong, including all their contact details. I took my phone and immediately called the number in Hong Kong. I spoke to a gentleman by the name of Alex Li – the potential customer. I introduced myself to the gentleman on the other end of the line. He spoke perfect English (thank God), but with a strange accent. After the formalities were concluded, he seemed very happy to hear from me. He then explained that he had an order from some guys in mainland China for these particular phones that were made only by Motorola. He asked me if I was sure I could source them and I replied positively. I told him I could get the phones, but I would have to check the latest price from my supplier first before getting back to him.

After our call, I sat in silence. Where the fuck was I going to get 183 Motorola phones from? More pertinently, where the fuck was I going to get the money to buy these phones, considering that each phone was £700? Multiplying £700 by 183 units meant I needed to come up with a whopping £128,100. The next few days were painful for me. I had promised Alex I would call him back with the full details but what could I tell him? As I was driving I received a phone call. There was no caller ID in those days, so I simply answered the phone, not knowing that I had a very anxious Alex on the other line.

"Can you give me the price please?" Alex asked.

I was stumped for an answer but my mouth was running faster than my mind at that time. "Alex, I have checked around and the prices will be around £1,000 per phone."

He didn't seem to be bothered by the number I had given him.

"It's OK. When can we get the stock?"

Of course, Alex didn't know me, so he followed by saying that the only way this deal would be possible was if he flew himself to London with the cash. He was adamant that he needed to see the stock first before he parted with his cash. I was in a tight corner here, but my guts told me to speak. I told him to come to London and I would arrange everything.

I was in a fix. A major fix. I didn't want to lose the deal but I knew that if I could not supply him, Alex would surely buy these phones from someone else in the UK because he seemed very specific with his request. With the strange number of 183, it seemed he had already sold them on. Alex had the order and the cash but I was not the only person in the UK selling phones. If he came to London and I did not supply, he would get them from someone else. He was not going to come all the way to London to only go back empty handed.

My word is my bond

After that call I went to work. I deliberately did not call Chester because, quite simply, I did not want to share the spoils of this deal with anyone. I felt no loyalty to him. It was my deal and it was up to me to make it work. I started frantically calling around and eventually I located a company, Midland Cellular, asking them if they could supply. They told me they could – but they wanted the cash up front. Now, that was the good news. The bad news was that I could not risk taking Alex to Midland Cellular because if he knew my source, I could kiss the deal goodbye. Introducing Alex to anyone was not an option.

I went to my family for help. I explained the merits of the deal but none of my family had £128,000 spare cash lying around. It was a quick back-to-back deal and I stood to make around £50,000 on it, but that was not enough to convince any of my family members to come up with the cash. I then went to speak to an uncle who was involved in international commodity trading to ask him for his help. Out of pity I think he decided to help me and he took me to see one of his big trade financiers, another Indian guy living in Leicester. We got on the train and went to see him. This guy was an Indian version of Chester, except much more polite and courteous. We met, and after I had explained the deal, he turned around and told me that he would be able to help me on one condition – I had to split the profit with him 50–50.

The guy was hustling me on my own deal because he knew I had no other option. He was a financier after all and he knew I was stuck. Alex was arriving in a few days' time and I needed an immediate solution. Reluctantly, I had to agree with him.

After a few days, Alex arrived, as promised, in London. The guy didn't even bother sleeping after his 12-hour flight. He called me straight from the airport early in the morning and told me he was coming to see me immediately. He arrived at my apartment in Mayfair and I greeted him. We had spoken a few times already, so it was nice to finally see what he looked like in the flesh. He was young-looking with glasses and he had two large bags with him. He walked into my apartment and put both bags down on the couch. He immediately opened one and it was full of crisp £50 notes. I had never seen so much cash in my life. I kept my cool as I didn't want Alex to think that I was a rookie in the game.

"Where are the phones?" Alex asked.

I laughed. Did he actually think I had 183 phones locked up in my spare bedroom?

I told him I needed his cash to pay the supplier as I was making so little profit that it was not worth my while to use my own money to bridge the deal. He didn't seem too happy about the fact that he had the cash but I didn't have the phones. I could tell there was no way he was going to let go of his cash until he saw the phones. I wouldn't have either.

There was some panic that morning with Alex sitting in my apartment. I had to make calls but I didn't want him to listen in, so I kept running downstairs to speak from my car. I had to prevent him from knowing the identity of my suppliers. I called the financier and asked him how best we could do this. I told him that the Hong Kong buyer was with me and I had seen his cash. Knowing this, the financier then suggested he open a letter of credit to the supplier Midland Cellular to guarantee them the payment. In parallel, a few days later I would have to then arrange to take Alex with his cash to the financier's freight warehouse in Heathrow in London; at least this way Alex would never know the source of the phones.

The financier was true to his word and applied for the letter of credit with his bank. It would take a number of days for all of this to be done before the suppliers would release the goods. I had to explain the situation to Alex. He was not happy because it meant him staying in London for a few more days. Unfortunately, the slow pace of the financier's bank, coupled with the slow pace of the suppliers confirming they had received the letter of credit, meant that two weeks passed. In those two weeks, Alex must have called me 20 times a day asking about the phones, each time with the same questions.

"Is the stock ready for inspection?"

"When can I go and see them?"

"Who do I pay this money to?"

The guy was a cross between a bulldog and a terrier. He simply would not rest. I could hear the desperation in his voice as each day passed with still no phones to show him. He had made his commitments to his Chinese buyers and he didn't want to screw himself in front of them. The day came when we finally got the call from the suppliers that they had received and accepted the letter of credit from the financier. They then dispatched the phones to be delivered to my financier's freight offices in London. For the first time in those two weeks I called Alex and I gave him the good news that the phones were ready for inspection. He rushed excitedly to my apartment and we drove to Heathrow to see the phones. Once we got there, we duly walked over to the warehouse where the phones were packed in large cartons. Both Alex and I breathed a huge sigh of relief. They were exactly as per the specification he had ordered, but still he insisted that he inspect each and every phone. I really was not in the mood to rush anything because I had waited for so long already. I had to remain calm.

Alex seemed satisfied and we then we moved over to the office. He had brought along his bag of cash and he started taking it out in its crisp bundles. The warehouse freight manager was given strict instructions by the financier not to release any stock until all the cash was counted. Prior to that, I had already agreed with the financier that he would collect all the cash and he would later give me my share as I did not want Alex to see me take it. I trusted the financier because he was an older guy and tied in with my family somewhere along the line. Besides that, I had concluded my part of the deal so he had to pay me.

One hour later, it was all done. Alex had already called his nominated freight company to collect the stock for immediate dispatch to Hong Kong, before going to China. He looked very happy and relieved when we walked out.

"You make me lose weight uh! I don't sleep proper for many days."

The poor guy had been stressed out about the deal ever since he had arrived in London. He hadn't expected it to be that rough. I had given him the runaround but at the end of the day he had what he came for; his 183 phones. He gave me his thanks and, upon departing, I clearly remember him saying, "You must now come to Hong Kong. I want you to be with me when we open these boxes in China." His tone was more like an order rather than an invitation.

I said yes immediately, not because of his order but because I was dying to see Hong Kong and I could officially claim that this would be my first international business trip since leaving university. I had just made a cool chunk of cash and had nothing to lose by accepting him. I called my mum and gave her the good news on the deal and told her I was going to Hong Kong. I think by now she had simply given up on me ever staying put. I was 23, but in her eyes I was still her little boy.

A couple of weeks later I arrived in Hong Kong and met Alex again. We had become much closer because I had delivered my part of the deal and he had clearly seen that I was a genuine guy, even though I was operating solo out of my apartment and had no company. I think he wanted me to meet his buyers to show them that his supplier valued their business so much that he had come all the way to China to meet them. This was my first induction into the Chinese culture and their way of doing business.

We went from Hong Kong to Macau and spent a night on the town. Alex entertained me with dinner, karaoke and the honorary VIP massage. We then moved onto a place called Zhuhai. This was my first time ever in 'red' China; in 1990 China was still very much a communist state and 'red' was the nickname I had heard somewhere. I clearly remember arriving at the port of Zhuhai with Alex and being met by 10 or so official-looking Chinese guys. I then saw some pallets on the ground, the same ones that I had last seen at the financier's warehouse at Heathrow. The phones had arrived, but then questions started to swirl around in my head.

'What if the phones are not inside?'

'What if they're damaged?'

'What if these are not our cartons ...?'

'What if ...'

Alex then instructed the Chinese guys in their language that they could open the wooden pallets. They got stuck in with hammers. What got me was the way these guys pounced on the cartons – like a bunch of vultures flying down on a carcass. The cartons were opened and they all stood back to let one of them (he looked like he was the boss) make his way toward the open cartons. He bent down and ever so slowly pulled out the first phone box. It was as if he was unwrapping an ice-cream lolly; he carefully opened the phone box and lifted the phone out of its box. We could smell its newness. He then looked for the battery and slowly tried to put it into the phone. I stepped in to help him as I had known these phones for more than a year by then; I inserted the battery and switched on the phone, handing it to him when the lights came on. He gazed at it with awe. He looked at the front, the back and sides. He then raised it up and showed it around like it was a World Cup trophy. Everyone cheered. He then looked at both Alex and me with a huge grin on his face. We had a happy customer.

There is nothing like a happy customer

For me, this was the first time I had ever truly understood the meaning of customer service. Here we were in China, delivering the product to a first-time customer who was clearly very happy with what we had delivered. Our job was done and oh how well we had done it.

That night we were invited to a large banquet. We sat at a large round table and somehow (maybe because I was the foreigner) I happened to be their guest of honour. No one spoke English except Alex, so he was busy doing all the translations. Every few minutes I was getting food piled on my plate and a Chinese guy would come up to me with a small glass of beer to say cheers. We then moved on to a karaoke bar. There was me, Alex and five of the Chinese customers but by now we were now surrounded by 25 young Chinese girls as our drinking companions. I couldn't believe that this was business entertaining in China.

That night the head buyer kept plying me with drinks and asking me to sing all the English songs on the karaoke screen. Now, I'm no singer but the fact that I could read and shout out every word on George Michael's *Careless Whisper* made me a superstar in that room. In fact I sang that very same song about 10 times that night.

As the evening ticked along, I kept seeing Alex deep in conversation with the head boss. I was in full merry mode as I had been given so much alcohol. My head was spinning, but in a good way. I had girls all over me asking me over and over again to speak in English. Alex, however, seemed to be quite focused. I could see he was not into the entertainment side of things. After a few minutes he fought his way across the bevy of females toward me.

Over the loud karaoke music he shouted in my ear, "This guy wants you to get him another 200 phones!"

I was not expecting that sort of news in the early hours of the morning.

I left Hong Kong with an order that had not even been in my plan when I left the UK. I had travelled there solely to give my thanks and see a new city. I had never planned for any sort of outcome. It had been a fun trip for me. I had made my money and I was happy. Little did I know that this first trip to Hong Kong and China would shape my destiny for many years to come. I had ventured out of my London comfort zone … and as they say, "Your life only really begins when you step outside of your comfort zone."

ARE YOU WILLING TO TAKE EXPENSIVE RISKS WITH NO GUARANTEES?

Short-term expenses can lead to lifetime gains

ARE YOU MAKING SHIT HAPPEN?

*When the student is ready ... the solution will appear;
you don't need to know how until you know you will ...*

WHEN OPPORTUNITY KNOCKS

shove a door stopper under the door and keep it ajar!

**DO YOU UNDERSTAND THE UNIVERSAL
LANGUAGE OF CUSTOMER SERVICE?**

Service the customer and the world is yours!

CHAPTER 5

ASIAN DECADENCE

T he year 1990 was a defining moment for me. I had just come back from Hong Kong with a second large phone order. I certainly did not want to use an outside financier again, but I would have to if there was no other option. I had to make some changes quickly and I needed to raise some money from somewhere. I decided to sell my flat in Mayfair – I didn't make much profit on it but at least I recouped my deposit. I also sold my car and put all my money into buying the phones. I told Alex that with regards to the new 200-unit order I would be shipping them out in batches of 50 phones at a time to help my cash flow and each time he was to remit me the payment. We therefore made four shipments over a few weeks. After a couple of months, Alex came back to London to see me, saying he wanted to buy more stock. The hard part was over as we were finding a routine.

By the time Alex left London I had decided it was better for me to be closer to the action than away from it. I went one night to tell my parents that I wanted to move to Hong Kong. I hadn't really gone back home to live since leaving university and now to make things worse I was moving 6,000 miles away. My mum was not happy, but she gave me her blessing. I think she knew that I was like a bird that needed to spread its wings.

Before I left for Hong Kong I used some of the money I had made from selling the phones to Alex to buy my own stock. I packed 20 phones into my suitcase. I had two suitcases full of clothes and one full of phones – and off I went to Hong Kong.

I didn't know anyone there other than Alex. I arrived and settled into the Emperor Hotel in TsimShatSui, the central shopping area of Kowloon on the mainland part of Hong Kong. I booked a room for three weeks to settle in before looking for a more permanent place. During this trip, Alex and I had delivered another batch of phones to Zhuhai and now I had nothing else to do other than show Alex that I had the 20 phones I had brought over in my suitcase. Due to the large size of the phone boxes I could only fit 20 units into my suitcase. I asked Alex if there was a way we could start some local sales of the stock instead of only relying on the orders from Zhuhai. Alex didn't seem keen to do one-off deals with small quantities; he was all about the big back-to-back orders from China. He did help me, though, and passed on my details to some Hong Kong electronics traders he knew who might possibly be interested in my phones. Alex said they could buy and, if they did, I should give him a small commission on each phone sold as a goodwill gesture.

One afternoon, as I walked back into the hotel lobby after wandering the streets of Hong Kong, I was met by three local Chinese guys. They looked like gangsters I had seen in those old Bruce Lee movies. One of them was called Mr Li Yu Chung. He spoke perfect English and until today remains a good friend of mine. Mr Li was the Chinese version of Chester, a real hustler with a wheeler-dealer air about him. He told me straight that he wanted to buy my 20 phones. I told him my price keeping in mind that I had brought them to Hong Kong and they needed to pay a bit extra.

"No probrem," he replied in an English Chinese accent.

They wanted to see the phones there and then so I took

them to my room. I didn't fancy showing off phones in the hotel lobby coffee shop so, yes, as dodgy as it may sound, I took three Chinese dudes to my room not knowing who they really were, but going with the flow as I had trusted Alex's recommendation. We unpacked the phones in the room and they turned each one on to see if it powered up. All the phones worked. We discussed the price and they promptly handed me the payment in crisp Hong Kong dollar notes. We shook hands and they left. Now, this was a whole different deal from what I had with Alex. With him I was buying phones for around £700 and selling for £1,000, but with these smaller quantities I was able to sell the phones at £1,500 each to the Hong Kong guys. On 20 phones only, I made a whopping £16,000. We did not even negotiate on the price. The Hong Kong guys wanted Motorola and I seemed to be the only show in town.

The next morning Mr Li called me to say he wanted to meet again. I happily agreed and in any case I had nothing much else to do. He told me to meet him in the Mongkok district of Hong Kong. After getting a bit lost, I found him waiting for me in a dodgy looking noodle house. I walked into the place, sat down next to Mr Li and by the time I had ordered a drink Mr Li had smoked about five cigarettes. Never have I seen anyone smoking in one hand while holding chopsticks and eating noodles with the other. A memory to treasure for sure.

"My friend … I have so many buyers for you," Mr Li said. "The people yesterday have already sold the 20 and now want 20 more. I have many people like this so we need to arrange the deal between you and me. I will bring you the buyers, they will pay you, but I need something. I am a local Cantonese guy – you will need me more than you think."

I thought for a minute and agreed immediately. Mr Li could make life much easier for me if I had plans to keep selling more phones. He was a pure local and he understood the streets. With him as my conduit, I could get a hell of a lot more done, much faster. I also liked him. He seemed genuine, although he looked as if he might have killed 20 people. He had that serial-killer look!

We got started. One week later I was back in London to buy more phones. The surest way to get them to Hong Kong was to pack them in my suitcase. This time I decided I would fill two suitcases with phones. Never once did I get stopped by customs and, besides, there was nothing illegal about taking phones into Hong Kong – it was, after all, still part of the UK!

The correct definition of what I had become was a 'suitcase trader'. Over the course of that first year, I shuttled between London and Hong Kong every few weeks. I also continued to receive good orders from Alex, which we arranged via our normal freight routes. I had also set up a bank account with Po Sang Bank, a division of the Bank of China. I had been instructed to set up an account with this bank by Mr Li and his Hong Kong traders. I don't know why, but that particular bank was a local favourite with the traders. The business got to the stage at which I would wake up in the morning to a call from Mr Li, who, not even bothering to greet me with a 'good morning', would simply come out with his classic one liner, "The money is in your account. Please deliver the phones."

Every other day I was in that bank, either depositing cash, collecting cash or just checking my balance. There was even a time when Mr Li met me to hand over a bag consisting of a cool HK$1,000,000. He seemed to be in a rush and didn't have much time, so we met outside one of the MTR (Mass Transit Railway) stations, where he asked me to count all the money. I told him he was mad to think that I was going to count that kind of cash in public, but it all seemed to be there. We had developed a pretty good understanding of trust.

After six months, I had started enjoying Hong Kong more and more. I did not want the hassle of travelling to London every other week and I figured out there was a much more convenient way to bring the stock in. I needed to have my own bulk shipments at least once a week and every Sunday night, without fail, I would excuse myself from hanging out to go to the airport to release my goods. I would then take the goods back to my apartment knowing in advance that first thing Monday morning there would be a couple of Chinese guys with a van outside, instructed by Mr Li to come to collect their goods.

This exercise was to go on for the next two years and they were probably my best years ever. The heavens had opened up to me. I had never experienced such a flow in my life. I moved into a harbour-front apartment in Causeway Bay and started forming a great circle of friends. I didn't fancy only meeting Mr Li and going to karaoke joints and mah-jong parlours. I wanted the nightlife I had experienced in London. I remembered a girl I had met in London and she lived in Hong Kong, so out of the blue I called her. NS was the first non-Chinese person I hung out with in Hong Kong and she quickly took me into her circle of friends; I guess she felt sorry for me because I was all alone thousands of miles away from home. She started taking me out and we would always end up in Lan Kwai Fong, the famous nightlife area in Hong Kong. It was always me, NS and her girlfriends, until one night a guy stepped out of a bar and NS immediately jumped on him.

"Doron!"

She immediately introduced him to me, even claiming that we somehow looked alike. Doron and I clicked in seconds and from that night on we became best friends – our friendship remains to this day. Doron is one of the few guys who has followed my path over the past 25 years and we speak every week. He was to become my partner in crime when it came to wine, women and song. Doron had left his home in Israel to live in Hong Kong. His first role was as a barman and very soon after that he joined his older brother in opening what is now a thriving and successful garment trading company. Doron and his brother Sam were one of the first true entrepreneurs I met. They had a garment start-up business and over the past 25 years, they have shown me the meaning of the words 'focus' and 'consistency'.

I spent much time socialising in Hong Kong, but I always made sure I was there for my customers. I have had meetings in some of the strangest places; smoky noisy mah-jong parlours, back-alley karaoke joints, box-like noodle cafés, big dim sum houses and massage parlours. Yes, many a time Mr Li and I would meet at some of the top Hong Kong massage parlours to chat. Everyone talks about the best deals being done on the golf course, well, the massage parlour was my golf course. They were the ultimate retreat for me; saunas and steam rooms, followed by sitting in luxurious surroundings eating fruit, enjoying manicures and pedicures and then the actual massage. Sometimes we even went in groups. This was the way my business was done.

Immerse yourself totally into different cultures.
It's the only real way to keep learning

My rule was to never let down any of my customers; I had come to understand the importance of making commitments and keeping my word. I remember one day I was called in the morning by Mr Li.

"The money is in your account. Now you must deliver the phones at 3pm by the seafront near Sai Kung. Not 2.55pm, not 3.05pm. You must be there exactly at 3pm."

He explained that some of the phones were being smuggled into China because the country had very high rates of duty and I had to deliver the phones to the port. He told me a boat would be there, but it would not actually stop by the jetty as it could not remain stationary due to some harbour laws. In the event, the boat rolled by very slowly and in those few precious minutes, several guys rushed over to me and threw the cartons of phones onto the boat. It was amazing for me to see this. Smuggling in its purest form. Everyone was making something out of this; me, Mr Li, his contacts, the throwers and the boat owner!

I fairly quickly garnered a reputation for reliability among the Hong Kong Chinese phone traders and by now, in addition to Mr Li, I had numerous other buyers I had met along the way. Most of them had heard about me and somehow they had managed to track me down. Everyone in the business came to me to buy phones. By the time I turned 24, I had amassed US$1 million in cash scattered between several bank accounts.

Opportunities then started coming my way. My harbour-front apartment landlord was desperate for money and offered to sell it to me for next to nothing. He kept begging me to buy his place – I couldn't be bothered.

Through some other contacts I was offered the chance to be part of a new chain of retail phone shops opening in Hong Kong – I couldn't be bothered.

In 1991, some people from India approached me to see if I was keen to not only supply phones to India, but also to be involved in some kind of MNO licence deal – I couldn't be bothered.

I just couldn't be bothered.

Why would I want to burden myself with all these headaches when money was just so easy to make?

Quite simply, I was too caught up in the glory of it all, what with the late nights, fancy weekend trips to Thailand, Bali, the Philippines and numerous other places, not to mention the copious spending on luxuries and the huge number of girls – everywhere! Why would anyone want to stop that kind of lifestyle? I was caught up in my own bullshit. By 1993, I was living in a very swanky apartment in the Mid-Levels area, a popular upmarket part of Hong Kong Island, where most of the expats would stay. I also purchased a nice customised Porsche 911, which I had shipped in specially from the UK.

I simply did not have the vision on why I should be taking my game to the next level. I never questioned where I wanted to be 12 months down the line; for me, it was all about *today*. I never questioned about tomorrow. Looking back, it was a case of ego. I didn't have any mentors or role models. My dad was there to send me shipments and arrange payments for me, but beyond that, I had very little interaction with him on how to take this game to a higher level. He never bothered pushing me, he just let me be. In a way, I think he had a lot of confidence in me.

By now it was late 1993 and I was also ignoring the competition that had started coming in. I was no longer making those crazy margins anymore because the game had started becoming much fiercer. All the major phone suppliers in the UK had decided that they, too, wanted to be in the market. I was still a one-man show, with no office, no staff, no infrastructure. I never even set up a limited company as everything was done in my own personal name. Every week I would see British guys at the airport picking up stock and there was nothing I could do about it because I had not built on the momentum I had created. Up until then all the demand had been for Motorola, but then a new brand had started emerging – a company from Finland called Nokia.

I had never felt this kind of threat or challenge before. I didn't really know how to handle the decline in orders as my once loyal customers had, quite naturally, started buying from cheaper sources. Some were even given credit lines by the big UK trading houses.

It was late 1993 when everything started to fall apart.

The decrease in phone business meant I had no choice but to look around for new angles to make money. Besides the numerous opportunities I had turned down, I did go for one in particular, Safebag. This idea was introduced to me by my contacts in Spain from my time buying phones there. Yes, besides the UK, I had also sourced Motorola phones from other parts of Europe. They asked me to look at a product called Safebag, adding that if I was keen, I could become their agent for the Asia Pacific region. In order to become their agent, I needed to show some commitments by buying a couple of their machines. Safebag blew me away. I immediately saw the massive potential in this product. It was a patented Spanish invention, a weird-looking machine placed at airport departure areas for passengers to wrap their bags before check-in. This was the original machine that securely wrapped luggage with plastic. I was in love with the proposition and immediately paid over the money to purchase the two machines. In exchange, I now had the rights to this technology for the whole of Asia.

All I had to do was to get each airport to buy one machine. In order to attract them, as soon as I got the machine I arranged to be part of an aviation trade show in Beijing. I excitedly went to Beijing only to find out that there was absolutely no interest in this machine whatsoever. I then presented the machine to the authorities at Hong Kong International Airport, who also showed no interest. The Safebag machines were big and cumbersome. They were not something I could store in my apartment and also, they needed to be housed in secure areas. I had to put them into special storage with my freight agents in Hong Kong – at a cost, of course.

I kept sending brochure after brochure and letter after letter to all the regional airports in Asia, but I received no positive feedback. It baffled me as to how the airports themselves did not see the potential in this product. To me it was an amazing invention. Imagine, every passenger could protect his or her bag from damage and theft. Imagine how every airport could earn additional revenues and every airline could also reduce its liability costs on damaged luggage. All in all, a win for everyone. Not so. No one gave a shit about this concept.

I made no progress after trying this for eight months. It

even came to a stage at which I stopped paying the storage space to house the machines. My freight agents kept asking me what to do with the machines, but I had no idea what to tell them. Even now I don't know what happened to those machines. Maybe someone somewhere made better use of them, tweaked the design and came up with a whole new revised look, but the point I'm making here is that today every airport in the world has these bag-wrapping machines. This is a billion-dollar business worldwide. Each time a customer wraps their bag at the airport it costs them an average of $5 per bag and *millions* of passengers worldwide use this service on a daily basis. Safebag was clearly way ahead of its time. It was a lesson that showed me that sometimes being first is not always the best option. This was a problem that would continue to haunt me over and over in the years to come.

Being first at something is not always a good thing

The failure with Safebag and the subsequent losses put me into a negative mindset. It also seemed that when it rained it poured. I got stuck once in my Porsche in the middle of a Hong Kong highway, only to find out that the guy who had sold it to me in the UK had used some engine parts that were clearly not genuine Porsche parts. The car ended up being sold for next to nothing. I then became partners with another friend and we set up a company to import beers and luxury cars. We had high hopes, but none of our efforts led to success. Both businesses were a write-off.

To maintain the lifestyle I had created, I was simply digging into what I had already accumulated. I remained in my apartment and continued socialising in the hope that there would be something good around the corner for me. By late 1994, I had spent or lost much of my savings nor had I made any investments with what I had earned. There was not even a mutual fund or a savings account somewhere gathering interest.

By 1995, it was crunch time as I had very little money left. I had no choice but to leave Hong Kong. I was in major debt with my credit cards and I had moved into a very small, cheap place, but even then, I was having a tough time just keeping up with the rent. The truth was, I had no business.

A man of sane mind would have found a job but that option never crossed my mind; after all, I had never worked for anyone. Ever. Had my head been screwed on right I would have joined a telecom company but, hey, not me. The nine-to-five life was not for me; not at university and not now. I had to do things my way and I paid the price for my stupidity.

My only way out was to look for the next hustle.

I left Hong Kong with my last $5,000 in my pocket, half of which was a friendly loan that had been given to me by my 'brother' Doron.

I left my heart back in Hong Kong. I loved the city. I left behind some amazing memories and friends, including my closest one, Doron. For me it was heart-breaking and I know he felt the same. We were brothers. We shared a favourite song back then called *It's So Hard to Say Goodbye to Yesterday* by the group Boyz II Men and oh how appropriate the title was.

Looking back, I see leaving Hong Kong as one of the biggest decisions I have ever made. Yes, things were tough, but I'm sure I would have figured something out. I had been there for five years. It was my city and I knew everyone. Bad times don't last forever, but something told me it was time to leave. However, had I stayed in Hong Kong I know I would never have had the family that I have today. God works in mysterious ways I guess.

I decided that from Hong Kong I would go to see some of my friends in California, USA. A few months before I left Hong Kong I had met a Japanese girl at the airport and we immediately hit it off. We kept in touch and she invited me to Tokyo, so I took her up on her offer and stopped with her for a few days on my way to the USA. After I landed in Tokyo I was simply in awe. This was *Blade Runner* all over again. It was completely different from Hong Kong – cleaner, elegant and with much more style. I returned a few weeks later after I had completed my journey to California and stayed with my Japanese friend. She was making good money, so I didn't have to spend much of my own.

I slowly started getting used to the Japanese way of life. There was one rule for the Japanese and one rule for foreigners. Nothing was written in English. I started going out on my own in Tokyo and had the city figured out within a few weeks. It was such a cool place to be and I had started meeting more and more people, mainly Japanese women. I decided it was best to leave my friend's apartment and I rented a cheap place for a while because I still had some money left over. I remember seeing an advert one day for native English speakers to teach private Japanese students. I immediately hustled the job by showing them my University of Hull credentials and speaking in my best Queen's English. I was signed up and started making Y10,000 per hour to teach English as a foreign language. Most of the clients were single Japanese women and the majority went from being my students to being my lovers. What more could a guy want? A paid dating service through which ladies came to me.

I was living day by day and spent one full year in Tokyo in the centre of town, in an area called Omotesandō. I never had a formal teacher training certification to teach English, but no one ever bothered to ask and I never bothered to bring it up. I was an English teacher with no clue as to what to do, so I simply bullshitted my way through by literally throwing away the English textbook in front of the students and telling them the best way to learn English was to have conversations verbally in different environments, such as in a coffee shop, at a bar, walking in the park, etc. I also broke down my teaching into accents to show the students that English was actually spoken in different ways across the world; accents like Cockney, American and Australian. The students found it hilarious.

I never took this work seriously. Teaching was just a side hustle to get by. I did not want to make it a full-time career. I was also quite brash in that I would cancel appointments at the last minute. I know that's not cool, but that's how I was back then. Even though things were tough, I couldn't really give a fuck. I wanted to do things my way. Looking back, I feel bad that one day I made a young Japanese student wait outside my apartment in the rain for three hours because I forgot about our meeting and couldn't be bothered to rush back home. I sometimes abused the simple politeness of the Japanese people.

In Tokyo, all I did was teach conversational English and fuck around. I was 30 years old and not concerned about my future. Besides the teaching hustle I had no grand plans on what to do next. I lost the vibe to make money and Tokyo was not a hustler's environment in the way that Hong Kong was.

That's when, out of the blue, my Nigerian friend and brother Deji called me from Johannesburg, South Africa.

DO YOU HAVE A LONG-TERM PERSPECTIVE?

While the sun is shining invest for the long term because you know at some stage it will rain!
Invest, invest, invest!

DO YOU REALLY BELIEVE IN YOUR VISION?

Don't give up too early ... you're gonna make it ... you're nearly there but you just don't know how close you are!

LEARN HOW TO SELL WELL

it'll make life much easier

CHAPTER 6

SOUTH AFRICA, THE EARLY DAYS

I had been in Tokyo for one year and by then I knew the city pretty well. The problem was that Tokyo was not a place to make big money simply because it was so closed off to foreigners. I enjoyed learning about the Japanese culture and the people, but I was always an outsider and no matter how 'Japanese' I tried to be, I was still considered a *Gaijin*. This meant 'foreigner' but I found out later that term specifically refers to white foreigners. Indians were called *Indojins* and blacks were called *Kokujins*.

When Deji called me out of the blue, he was just checking up on me. He told me he had moved to Johannesburg in South Africa and that I should go out there and join him as there seemed to be masses of trading opportunities. For me, South Africa was a place that had never been on my radar. I had never once thought of visiting the country. It was a place that I had only seen through the media. All I knew about it were the images of apartheid, Soweto and Nelson Mandela.

I was in two minds about going, but Deji was convinced that Tokyo could never be as lucrative as Hong Kong. He was right. I was doing fuck all in Tokyo. I needed to get back on my feet. It wasn't that hard for him to convince me to go to South Africa. I had a temporary rental in Tokyo, no possessions, other than my two suitcases of clothes, and no ties to Tokyo. I wasn't sufficiently in love with any of my girlfriends for me to stay on. Basically, I had nothing to lose by going to see South Africa. As many foreigners who have lived in Japan might tell you, after a while, you start feeling alienated.

We discussed my plan for a while and eventually agreed that it would be a good idea for me to stop off in Hong Kong first to see what I could buy for selling on to South African traders. At that time, we weren't exactly geniuses in coming up with something hot to sell but I remembered my Tangier days and, if anything, we had to invest whatever money we had in buying branded goods that were going to be easy to sell. We agreed on buying discontinued designer clothes and we tracked down a stock lot of Tommy Hilfiger jackets through one of my Hong Kong contacts. Deji sent me some money for his share and I then flew to Hong Kong, where I stayed with my friend Doron. He was happy to see me but sad to see me, once again, only in a transitory manner. I inspected the jackets and promptly made the payment. There were some amazing styles. We spent $2,000 to put the parcel together and I had estimated that most likely we would be able to double our money.

In early 1997, I landed in Johannesburg after a 15-hour economy flight. Johannesburg airport was so small in comparison to Heathrow, Hong Kong and Tokyo airports. I was met by Deji and we drove to Sandton, the upmarket area of Johannesburg. I was pleasantly surprised by how 'non-African' the place looked. The roads were perfect with beautiful mansions everywhere. We stopped to buy some groceries and I immediately realised how cheap the food was compared with Tokyo! When we arrived at Deji's apartment we immediately opened the bag containing the jackets. Deji was of regular build in physical terms and he immediately tried on one of the jackets. The jackets were all large sizes, but for some reason the jacket he tried on was too tight and he could not get it to fit him. He tried another from the box – too tight again. He tried on a few more, again with no luck. He looked at me.

"I think we fucked up here."

I realised then that I had made a fatal mistake in assuming Chinese large sizes were the same as South African large sizes. Oh dear. We would have a tough time selling these to an adult crowd.

*Always do the research
so that you have covered all the bases*

The next few weeks were spent hounding the malls and pavements of Johannesburg. We went from one clothing store to another, offering them our Tommy Hilfiger jackets. One of the owners even kicked us out of his shop for showing him what he described as "body condoms".

Many buyers said the jackets were simply too small but we managed to click with a few retailers in Oriental Plaza, the main Indian shopping mall in Johannesburg. All of the retailers there were Muslim Indians and they reminded me of Shoey. Some decided to take our merchandise and sell them as children's jackets. The only problem was that it would be hard for any parent to fork out that amount of money for a designer Tommy Hilfiger jacket for their kids. We tried for many weeks and eventually after a couple of months we managed to sell everything, but not making anything close to the money we had assumed we would make, let alone thinking it would have taken so long.

With the small profit we made we paid for our upkeep and secured a bargain deal with a landlord who had a massive empty house in the Rivonia area that he was desperate to let. It was the same price that Deji was paying for his two-bedroom apartment, so, without even thinking, we signed the lease and moved into this place. The house had a small cottage at the side that we decided to convert into a clothing and record store. We were not keen on buying anything from Hong Kong anymore, so this time we decided to buy a brand that was owned by our friend in California; it was called Rudeboy – hip-hop streetwear.

There was no money to market the brand, so we started spreading the word in the nightclubs we were frequenting. I had never seen clubs like the ones in Johannesburg. South Africa has four distinct racial classifications and I could not believe how racially segregated everything was, including the nightlife; there were white clubs, Indian clubs, coloured clubs and black clubs. Coloured is actually a racial classification in South Africa, meaning a mixed bag of races. Deji was black and only had black friends in Johannesburg so we would spend most nights in black clubs, with me always being the only non-black.

Black urban youth in South Africa had their own distinct sound and street culture. The style of music that defined them was known as *kwaito* – house music beats that were then slowed down on the turntables. On top of the beats, they would then add their local language and slangs. *Kwaito* originated from the black townships and it was a music genre that I fell in love with pretty quickly. We got in tight with the *kwaito* crowd and very soon we got to know the major *kwaito* artists of that time, such as Bongo Maffin, Skizo and Thebe. Some of the most prominent artists became our friends and started coming over to our showroom to buy our clothing. It was a perfect fit.

Selling clothes did not help in paying our bills on time. It was more a way for us to get noticed, be invited to all the parties and build up a network of contacts. In reality South Africa was not the land of milk and honey. The promise of making quick easy money was not how Deji had made it sound, but I was there and I had to make the best of it. Deji was always much more serious in terms of business than I ever was. He was keen for us to keep moving forward and he came up with the idea that we should invest some of our meagre funds into buying laptops from London, then selling them back in South Africa. We could make more money selling a single laptop then we could by selling several pieces of clothing. When we did the calculations for buying laptops from London and selling them in South Africa, we figured that our prices would probably be the best compared with what was on offer locally. Due to the fact that we had very small quantities, the only way we could market them was to place small adverts in the classified section of the local newspaper. We did exactly that and our phones never stopped ringing with enquiries. We managed to sell a few and the returns were quite impressive.

On one occasion, Deji had gone to go to London to buy some laptops, as he had arranged to borrow some money from his uncle to help us buy more stock. Meanwhile, I was left back in Johannesburg holding the fort. I then got a call from a guy who wanted to buy three laptops. I jumped at this chance because it was easier to sell three together than one at a time. I merrily went along to his farm just outside Johannesburg. It was a large property surrounded by barbed wire; I noticed the heavy security and the even heavier group of dogs barking at the gate. It reminded me of the time I went to sell that kitchen I wrote about earlier. I was invited in and the owner seemed to be a very charming elderly man. He kept me waiting for a while and it was obvious that he was showing off about who he was and the big house that he owned. But me, I just wanted to sell the damn computers.

One thing led to another and he sweet-talked me into accepting a cheque. Who was I to question him? He seemed to be a wealthy guy with a farmhouse mansion and, in addition, he had a really hot wife. We shook hands and I left. As soon as I got into the car I called Deji to give him the good news that all three laptops were sold. He seemed relieved as the guy had paid our price without haggling. Deji asked me if I had collected the cash to which I replied that the buyer had given me a cheque instead. He didn't seem too happy about that for some reason and he was right to think that way.

A week later the fucking cheque had bounced!

When the bank called to tell me that the cheque had bounced, I had no option but to call Deji to give him the bad news. In my excitement to sell three laptops, I had fucked up by getting carried away with the perception of *who* the buyer was rather than *what* the buyer had. It was my fault. Deji flew back to Johannesburg and I knew he was disappointed with me. The main issue for us was to see how we could immediately get the situation rectified so we called the guy and asked him politely to please pay us in cash as his cheque had bounced. We said we either needed the payment in cash or our laptops back. He asked us to meet him the next day on the side lane of one of the freeways. The following day, as arranged, we made our way to the freeway and parked our car. We turned on the hazard lights and walked to his waiting truck. We got inside and started to talk. We ended up begging him to pay us or to give us our laptops back. He then started acting funny and told us that we were not getting our computers back nor any cash and that there was nothing we could do about it. The same guy who had charmed me had become the devil in disguise. We had been defrauded and now he was laughing at us. He made us look like pieces of shit. An argument ensued. Deji was desperate because he had borrowed the funds from his uncle to help us with ongoing laptop purchases. His main concern was how to pay back his uncle. The argument started to get out of hand. Then, out of nowhere, the old guy pulled out a gun and pointed it straight at Deji and me.

Fakkkkkkkkkkk!

He started shouting in a mix of English and Afrikaans. He told us straight that he would shoot us if we ever bothered him again and that we should get the fuck out of his truck. NOW!

We jumped out of the truck and bolted back to our waiting car. I had never had a gun pulled on me and this was not the kind of meeting we had envisaged. We had been scammed, pure and simple. As we sped onto the freeway we decided to go straight to the police station. All I could hear was Deji asking me over and over again how I could have made such a mistake. How could I have fucked up so badly?

When we arrived at the police station we showed our UK passports as ID, which made the cops immediately straighten up for some reason. I told the cops what had happened and how we'd had a gun pulled on us. I also said that the only reason we had accepted the cheque was because we had believed South Africans to be honourable people, but this episode had left a bad taste in our mouths. I even added that if we didn't get our laptops back, we would be lodging an official complaint with the British embassy in order to seek their assistance. Of course, we didn't have a clue where the fuck the British embassy was, let alone what they would do to help us. The cops looked at us and knew that we were not part of a local crowd. They kept asking questions and we explained who the guy was, where he lived, what car he drove and how he looked. We also showed them the bounced cheque that the bank had duly returned to us.

"Eish, man," said one of the cops, laughing whilst looking at the cheque.

"This is David again, up to his usual nonsense." The rest of the cops started laughing.

"We know this guy." The laugher continued.

"We know him very well. You mixed up with the wrong guy here."

"Yes, officer, we know but how are you going to help us, especially if you know him so well?" said Deji.

The cop immediately picked up the phone and dialled a number. He still had a smile on his face.

"David. Detective [whatever the cop's name was] here. How are you?" We could hear the guy's voice on the other side.

"I have two gentlemen from London who are lodging an official complaint of theft and being threatened by a firearm. They say you bought three laptops, but the cheque bounced on them."

We could hear the guy on the other side of the line.

"You are a grown man, David baba. Why are you playing with these young boys eh? Why did you pull your gun out?

77

Was your life in danger? No. Baba, stop this nonsense game and bring those computers back."

Then the cop started to laugh on the phone. "Eish, man. You can't play games like this *China*." ('China' is a slang term for 'mate'. It comes from 'China plate – 'mate' in cockney rhyming slang.)

The cop put down the phone and looked at us with a grin on his face. "Come back tomorrow morning to this station; your computers will be here."

The next morning, as promised, we turned up at the police station and there before our eyes were our three laptops in their original boxes. We breathed a massive sigh of relief, thanked and hugged the cops. They had really saved our asses. A lesson was learned. We decided there and then to sell all the laptops and not to bother with this exercise again.

So, now what?

All this time we had become ever more entrenched in the South African music and nightlife scene. We made a deal with a bunch of guys and decided that we should open our own nightclub; however, none of us had any money to rent a decent place in the middle of Sandton and then put in sound systems and decorations. The only option we had was to rent a house, but it had to be a house in the countryside due to the noise and the numbers of revellers we were expecting via all our contacts. We had seen others use houses as bars and clubs and we figured we could do the same. We scoured the papers and found an interesting place, a property in Midrand – a 20-minute drive out of Sandton. We made an appointment with the landlord and I went alone wearing my best suit. Had I gone with Deji or any of the others it would have been meant a straight decline.

South Africa was still very much racially segregated and from my phone conversation with the landlord it was obvious that they were white. We didn't want to frighten them with four blacks and an Indian guy turning up on their doorstep, so we all agreed that if I went alone I would stand a greater chance of securing the property. I would wear my suit, carry my briefcase and speak in my best Queen's English, while flashing my British passport. I was used to going to strangers' houses from my kitchen selling days, so for me it was no big deal. Once I was in the house, I inspected the property and slowly started nodding my head in approval. I had managed to convince the owners that I was an international businessman from the UK who needed a residence in South Africa for my frequent travels in and out of the county and, because London was so congested, I really wanted to stay on a large plot of land and be at one with nature.

'What a load of bullshit,' I said to myself.

The bullshit worked and I managed to convince them to rent me the house. After paying the deposits we secured the keys. We immediately put some artwork together and created our music venue promotional flyer. I had already decided on the name – Club TKO (abbreviation for 'technical knockout') – and it would be open only on Fridays and Saturdays. The property was a country farmhouse manor, sitting on 20,000 square feet of land, and the house alone was easily 10,000 square feet with six bedrooms and a massive thatched roof. We didn't want to play small as we knew so many people. We wanted to get started with a bang and the pre-opening promotions were a frantic pace of activity. We wanted everybody to know that Club TKO was the hottest spot in town and they all needed to be there.

Our first night was heavily promoted. By this time, everyone knew about our new club and that night we made a shit-load of money because we had bought our own alcohol for resale in the kitchen part of the house that we had converted into a bar area. The open mezzanine study area had been turned into a DJ booth and the dancefloor was the former sitting room and dining room. In addition, we had placed some speakers outside by the pool. The idea was that when they entered, we wanted people to think that they were walking into a mansion from a hip-hop music video.

The next weeks progressed well. On our fourth Friday, we promoted the party even more heavily and there were hundreds of cars piled up down the driveway and along the dusty rocky road leading to the club. This house had no neighbours, so we thought everything was cool. We had turned a predominantly peaceful white rural area into a crazy weekend party central with 1,000 people. It was only a matter of time before we got into trouble. We just did not expect the kind of trouble it turned out to be.

On that Friday night, everything was running smoothly. Deji was on the door collecting the entrance fees, I was overseeing the bar and our other partners were looking after the music. We made sure that Deji and I were in charge of places where cash was being collected – the door and the bar. We also employed some serving staff and cleaners and once in a while I would leave the bar area to check up on things. As the party started to really rock into the evening I popped out to catch up with Deji to see how much money we had collected. We were then taken aback when, from out of the darkness, 20-odd paramilitary camouflaged soldiers rose up from the ground. No one had even noticed them coming over the walls.

"Shut this fucker down *now!*" yelled one of the soldiers.

No one could hear them inside the building as the DJ was in full swing, the music was loud and the crowd were busy cheering. A few of the soldiers then ran up to the house with bright flashlights. They entered the dancefloor and the next thing we knew there was pandemonium everywhere. All of a sudden from outside we heard the music abruptly stop and then the soldiers shouting.

"Everyone get out of here *now!*"

"Who is in charge here?"

I raised my voice but not my hand. Technically I was in charge as I was the name on the lease as the tenant.

By now our revellers had quickly started to vacate the place. The driveway was suddenly full of cars reversing, but what made it worse was that there were more cop cars, with sirens blaring and blue lights flashing, coming up the pathway. It was a total mess. The soldiers rounded up me, Deji, the DJ and the workers. Everyone else was allowed to leave one by one. Luckily, no one got stopped and checked as I'm sure there must have been at least 200 people at that party with pockets full of Swaziland's best marijuana.

They then started checking all our IDs and, unfortunately for the workers, they were all found to be illegal immigrants from Zimbabwe and Mozambique. One of them was crying as the cops pulled him into the van. I will never forget his face.

"Please, boss, please, please tell them to let me go, I cannot go back to Zimbabwe. Please, boss, please tell them," he pleaded, looking at me.

I was helpless. I was speechless. I felt so bad for those

workers and especially for that crying guy, because he had come to do an innocent job of cleaning the kitchen and would never have guessed that on this night he would be facing deportation back to his country. I couldn't do anything with a soldier staring me down with a big rifle in my face.

That night we knew Club TKO had literally been TKO'd! We knew we could not carry on. We had assumed there would be no complaints but the music and noise in the countryside at night had travelled far. Neighbours had called the cops complaining about hundreds of cars pulling up to our house every weekend. I guess enough was enough for them. We had to give the house back to its owners. I was too embarrassed to face them eye to eye, so we had one of our guys drop off the keys. We'd had a good run for those initial four weeks and had made some money, but there was no way we could continue.

Clothes, laptops, nightclubs. We were running out of options for making money. Both Deji and I were disillusioned with our stop-start experience in South Africa. This was when the friction started between us. He was not happy with the way things had worked out, including my *ad hoc* recklessness, as he saw it.

I kept telling him, "You were the one who told me to come to South Africa. I was quite happy in Tokyo."

At times, we simply would not speak to each other, even though we were living in the same house. I saw the writing on the wall. Deji wanted to do his own thing and I knew I wasn't going to be part of his future plans for much longer. He had quietly decided to spend more time trading in Nigeria and London and only once in a while would he come back to South Africa. I was left on my own to figure out my own shit. With Deji gone, I had nothing to do. I had always relied on him to help sort things out but now I was on my own. All I could do was to keep hanging out with my South African friends. I started falling deeper into the South African music scene, but once again I remained the outsider; a British Indian guy hanging out in black clubs in South Africa.

I hung out with some of the younger guys and for a while they became the younger brothers I never had. They looked up to me and over time we slowly came together to see what we could do. I then decided to put my hat into the ring and start a South African R&B group, with me as its manager and executive producer. Nobody was doing R&B music in South Africa in the late 1990s. *Kwaito* was the rage, but I wanted to bring the London soul sound to South Africa. I thought that three of the young guys I was with would appeal to the crowd. They were decent-looking, presentable and I noticed how the girls were always all over them. Two black guys and one coloured guy – Freddie, Blondie and Lance. I named the group Reign.

I contacted my DJ friend in London to see if he had any beats and he promptly sent them through. I was introduced to Alexis Faku, one of South Africa's hottest producers, and we immediately hit it off. I explained the vision and we quickly arranged to use his studio. Alexis didn't charge us anything, purely because he loved what he was doing and he believed in what we wanted to achieve. We started work on an EP with three tracks and in a matter of days we had our final cut. I now had to figure out how to produce the CDs, the photoshoot and, of course, the music video. I had some money left over from the club gig and I also asked the three band members to contribute.

"You want to be famous, then you need to pay a price," I told them.

That was how we raised some of the initial cash to fund ourselves. After the music was done I went to the CD manufacturing plant in Midrand to order the first batch of 1,000 discs. We had already done a nice photoshoot and there were some clothes left over from our clothing showroom which I had to use. I knew there was no chance of us getting signed by a major label and besides, we wanted to be independent, so I tracked down the largest independent record distributors in Johannesburg and they agreed to sell our CDs.

What I really wanted to do was to expose these young South Africans to an international market. We sent our CDs to a few record companies in London, but never heard back from them. I then remembered that Japan was big on black music. It was the only country in Asia at the time that loved hip-hop and R&B music. I flicked through my contacts and located my friend Takeshi in Tokyo. By day, he worked at Dentsu, the largest advertising agency in Japan, but by night he was a budding DJ. Maybe he could do something? I reckon Takeshi agreed to help me promote the CDs in Japan out of pure Japanese politeness. He agreed to actually buy them and he personally would sell them to his friends and to the record stores he knew in Tokyo.

It was an awesome feeling when we received our first 1,000 CDs. We now had a product. This was the first time I had actually hustled my own project rather than being a trader. We then went through all our contacts and shot a cool video in a derelict downtown Johannesburg warehouse. We even borrowed flashy cars from our friends and put a whole heap of pretty girls in the video. Apart from the filming, we didn't pay for anything. The guys wanted to see their own cars in the video and the girls wanted to see themselves. The power of ego worked for us.

We did not become an overnight sensation. Far from it. Things were tough. South Africa was not used to this kind of music and it was hard work to convince radio stations to play our music, so we needed to push the sales via the independent distributors. There was no money for marketing the group so my job was to secure television slots for free live performances. The group was then booked by some clubs outside Johannesburg and we made some small amounts of cash via these live appearances. Before too long, we were being played on the radio and at one point we were in the national top 20 charts. I made sure we collected all our press mentions, television clips and radio interviews, as I knew this would all come in handy one day.

It did.

At this time, I was introduced to a gentleman by the name of Ernest Adjovi. He was the founder of the KORA All Africa Music Awards. I lobbied him to see if he could allow Reign to perform at the 1999 KORA Music Awards. He checked out all our press and confirmed that we could. He wouldn't pay us but I didn't care; I just wanted the exposure. The KORA All Africa Music awards in 1999 were held in the glamorous holiday resort of Sun City –some two hours by car from Johannesburg – known as the Las Vegas of South Africa, with its casinos, golf courses and nightclubs. The KORA weekend was like an NBA All-Star weekend. All the celebrities were there and we were pumped up by getting the name Reign out there. Reign was going to perform in between the award ceremonies and, little did we know, Reign would be performing live in front of two of the most famous people in the world – Nelson Mandela and Michael Jackson.

Unfortunately for us, we lacked the discipline required to shine in the music business. I was not experienced in the industry and our three artists did not practise regularly. That night on stage was the biggest moment for Reign; either we went big or we went home. I was their coach and no matter how much I spoke to the guys about the importance of this occasion, my message did not seem to get through. They thought they were already superstars.

When the time came and Reign was introduced to the stage, the boys simply did not perform. Their performance was weak and lacklustre. I was sitting in the back and knew immediately that it was not going too well. I could feel it from the reaction of the crowd. They simply were not energised. I recall sitting in the audience and seeing Blondie trying to take off his shirt, only for his cuff to get stuck at his wrist. He sang the whole song with his shirt hanging down from this sleeve. No one had told him to take off his shirt and it was not part of the routine! We definitely did not get a standing ovation and I realised that we had missed our great opportunity to really shine. How could we fuck up so badly when we had Michael Jackson and Nelson Mandela sitting in the front row? Artists would die for an opportunity to perform in front of these two legends.

When it comes to stepping up to the mic,
you'd better be ready

I knew then that no matter how hard I had hustled to get the press, sell the CDs and promote the guys – their hearts were simply not in it. I could prepare them to the best of my ability but they were the ones who had to make the final performance. I learnt then that if your heart is not in it, no matter what you do, you won't be able to guarantee results. We might have been hanging out in Sun City and mingling with the crowd, but we had missed our chance to shine that night. I didn't show it, but it hurt me inside.

I persevered with Reign – after all, I had nothing else. I had put my heart and soul into this group. We did some more appearances and then had to cancel some as on occasions I simply could not find my guys. They would literally go off the radar. Takeshi had also stopped ordering from Japan. I had set our ambitions too high I guess and by now I was really getting stuck for cash. My rent was very late and every few days Avis, the company I had rented my car from, would be calling me.

"Mr Patel, you are way overdue on your car rental fees, when are you coming to pay us?"

My reply was always the same. "I am around the corner. I will be there shortly." Of course, I was never around the corner.

So there I was, running from creditors again, but I still had to figure out how I could promote my group. Early in May 1999, I was invited to the launch of the new BMW Z4 by one of Johannesburg's top model agents. It was just another party with celebrities, but I was there to promote Reign and to see if anyone wanted to book them for an appearance. I told Blondie to accompany me that night so that I could at least show that I had one of the group members with me. The event was a crowded affair. The new BMW itself was hidden under a black satin cover. Music was playing and the MC came on for the event. He did the formalities and invited the guest of honour to unveil the car. There were gasps everywhere. The Z4 was surely a stunner. This was its first launch into the South African market. I kept looking at the car. If only I could drive this home rather than the beaten-up Avis rental I had parked outside. Oh well. I just shrugged my shoulders in silence.

Then someone walked by me and I took my eyes away from the car for a minute. My breath was taken away.

There next to me was the most beautiful girl I had ever seen in my whole life – London, Hong Kong, Tokyo – I swear nothing I had ever seen before came close to this female standing near me. I was like that cartoon character where the eyes pop out of your skull and your tongue hangs on the floor.

My whole life changed that night. The girl who walked past me was to be my future wife and the mother of my kids.

Rene.

ARE YOU DESPERATE?

All that glitters is not gold.... Don't let desperation get the better of you and don't be fooled by sure things

ARE YOU WASTING YOUR TIME WITH TYRE KICKERS?

Know when to drop losers like a bad habit or take a different business direction

DO YOU BUILD NETWORKS AT EVERY LEVEL?

Build and nurture contacts of every type at every stage of your life journey. You will be able to leverage these blessings in disguise in the short and long term

CHAPTER 7

RENE

I was 33 years old and had been single most of my life. I had dated a couple of girls for a lengthy period, but most of my relationships were either one-night stands or two-week shenanigans. I had never felt close enough to anyone to make a commitment. Making the kind of money I was used to meant that girls were very easy to get and even easier to let go. I'm not proud of some of the things I did or how I treated women. I didn't do anything bad, though. I suppose I was a likeable rogue. With my lifestyle in London, then Hong Kong and Tokyo, there was never a shortage of women. That's one thing that I have never had a problem with. Women.

Luckily for me that night, Rene had come to the event with my friend, the model agency boss. We were then introduced, but I couldn't even come out with a simple, coherent 'hi'.

I was simply dumbstruck.

As the evening progressed and the formalities were over, I recall sitting at a booth table with me at one end, Rene at the other and about seven people between us. This was when I knew I had to get my charm on. I had to make my move, but I didn't want to make it too obvious. I was also not keen on the idea of walking blatantly to the other side of the booth, only to be rejected. Girls had done that to me before and I wasn't in the mood for that. The only way to engage was via the seven people sitting in between us. I had to join the group conversation, so I started asking loud questions and getting replies. I asked each person on the table for their reply to my specific question and finally we got to Rene. She *had* to answer me.

This went on for a while and the questions then started getting ever more directed toward Rene only. I think the others got the message that I wasn't keen to include them in my Q&A session. About 45 minutes later, one by one, they had vacated the table leaving me in the booth with Rene on the opposite side. Each time I asked a question, I would subtly shuffle my way to get closer to her.

"It's very loud in here! I need to get closer so I can hear you clearly," was my excuse. We spoke for a good 30 minutes and I then asked if she wanted to accompany Blondie and me to a club. I was surprised she said yes so quickly. Normally, you would have thought that a girl might have been worried about getting into a car with two male strangers, but I had assured her boss that I would take care of her and drop her off at the model house a couple of hours later. We drove (yes in my Avis car rental) to Johannesburg's hottest house music club, Foundation, in Rosebank. I bought the first round of drinks and we sat down and talked and talked. After a while I noticed that the drinks had finished. It got to a point where the lemon slice itself had disintegrated in the glass.

There was one major problem. I only had R10 in my pocket. That's the equivalent of $1! With that kind of money, I couldn't even buy the lemon, let alone the drink to go with it! I had no credit cards back then and as I wasn't prepared for meeting anyone like this, I had never bothered to ensure I had enough cash on me, particularly as most of the events I attended offered complimentary drinks.

I simply had no money to buy a second round of drinks. The only things I had in my pocket were the car keys and my house keys. I knew for sure that Blondie had nothing either. I couldn't get myself to ask Rene to buy the drinks because I was old school in that way. It just wasn't my style to have a girl pay for the drinks. I started squirming in my seat as I could see she wanted another drink and was waiting for me to ask – but how could I? I nervously took my gaze away from her and started looking around. To my pleasant surprise I spotted my friend DJ Pepsi at the bar. I jumped up and happily ran over to him to greet him. I tried to maintain my composure, but the words just came out of my mouth.

"Bro, I need an urgent favour please. I'm with a really *bad* chick ['bad' was slang for 'better than good'] and I need your help to buy me some drinks please. I just don't have any cash on me."

Pepsi knew me well. He was the ex-partner and the resident DJ of Club TKO and I knew he couldn't refuse me but my statement made him get cocky.

"Where is this chick? I want to see her," he said in an arrogant manner.

He was now in control of how my night might evolve.

"Look over there on the corner table." I didn't point with my fingers but more with my eyes. His jaw dropped.

"Gaddam, Pesh…*Wow. Wow. Wow.* That is one seriously hot chick."

I looked back at him and my eyes conveyed my reply. "I told you … so can you help me or not?"

He asked me what we were drinking and then ordered the drinks from the barmaid. He handed them over and gave me that look as if he was my dad and I was off to summer camp

"Enjoy, bro."

I thanked him several times but didn't want to waste time talking to him further as I saw that Rene was sitting alone. The last thing I needed was some other dude coming up to her to strike up a conversation. I had a confident feeling that she would have shut any other guys down, but I wasn't prepared to take any chances. I breathed a sigh of relief as I returned to the table. We raised our glasses and said, "Cheers."

Rene never guessed that I had no money in my pocket and that the car I was driving was an overdue Avis rental. She knew that I was in the music business and I had always made an effort to look as good as I could. My style and fashion were central to my soul. I had always been into style ever since I was a kid, so I certainly never came across as a broke hustler.

I did bullshit Rene. I said the group was doing well and that we had received good CD sales, blah blah blah ... It was all bullshit. I was not going to tell her right there and then that I didn't even have a pot to piss in. My life up until now had been full of ups and downs; I was just in a temporary down phase.

The following day, PK, another very close Nigerian friend of mine, was visiting me from London. I wanted to show off Rene to him, so we picked her up together to go for some coffee. I remember the look on his face when he saw her walking toward the car. At the coffee shop Rene excused herself to go to the bathroom and the minute she was out of sight PK grabbed my arm.

"This is your girl, Pesh ... I know it. This is your woman for life." In no uncertain terms, he was telling me that this was the girl I was going to marry.

My purpose for writing about Rene is not to take a 180 degree turn and turn this book into a soppy romantic novel.

The reason I talk about her is because the period after we met was the first time in my life that I had ever felt a sense of calm. She made me feel centred when everything around me was so erratic, *ad hoc* and unpredictable.

I continued with Reign for a few months, but was still dodging all the bills. Rene had won Miss Clifton that year, a popular Cape Town beach contest. She was a model, but, in essence, she was actually a true beauty queen. She had been in more than 30 competitions and had won many prizes. Even today she maintains her beauty, further confirmed by the fact that she has just been crowned as the official Mrs Africa 2016. Her prize for winning Miss Clifton was an all-expenses paid trip for two to Spain. She told me about it and said she would be taking her mother as her partner. I immediately stopped her.

"I don't think that's a very good idea. I think you need to take someone like me who knows Spain very well. I speak some of the language and your mum is going to go to sleep early every night, so who are you going to go out with at night to enjoy all that amazing Spanish nightlife?" Again my bullshit worked.

Rene agreed immediately and off we went to Spain a few months later. This was the first time in many years that I had been on holiday with a girl. What made it really great was that I actually felt something for this one. We had been together every day since we had met. Rene soon figured out that things for me with Reign were not working out, as she would be with me when I got calls from Avis who were still waiting for me to turn up and pay the overdue bills. The whole holiday was paid for by Rene, including flights, hotel and spending money. I had never experienced that before, because I had always been the one paying for everything in the past.

We had an amazing time in Spain and I decided that Rene would be my girlfriend. I shut down the other girls that I was seeing to fully focus on having this one girlfriend. She didn't come with me to the KORA Awards, but I gave her the bad news that the show was not a success for us. I was straight with her and told her that I was flogging a dead horse with Reign. I also confessed to her that I simply had no money.

Learn when to move on

Call it what you may, I believe Rene was my Lakshmi – in our Indian Hindu religion the goddess of wealth is called Lakshmi. Rene confirmed to me that there is such a thing as 'lady luck'. As soon as I got back from Sun City, I had a call from my brother in London. He was working at Motorola and he was calling to tell me that his ex-boss had now become the director of EMEA (Europe, Middle East and Africa) for a company called Harris Corporation, a large billion-dollar American defence and telecommunications equipment provider.

"They are looking to hire a guy for Africa," my brother told me. "They wanted me, but I've got something good with Motorola. Do you want me to recommend you?"

I let it sink in for a minute before I replied.

A job? *Me* in a *job*?

I was desperate and needed the money badly, so I told him, yes, I would be happy to look at it. I asked him how much they were paying, but he didn't know. All he told me was that he would get his ex-boss to call me.

"Be ready for the call!" he ordered.

It duly came through and within a week the director's deputy was on a plane to South Africa to meet the small local team and to interview me. It wasn't a formal interview and I figured that my brother had already put in a very good word for me. He was a star performer under his ex-boss so he sold me on a 'peas from the same pod' kind of basis. I put on my best suit and met the Harris manager at the Michelangelo Hotel in Sandton. That day my skills in conversation were on top form and we agreed that we would take things to the next step. I received a follow-up call from my brother's ex-boss.

"If you are as good as or better than your brother then you need to be on my team. I want a runner. I want someone who is willing to run around the whole of Africa getting us business."

My reply was very simple with a hint of arrogance. "I have run around the globe several times. This is nothing new."

My confident attitude disguised the fact that I didn't have a clue about the technology I was meant to be selling.

Within two weeks I had my first ever corporate job offer. It was a UK salary package, but I was to remain in South Africa, which worked out well as I was falling ever more deeply in love with Rene and I wanted to be with her all the time. I started work immediately and when I got my first pay cheque, it was more than the total I had made with Reign in the previous nine months. One of the first things I did was to go to Avis and pay my several months of overdue bills.

"I *was* always around the corner, but the corner was just far, far away," I told them in a joking but nervous manner.

I had hustled my way out of a dire position to claim a spot with a top US firm. The new millennium was the year I started my FIRST corporate hustle.

WHEN LOVE COMES CALLING DON'T HANG ABOUT
grab it with both hands and don't let go!

CHAPTER 8

GOING CORPORATE

I was 33 years old and joining Harris was the *first* corporate job that I had ever taken on. Since graduating in 1988 all I had ever done was hustle my own game. For 12 years I had survived by doing my own thing but right now I needed to cover my bills, which meant I had to take up the job. I was an employee of a major company and little did they know that the job was a lifeline I was very much in need of. I had a girlfriend and wanted to take care of her. Running in the music game simply did not pay me well. I knew I had done my best with Reign, but my best was not good enough to survive.

Joining Harris also gave me my first real taste of doing business in sub-Saharan Africa. I grew up in East Africa and had visited Nigeria a few times on holiday, but now I was set to explore the whole continent. I had no set mandate other than to get out there and meet as many Mobile Network Operators – MNOs – as I could and sell them microwave radio transmission equipment. The problem was that Harris was the 'Ferrari' of all microwave radio providers in the industry and I was tasked with selling some of the most expensive equipment to some of the poorest countries in the world – a challenge and a half for sure. Throughout my first year with Harris I was on a plane every two weeks. I visited many countries that year; just me, my business cards and a suitcase full of glossy corporate product brochures.

I didn't know a thing about technology. I had never been a technical guy, but there I was trying to sell some of the most complicated pieces of equipment to large well-established MNOs. I had to first engage with their technical departments by speaking with their chief technical officers (CTOs). These guys were engineers and they knew what they wanted, so there was not much bullshitting I could get away with. The product either met their specification or it did not. If they found something of interest they would then recommend that their company buy the product by moving the paperwork to their procurement department, which then had to ensure they had the budget to pay for the goods via their finance department. I had to learn the art of 'strategic selling'. I had to cover all the bases. This was not a world I was familiar with. My boardroom had always been massage parlours, coffee shops and evening events.

I remember visiting Rwanda for the first time to meet an MNO who clearly was not happy with the way they had been jerked around by Harris in the USA. I was the first Harris guy to visit them in person. They explained their problem and I told them I would do what I could to fix the problem. I knew if I could fix their problem with some old Harris radios they had, it would show me in good light, making it easier to ask them for a new order. Part of their network needed to be upgraded and when some of their radios didn't work it meant that they had network downtime. This led to big losses because they could not pass customers' calls through their channels.

"We paid top price for Harris!"

"You guys are the most bloody expensive equipment providers and we know the quality that Harris stands for, but for God's sake get your act together please!"

This was what I kept hearing over and over again from the CTO of the Rwandese MNO.

It was clearly a matter of stalled communications between them and someone in Harris USA. I called the Harris UK office, which then referred me to Harris USA. Somehow I managed to get through to the right person, a service engineer sitting in Redwood Shores, California. I told him I was with Harris Africa and needed an urgent favour. I spoke to him in my own way and that very night he sent me an email confirming what they would do to fix the problem. I told him we had a big order pending and if could they help me fix an old problem first, it could mean getting that big order next.

The next day I received some emails with some software configurations to pass on to the MNO CTO. I advised him with written instructions on what he needed to do to fix the old radio's software configuration. If he did that, then the radios would work. He called me back in the evening and told me everything seemed to be working. The very next month I received the order that had been stalled and I was also going to get my first commission pay cheque as well.

I then managed to pick up a nice $1.2 million order from a Tanzanian MNO a few months later. Again, that was a crazy deal. We were sitting in a hot steamy boardroom in Dar es Salaam and I had taken my installation team with me so we could address all the questions in person. I hated flying several times to see a customer over and over again, so I lobbied my manager to let me take a technician along to allow us to answer all the commercial and technical questions in one go. I wanted to close the deal, but it was a long, hot afternoon of tough negotiations. I had to keep leaving the room to call the UK office for price approvals as the CTO and the procurement head of the MNO were acting as if this was a sale in a market.

They did not stop haggling. They knew I wanted the deal so they tried pushing their luck as much as they could. We eventually sealed the deal and I even accompanied the administration lady to the computer to type up the purchase order. One of the things I learnt was that in Africa you have to get your order while you are there. The minute you leave, the order will be delayed. This was my first big deal for Harris and my commission on this deal was not a cent less than $25,000.

I did pretty well at Harris and pleasantly surprised myself by bringing in regular orders. I travelled right across Africa, but most of my orders came from Rwanda, Kenya, Mauritius, Ghana, Tanzania and Nigeria. The sales cycles, though, were very long and boring. I came to appreciate – and slowly started learning – the full meaning of the word 'patience'.

This job helped me to discover not only how Africa and its individual countries work, but also how big companies function. I started learning how corporations organise themselves in such a way that it becomes a maze for any outsider to figure out. You are constantly moving from one department to another. Working with MNOs in Africa was like putting together a jigsaw puzzle. You could see the individual pieces, but to get the picture you needed to put the pieces together in the right places. Bit by bit, I managed to work out their internal systems. I figured who it was I needed to speak with and what I needed to do. I made sure every time I visited an MNO I would first give the receptionist a warm greeting, then I would greet the CTO, followed by a stop at the procurement department to make myself known. I would follow this with greetings at the finance department. My most important alliances were the ladies who typed the purchase orders and the finance guys who issued the payments.

On its own merits Harris was a class above the competition, so I couldn't add much more to the product in terms of sales value. My only winning hand was my personality and really it was the only thing I had. I was a people person and having experienced different cultures I was quite adept at engaging quickly with people. I knew the questions to ask and I knew how to make people feel good. I made sure to always smile at the ladies in those office cubicles. I never bought them expensive gifts, because I never have and never will bribe anyone, but when you buy a 50-year-old woman a nice, cheap $20 bottle of perfume from the duty-free store it makes her day. I don't see that as a bribe. She was not in a position of authority and she did not control the purse strings of the company – rather, what I needed from her was *speed*.

I had been in some offices where an order was approved and then needed to be typed up. In some parts of Africa, if you were not there in person it could take weeks to get that order via email. I have been in many offices where I would literally stand next to the lady typists, laugh and joke with them and get them to finish faster, accompany them to the printer, print the purchase order, then walk with them to the finance department to get it signed and stamped. Sometimes this exercise would take hours, but I preferred to spend a few hours doing this rather than sit and wait for weeks, as would have been the case had I not been there in person.

This was one of my first lessons in doing business in Africa. You needed to be on the ground as much as possible. The moment you were on the plane back home, some Chinese dude would be flying in ready to hustle his own deal.

If you are not next to your customer ... someone else is!

Yes, this was also the first time I started feeling the pressure of the Chinese coming into Africa. Harris was expensive and my sales tactics were pretty transparent. I would ask the customer for the order based on the merit of the product and reputation that Harris had, but Africa was becoming fair game for the whole world. This was when the Chinese started arriving and they were offering very similar products at much cheaper prices. I had to increase my salesmanship because even though quality and 'Made in America' was a great label, when it came to corporate budgets – price was always a key factor. For the same money the customer spent on Harris products, they could buy double the quantity of microwave radios from the Chinese. Double the number of radios meant double the network coverage and double the potential customer subscriber base. We simply could not fight that price battle. I had to keep going and I started looking for new customers in markets the Chinese had not thought of. I knew Africa pretty well and I knew the terrain better than the Chinese, so for once I was faster than them in getting to new customers. Most of them couldn't even speak proper English.

A lot happened in the year 2000. Midway through the year Rene and I decided we wanted to live together, so we moved into a nice new place and I bought myself a decent car. Dealing with Avis was a thing of the past. By then I had decided that I had the best life partner I could have ever asked for and I was ready to settle down. I called Rene's father to ask him for his permission to marry his daughter. He agreed immediately and the very next day I went to the jewellery store and bought a beautiful diamond ring. That afternoon at home, at 5pm while we were watching the news, I proposed to Rene. It wasn't exactly a whirlwind, well-planned, or exquisite proposal ceremony but, hey, I was never one for emotions. I just wanted her to say yes. We planned to get married in December 2001. My life had become greatly improved and for once I could actually breathe. I was working, travelling, getting orders and being paid!

My salary was in pounds sterling, but my commission would be based in dollars as we sold equipment in that currency. My commission would then be converted into pounds to be paid on top of my salary. We started living a decent life in South Africa and Rene and I decided to buy our own house in Cape Town, a lovely three-bedroom detached house at the base of Table Mountain overlooking the city.

We started our wedding plans in June 2001. I remember walking at the V&A Mall in the Cape Town waterfront and, without any hesitation, buying my first Rolex watch. I remember looking at all the wedding venues – I wanted the best for us. We booked the Bay Hotel in Cape Town for our wedding and all was set for December 2001. This was going to be one of the biggest parties of the year. We actually had many weddings planned. Our civil official legal marriage date was planned for 19th December, after which we had a traditional Hindu wedding planned for 20th December. This was followed by a Christian church wedding and a reception on 22nd December. There were no conflicts with any of these, even though I had been born a Hindu and Rene a Christian. Religion never came into our discussion. We always went to both churches and temples.

I had to make my 50% wedding deposit payments in June 2001 when the South African rand was R10 to the pound sterling. Then South Africa went through some kind of crisis for the rest of the year and on the day of our wedding in December I had to settle the 50% payment balances. Luck shone down on me that day as the rand had gone to R20 to the pound sterling. I was paying all the bills out of my UK account, so I actually got my wedding for half price. That was an unpredictable hustle right there!

Throughout the latter half of 2001 my focus started shifting increasingly towards the wedding and I started to ignore parts of my Harris duties. I began to feel bored with the monotony and the long sales cycles. There was also the increased competition from the Chinese that I was constantly fighting. My frustrations had also started internally with the company. This was my first corporate role and I was working for an American company – I learnt how stubborn American companies can be. They were simply too slow to react to market conditions and with the incoming competition from the Chinese, they simply assumed a stance of arrogance that their product would sell because they were American. I kept telling them this was not the case in Africa and that we needed to be more flexible and provide innovative ways for our customers to continue doing business with us. I was fighting an uphill battle.

We were now reporting into the European head office based in Paris and I had frequent visits to that city (one of my favourites I must say). I noticed how caught up everyone was with internal affairs. Our corporate HQ was in the USA but our EMEA sales office was now based in Paris. There was always some kind of politics or drama going on between the two offices. Maybe it was French–American 'thing'. A case of two arrogant business styles does not make for quick results. I also noticed how the French were sticklers for timekeeping. By 5pm all the offices were dead. The French really valued their time out. They actually know how to enjoy life I guess.

I was in Paris on the day of 11th September 2001 when the world changed. I'm not even going to bother starting on my story but very simply I was at the airport about to take a flight to London when the towers came crashing down. I wasn't in the cosiest of places. All I remember was that it was a very messy and ugly day, but what pissed me off big time was that all the black cabs at Heathrow had jacked up their rates by 200% just so they could make money out of the situation with everyone just wanting to get home in the quickest manner possible.

In December 2001, God had *blessed* me again and brought me out of the wilderness for our wedding week. I could have not asked for a better setting and I was so happy that I could invite my friends from all over the world to come and celebrate a week of festivities. I had some money now and I made sure I had one of the best weddings ever. As a man, I can tell you the joy we men have when we know 'we have taken care of things'.

Over 2002 I continued with Harris and we had a new director who was an American Iranian and one of the toughest guys I had ever met. A seasoned sales pro. By now I had started to think about other things and this was made all too clear by my dwindling performance at Harris. As I had some money, I thought I could start doing other things and that's when one of my best friends from London and I spoke about setting up a *proper* clothing store in Johannesburg. He would manage it and I would fund it as I still had my day job. I didn't see how we could lose, because my friend was very experienced in clothing while I had a love for style and had done clothing before in Johannesburg; plus, I still had all my old fashion and music contacts in place.

We located a space and my friend flew down and we started putting things together. I gave him the funds to go back to London to purchase our first collection of clothing. He did a great job as he had a great eye for style. His name was Bosun Eugene Thomas – we called him Bosco – and he was a rare breed of a guy. The guy had so much style and flavour that celebrities themselves would look at him and acknowledge his presence. That's how cool he was.

In late 2002, now with a heavily pregnant wife, we opened a store in Rosebank in Johannesburg that we called 'Wardrobe' and without much fanfare we started business. Our store was way ahead of its time for South Africa. It was clean, minimalistic and had the hottest music playing, with the bonus that our staff were some of the prettiest girls you could imagine. We were portraying our lifestyle. Unfortunately for us, the local crowd did not see it that way. This was when I understood how the power of big business and how South Africa really worked. People back then were simply not into style. Over the years I have seen South Africans develop a sense of style, but in the early 2000s I am sorry to say South Africa was quite simply not a stylish place. It was not like London or Paris. South Africa was never famous for its fashion styles, so who were we to change that?

We had our first child, our daughter Shanti, in January 2003.

I was now a father and I couldn't have been happier. I had managed to come through my struggles to find a good wife and now I was also blessed with a daughter. We were still staying in Cape Town, but every week I was in Johannesburg, not only for Wardrobe but also still working at Harris. I was juggling a lot of things, but I wanted to really make Wardrobe a success. I invested more of my savings for us to open a second store at Southgate Mall, which was on the south side of Johannesburg. By late 2003 we had three stores in Johannesburg, but I realised it was a case of over-expansion and that apart the odd eccentric fashionistas, we did not have a dedicated following of loyal customers. We tried to hold events and private shows and people would come to show us support, praise our styles, ask us to give clothes for music videos and so on, but none of them ever put their hands in their pockets to actually *buy* something. Customers would end up buying clothes at major department stores, because in South Africa most people live on credit. In-store credit was easily accessible, so why would they pay a few thousand South African rand outright for a jacket when they could buy a jacket on credit at a major department store and pay it off month by month? We tried speaking to credit providers to enable us to offer in-store credit but they simply shut us down. As I have said, the power of big business was something I had started to learn about.

Bosco himself was not a businessman and I had to try focus as much as I could on Harris. It was my lifeline, my monthly pay cheque. I had to leave the management of Wardrobe to him. We were not selling enough clothes to cover all our expenses and I felt myself slipping again as now both Wardrobe and my Harris jobs were suffering simply because I was not focused on doing either of these things well. I wanted to be the master *and* the jack of all trades.

Unfortunately, Bosco was also a heavy weed smoker and he couldn't go a day without lighting up a blunt. I saw how this affected his productivity and we started feeling the pain of running a business. I had invested close to ZAR700,000 in Wardrobe but simply could not handle all the pressure alone. I also had a monster sales boss from Harris breathing down my neck daily looking for his sales figures, which meant I had to keep giving excuses as to why the sales were so slow. To be honest, I never really had the passion and love for Harris. Selling network equipment to a bunch of boring tech guys was not the real me. Yes, I did well for a while and it was fun in the beginning because of the travel and the excitement of doing the deals, but the real essence always comes through sooner or later. In reality, I was more in love with the idea of building a clothing business than I was with selling network equipment. However, clothing did not pay and with a child and a new house, I had to keep the money rolling in at all costs.

Passion does not equal profit

In November 2003, it all finally came to an end when I had to visit San Francisco for a Harris team meeting. Before leaving, I had advised Bosco that I simply could not continue bankrolling the Wardrobe project and there were not enough sales coming in to cover all the expenses, including his upkeep. Bosco knew I was right and that things were tough, so he agreed to start closing down the main store (we managed to close down the other two within a matter of months). We told the landlords that we could not continue because they had lied to us about the foot-traffic statistics. This was our way out of the lease agreement. Luckily for us, they let us off the hook and we avoided all the legal implications of breaking our tenancy.

Bosco had decided to move to Nigeria to see what he could do there with Wardrobe. I could not afford to have him stay in South Africa while I had all these other bills to pay so by November 2003 we had closed the shops. It was another disappointment on a long list of failed accomplishments. Then the double whammy came during my trip to San Francisco when after three days of excellent team meetings, great dinners and great conversations my boss called me into the room and dropped the big one.

"Due to the downturn in the business we are going to close down the South Africa office and hence we will be terminating your position immediately. We will focus on Nigeria only and we will run that out of the USA for now."

My heart sank.

This was the first corporate job I'd had and it was also the first time someone had terminated me. I didn't take it well. I was gutted. That night we had all planned to go out for dinner but I was so distraught that, as we left the hotel driveway, I told the driver to stop and let me out. I told the group I wasn't feeling well. I just wanted to be alone and to go home to be with my young family. I returned back to South Africa dumbfounded. Here I was now with no job. Harris did not even give me a payoff. They just terminated me there and then. I had already bought a new second home in Johannesburg, Rene was not working and my daughter was about to turn one. It was not exactly the situation I had planned.

But I had been here before.

I simply relied on the fact that none of this was new to me. I had been worse off in the past and at least I had some money now to cover our expenses for a few months. I had to think rationally, though. I did not have any fresh business ideas, nor did I have any spare cash to invest in anything and now I had a family and two mortgages to pay. I told my brother what had happened. He was still with Motorola and he started making enquiries on my behalf. He told me there might be a position within Motorola Africa and he would let me know. He passed me the number of the human resources (HR) manager at Motorola South Africa and I managed to get hold of him, tactfully informing him who my brother was. The HR manager told me that they did have a headcount approved for a business development manager for Africa and I sent in my CV.

He called me a week later and told me he would push for me to meet with the country manager in charge of the hiring. By now this was early December and in South Africa the main holiday season had begun, because everyone takes their long annual holidays from mid-December to mid-January. When the new year of 2004 arrived, I continued pushing the Motorola HR manager to see if anything had materialised for me to meet with the country manager.

No news.

I did not hear back from Motorola until mid-February and by now I was getting nervous as I had not bothered to look for any other work. I had not even submitted my CV to any recruitment companies. I was genuinely worried, not only because I hadn't secured a job but also because I had just found out that my wife was pregnant again with our second child, due in September

2004. I waited and waited and finally got the call back from the Motorola HR manager that the country manager was now ready to meet with me. At the meeting we spent one hour talking and I spoke about my Harris experience, plus my days as a Hong Kong phone trader when the only phones I ever sold were Motorola. I told him that for me dealing in Africa was not an issue as I had been doing it for a number of years.

Motorola South Africa was the African HQ for Motorola Inc. The business was split between South Africa and then the Rest of Africa (ROA). The South African team was comprised of about 50 people and the ROA team was basically zero. The management had received HQ approval for them to employ a business development manager for the ROA region. They could have recruited a local South African for the job but I don't think they had any takers. Surprisingly, South Africans at that time did not understand Africa (in a way they still don't). There was an air of arrogance with them when it came to dealing with the rest of Africa. I think the manager realised that he simply did not have the right person in his local team to do the job. Without sounding obnoxious, I told the manager that if they wanted to go hunting, they needed to go with a hunter and that was exactly what I was – a hunter!

I was very forward with the manager and we got along very well at the meeting. When I left I had the feeling that all was going to be well. The very next week I received my job offer letter. I was to be the new business development manager for Motorola Africa. My salary was decent, but it was paid in South African rand and this was my start of being localised. I didn't need a work permit as I already had permanent resident status due to being married to a South African. Both Rene and

I breathed a sigh of relief. I had a new job.

I swore to myself in silence, 'Don't fuck this up.'

I knew in my heart that Motorola could not have found a more suitable person than me for the role. I knew I would be much happier at Motorola than I was at Harris for a few reasons:

a. I had a head start on most people with my African telecom arena knowledge

b. I was now selling consumer products and not B2B products

c. I could get involved in marketing

My first day at Motorola was in April 2004. In their previous financial year, they had completed around 40,000 phone-unit sales in ROA. We all agreed that it was a dismally low number for a great brand like Motorola. It wasn't the products at fault, though; it was the fact that they had never had the right guys in place who could actually sell the products. A week after I had joined we were whisked away to a three-day team event in Sun City. I was excited because it was my first chance to meet the rest of the team, interact with them and start developing relationships. I had my time slot to present my Rest of Africa forecast, which was a few minutes right at the end of the other presentations. None of the crowd was in the least bit interested in what I had to say about our ROA goals; some of them were busy chatting during my presentation. I knew they didn't give a shit about whatever I was saying as they were far too caught up with the South African part of the business. Motorola in South Africa got its orders solely from the local South African MNOs. During my presentation to the 25 people in the room,

I explained my immediate targets for the next six months and when I was asked what number of phones I had planned to sell, I simply blurted out,

"50,000 units is my target."

The whole room then erupted in laughter. Even my boss laughed at me.

"We did 40,000 all of last year so how are you going to manage to do 50,000 in the next six months? Where are you going to get these numbers from?"

I looked at him straight in the eye and I then looked at the rest of the room. "I will get them. I *will* get them."

I had set myself a task to bring in the numbers or risk being majorly embarrassed, not only with my boss, but also with the other 25 South Africans. I knew they looked on me as an outsider as I was one of only two non-South Africans working in that office. At the end of the day, one thing I have always realised being in South Africa is that you can be friends, you can hang out, you can work together, but if you are not South African – you are simply not South African. Period.

I wanted to prove a point and by hook or crook I was going to make my numbers.

I was ready for the Moto hustle.

STAY CLOSE TO YOUR MARKETS FROM THE GROUND UP!

YOU DON'T NEED TO KNOW EVERYTHING
but you need to be prepared to do everything

CHAPTER 9

THE MOTO HUSTLE

B eing the original Motorola guy from way back in 1989, I was kind of re-entering the business of mobile devices after a 10-year absence *and* to top that I was entering with a brand that I knew very well. After my Hong Kong trading and the Harris Africa episodes, I was merging my two experiences to ensure Motorola was going to succeed in Africa. I also now had the support of a massive company behind me, which, of course, made things a bit easier. In reality, I had to fight to gain the respect of my South African colleagues. I was the underdog from day one.

I fell in love with my Motorola role very quickly. I never loved Harris the way I loved working at Motorola. There was just something about Motorola that just got me going. Even to this day, no other phone company has come close to the originality of Motorola. They simply made the best-designed phones.

My targets were quarterly, so there was no time to waste. I immediately went about my business. My manner and style were very unconventional to the South African office crowd. I had my small assigned cubicle but I have always been a naturally loud talker. My exuberance showed, especially when I was cold calling customers. I was calling all my old MNO contacts from the Harris days and our conversations were always loud, mainly because the quality of the phone connection was so poor. I started arranging meetings and forced my boss to approve all my travel plans. I had to hit the road.

The Motorola South Africa team did not understand that Africa was, and still is, very fragmented. There were no formal rules on distribution. The electronics and phone distribution market in Africa has traditionally been controlled by the Indian traders – these were the guys I needed to engage with as they would be able to get my products into the distribution channels and finally onto the shelves of independent retail stores. These seasoned Indian traders were not used to dealing with corporate types and, vice versa, the corporates did not understand these Indian traders – how they thought and how they acted. My job was to marry the two extremes. It was the traders that I had to get on my side if I was to move the numbers. I entered a world I knew well, but which I had to slowly sell internally to an organisation that simply did not understand the 'trader' mentality.

As I began to settle in, I also started to become more vocal in the office, especially at our Monday morning team meetings. Whenever I laid out my plan for achieving the numbers, there would be some smartass comment from the team on the impossibility of me achieving them. My response was always, "Hey, you want the numbers? Then you let me do things my way!"

Yes, it was aggressive and, yes, it pissed off some of the local crowd, but, honestly, making new friends was the last thing on my mind – I wanted to make the numbers. There were constant internal battles at Motorola. Everyone wanted a piece of the marketing budget pie. I kept lobbying for my own marketing funds, specifically for ROA, but I was constantly shut down. There was one budget for the whole of Africa and South Africa was used to taking 100% of that budget. Now they had to share it with the ROA region and with me, a solo guy with no numbers under my belt. I was negotiating from a very weak position.

I knew the *only* way to convince the management to allocate marketing funds to Africa was by bringing in some orders. Talk was cheap – I had to make some moves. I knew that the Indian traders couldn't give a fuck about marketing; they just wanted the best prices, so I called around and, using the power of the Motorola brand name, I finally managed to sign up some traders, securing the first few purchase orders. I would only show one order to Motorola, though. The rest of the orders I kept in my back pocket. When it came to our Monday morning meetings the shouting match would erupt again due to everyone arguing for a piece of the marketing budget. This would be when I told them about the other orders I *could* get *if* I had a slice of the marketing budget.

"If I was to get $X in marketing, I can guarantee that I can get more orders within the next 48 hours."

Little did they know that I already had the orders in my back pocket. They had no choice but to approve my request and within a few hours I would simply present my orders to the firm. The Motorola office needed my numbers and I needed the marketing budget. With this budget I could better promote the products and, in doing so, increase the rate of stock turnover of the phone inventory. This would then lead to more orders to replenish stocks. In this game it was all about 'sell through'. You were only as good as your last order. To everyone's surprise, within six months I had hit my 50,000-unit target. I became quite vocal and many will tell you there were numerous shouting matches in the office, but really, I was simply fighting for my ROA market. I wanted my area to receive more recognition as well as more investment. There were 25 people chasing two MNO carrier accounts in one country (South Africa), while I was this solo guy chasing business from 50 African countries. It just did not make sense to me.

Then I did a deal that changed the game. I reached out to the CEO of Safaricom Kenya, Michael Joseph, a man known to be direct and ruthless. I managed to get an appointment with him to discuss a large order, – 100,000 phones in one shot. One single order. This order was worth a cool $5 million. It could be the biggest single order for Motorola from the African region. If this order had been from an Indian trader then I'm sure the eyebrows would have been raised and there would be suspicions all round, especially from the already antagonistic South African co-workers. The Indian traders did not command the respect that an MNO commanded.

After I returned from Kenya nothing much happened, but I remember the day something *did* happen. My boss knew that we had submitted our bid to Safaricom a few weeks previously. He knew I was working on it, but he wasn't on my case every minute of the day asking me about it. We had left it as a longshot anyway.

In the afternoon, I called Michael Joseph to ask him about the progress of the order and he told me the order was being processed. I then called the Safaricom order processing department. They told me that Michael Joseph had signed off the order and that they would be faxing it over soon. In the Motorola office, we had a big fax machine that was openly accessible to everyone. I did not fancy someone else picking up the fax and shouting about it around the office. I didn't want anyone interfering with my business, so that afternoon I loitered around the fax machine for one hour or so waiting for the order. I was teased a bit as other random faxes were coming in but none of them were mine from Safaricom.

When it finally came through, I saw the Safaricom letterhead and my excitement rose. I didn't even read it, but rather quickly ran back to my cubicle to sit down and go through it in detail. I must have read the order 10 times, praying that there were no fuck-ups on the wording or the numbering. It was all 100% correct as I had expected. I then took a deep breath and confidently walked down the long hallway to my boss's office on the other side of the building. He maintained an open-door policy, so I knocked and simply walked in. Saying nothing I handed him the paper.

"You ready? Look at this."

He nearly fell of his chair.

The smile on his face was the biggest I had ever seen. I knew I had made his day, his week, his quarter and his year. What made it even sweeter was that the order came from one of Africa's most respected network operators. The word had spread by that afternoon and my boss immediately called the UK and USA to give them the good news. This is when I started earning the respect of my colleagues. This is when my name within Motorola started to grow.

Within the first year I had fully settled in. The initial animosity that I had faced with some of the South African office staff had completely disappeared. I had now started to develop some really good relationships with my colleagues and we had become one big happy family. Yes, we always had our heated debates, but my colleagues were the most loving and supportive people and by now they were all fully behind my vision to make Motorola the number one brand in Africa.

On 8th September 2004, God gave me my second child – another daughter, Omala. I remember being at the hospital to welcome her into this world, but despite being so excited, I went straight back to my office as my customers were waiting for me to send information. My dedication to Motorola could not be questioned.

When you love what you do it shows

The business grew from there. The first year was amazing and the second year was even bigger. Motorola had also started bringing out some very cool products and there was a sense that this giant was now coming back to claim its rightful throne from Nokia, our biggest competition. My task was to ensure we grew our sales numbers and, more so, that we grew our presence on the continent by constantly expanding into new markets. Every few days, I was flying all over Africa. With my constant travels and ever-increasing order book, by mid-2005 I was in full control. I knew exactly what I was doing and everything worked like clockwork. Funnily enough, the last time I had felt like that was when I had the phone business in the early 1990s in Hong Kong. I guess God gives us our moments to shine and we need to make the most of it. The challenge is to know when you are on a roll and to make it work. I was ambitious and wanted to move up the ranks, but to what? I was the only guy in my immediate team.

The more I investigated the business, the more I learnt that the *real* action for phone distribution was actually in Dubai. The city was full of traders and the centre of the global phone trading activity. Millions of phones were moving in and out of Dubai every day. One day, out of the blue, I received a call. My receptionist informed me that there was a guy from Dubai who wanted to talk to the head of the Africa market. The Motorola receptionists were great and I always treated them with love and respect. I also wanted to ensure that any cold calls from anywhere would come to me first.

The guy on the line introduced himself and went straight to the point. He was looking for 20,000 phones as a one-time order, but he was not a distributor. He asked me what I could do to help him. I told him our rules, that he could only buy stock via my authorised distributor in South Africa. Within a few days, the order had come in through this distributor. Another big win for me.

The Dubai buyer then invited me to Dubai. I managed to convince my boss that I needed approval to travel to Dubai to meet with one of the biggest trading houses. Every Dubai trader was dumping grey stock in Africa (also known as parallel imports), so why could we not supply them with *bona fide* authorised stock at the same prices and turn their 'grey parallel' business into an official one? My boss agreed and within a week or so I was in Dubai.

It was mid-2005 and this was the first time I had ever been to the Middle East. I was immediately fascinated by the place. I spent three days with the Indian traders and it brought back memories of when I was dealing with the Chinese. No formal offices and meetings over dinner in Indian Mujrah dance clubs. These clubs were like strip joints, but the dancers were fully clothed and danced to Bollywood hits. The crowd would exchange cash for white cards and whichever dancer enticed them the most, they would simply shower with these white cards. The better the dancer, the more cards she was showered with. I had never seen that before, but it was certainly very funny. The traders' world was completely different from the Motorola corporate world. It was something that I knew well and by now I could easily switch between my two worlds of traders in dens and suited guys in shiny offices. I was a chameleon; I adapted my personality, my poise, my mannerism and my gestures according to my environment.

I came back from Dubai with a massive sales order forecast. I showed my boss and told him that we needed to sign these guys directly as we couldn't keep dealing via our third party local distributor; besides the Dubai buyers had loads of cash but wanted to be safe and pay Motorola directly. My boss was in two minds. He had to be conscious of the fact that we had a Motorola Dubai office as well which would naturally want to claim these numbers as its own. Technically, even if the stocks had been for Africa, the purchase order had been generated in Dubai and Motorola Dubai would therefore want to claim its numbers on any orders generated in its territory. The other half of his mind was that the Africa office needed to increase its numbers. The local South African market was simply not reliable, especially as we only had two customers, the two major MNOs, and they would never give orders on time.

My rationale to my boss was simple. "The guys at Motorola Dubai are simply not addressing these trader guys. These traders supply to Africa and they need support for their sell through marketing activities in Africa. We can't allow the

Motorola Dubai office to claim these numbers while we have to spend marketing money in Africa from our budget."

In my mind, I was not prepared to hand over the biggest Dubai traders to another office. My buyer had told me that they had called Motorola Dubai first, but no one had got back to them.

"Tough shit."

I had to make a plan to get a further buy-in, not only from my boss, but also the guys above him. We were in sensitive territory. The different Motorola offices were all very protective of their own patches.

At the end of each quarter there would be a frenzy to secure purchase orders from customers. Being a US company, everyone and everything was programmed to work in quarters and come the last day of the quarter all hell broke loose in the office as other sales guys' orders were delayed, never came in or were simply bullshitted. Some of the guys in the South African team sounded like broken records.

"The order is coming. The order is coming ..." Their orders never came for months.

I knew this issue would arise, so my plan was to get some orders from my Indian traders in Africa and simply hold them until the very last day of the quarter. It was my negotiating tool and the only one I really had. It was the ace up my sleeve. I used this tactic regularly, not only for my own platform, but also to bail out the South African numbers due to their own order shortfalls. To really change the game further, I also took orders from Dubai without anyone knowing. I simply asked my Dubai buyer to send me a draft purchase order via our local authorised distributor. I wanted to show this to my boss, because I knew once he saw an official draft order he would do whatever he could to make it happen.

I knew he was under pressure as his boss was the biggest bully around and everyone was shit scared of him. Even I was a bit intimidated by the higher echelons of Motorola but, at the end of the day, the only thing these guys wanted was the numbers so they could look good in front of their bosses. In Motorola, everyone was your best friend on the last day of the quarter, but on the first day of the new quarter – no one remembered shit! I didn't even get a thank you from the upper bosses, but I was cool with that. As long as my shit got approved I was OK.

I had been in Motorola for 18 months and in that time I was promoted from business development manager to director of sales, ROA. My numbers were simply astonishing, even to me. In 18 months I had clocked close to $50 million in revenues for Motorola and this was because I was always near or in my markets. I was travelling every week into markets like Kenya, Uganda, Tanzania, Zambia, Mauritius, South Africa and parts of West Africa. I saw very little of my family back then. On the marketing side, I had teamed up with some very creative independent agencies. Motorola Africa gave a massive chunk of its budget to big firms like Ogilvy South Africa. I simply did not have time to sit with a South African advertising agency that did not have a clue about the ROA, so I went out on my own and located smaller local agencies in different countries. They were quicker, cheaper and more in tune with their markets. The coolest project we did was with Channel O, an African music television offering. We conceptualised, produced and marketed a 13-episode lifestyle music series, filmed in 13 different African cities. It was *the* show that would get us pan-African coverage for the brand and, in a way, bring Africa together. I did this with an old contact of mine, Nicolas Regisford.

Nicolas and I had met via Rene. When Rene moved to Johannesburg as a model she was appointed as a gladiator on *MTN Gladiators*, the famous weekly show in which contestants battle against gladiators. She was known as Lightning and even had her own doll. One of her colleagues was a girl called DT and her boyfriend at that time was this guy, Nicolas Regisford.

By late 2005 I was starting to spend increasing amounts of time in Dubai, because by now approvals were being granted for me to explore the massive trading channels from Dubai to Africa. I figured that if Africans got on planes and packed their suitcases full of phones, then why couldn't we supply to those same Africans from our distributors' Dubai warehouses? To make it easier, each time the Africans came to Dubai to buy our Motorola phones, they would also get a chunk of marketing promotional material like t-shirts, pens and posters. Our aim was to ship them a 'business in a box' solution.

I developed a very good working relationship with my buyer in Dubai. I just loved their style of doing business. Everything was done as per their word and there were never any issues when it came to the payments they had to make to Motorola. They were always on time. Every time. They were a tight Nepalese Indian family business and hours spent at their office would mean big orders for me. They were very religious and had the kind of office in which you took off your shoes, were fed snacks, drinks, cups of masala chai and spent hours discussing everything. They had created a massive trading empire spanning many countries and had offices all over the world. I was spending more and more time in meetings with them and they were giving me more and more orders for Motorola phones.

The main buyer also invited me to his wedding in Nepal and a group of us had planned to go. I had never been to Nepal and was dying to see Mount Everest in the Himalayas. A couple of nights before we left for Nepal, we were in a Dubai nightclub when my phone rang. It was Bosco from Nigeria. I hadn't spoken to him in a few months and was so happy to hear from him. I ran out of the club because it was so loud inside and I wanted a proper chat with him. Regardless of what had happened with Wardrobe, Bosco was like my younger brother. I had his back and I knew he had my back.

"Pesh, what's crackin'?"

"Bro, I'm in Dubai, heading to Nepal for a wedding."

"Ahh, you are chopping life." In the Nigerian pidgin dialect this means you are 'eating life' as in enjoying life.

"Somebody's gotta do it." I said, jokingly.

"Listen, Pesh. You still have all my stuff in your garage back in South Africa?"

Bosco had left most of his possessions, clothes and all his vinyl record collection with me before he had left for Nigeria because he had no fixed abode there. I had agreed to hold his things in my garage until he got settled.

"Do me a favour, Pesh. When you get back to South Africa, please go through my clothes and take out all the crap. Just keep what you think is the good stuff and the rest just give to charity, but don't get rid of my vinyl records."

"Yeah, sure, bro, no problem. Don't worry about that."

"Let's speak soon then," he replied.

We exchanged a few more pleasantries, I dropped the call and went back inside the club to continue chatting with my buyer and his team.

I remember I was then staying at the Park Hyatt Hotel at Dubai Creek. The following day in the early evening, I got a call from PK, my friend in Nigeria.

"Pesh, has anyone called you from Nigeria?"

"No, why?"

"Pesh. I'm sorry to tell you this but ... Bosco is DEAD!"

Bosco is dead.

Bosco is dead.

Bosco is *dead*?

I was in a daze. I had only spoken to Bosco less than 24 hours earlier. He had asked me to take care of his stuff and give some of it away to charity. Did he know then about his next few hours? Did he know he was about to leave this earth and was his call to me some kind of cryptic message?

I asked PK what had happened and he told me that Bosco had messaged him that he was going to go for a swim and would then meet him later for a drink.

"God willing," were Bosco's final words to PK.

He had decided to go for an afternoon swim in the pool in his apartment complex. Usually there was a lifeguard there but for some reason that day the lifeguard had not turned up to work. Bosco's body was found floating in the pool with a gash to his head. It was decided that he had been swimming and must have bumped his head somewhere in the pool, rendering him unconscious so that he drowned. I was in utter shock. In my 38 years I had never lost anyone close to me. It was the first time that someone so close to me had died.

After the call with PK, I sat on the edge of my bed trembling!

I then immediately called Deji, who only confirmed to me that Bosco was gone. I was numbed with shock. I slowly walked out of my room to my buyer's room. As I walked up to his hotel door, all I could hear was laughter, loud voices and Indian music. The door was slightly open, so I walked in and broke the bad news to all of them. The music was turned off immediately. They did not know who Bosco was, but they immediately felt my pain. I then frantically started calling round. I wanted to cancel the Nepal wedding trip because I needed to go to Nigeria immediately. There was nowhere else I wanted to be in the world, other than with my friends in Nigeria to really find out what happened and, more so, how the fuck this could have happened.

I called the Nigerian Embassy in Abu Dhabi to see if I could have an emergency visa – the phone just rang and rang – no answer. The only way I could enter Nigeria was with a visa but it was seemingly impossible to get one. This was one of the difficulties of moving around in Africa. You couldn't just get up and go to Nigeria. It had to be arranged in advance and, of course, I had not planned for this to happen.

I had two types of pain that day. The heartbreak pain of losing Bosco and the frustrating pain of knowing I could not go to see him off at his funeral. My buyers that night took us all out for dinner and tried their best to cheer me up, but all I could do was cry. I cried in the car, I cried at the dinner table and I also went to the bathroom of the restaurant to cry alone. The next day we all departed for Nepal and for the next four days I went through the most excruciating pain. Of course, I had to appear happy for my buyer's wedding, but I could not get the loss of Bosco out of my mind.

The Nepalese are some of the most hospitable people I have ever met. They showered me with garlands as soon as we landed at the airport. It was a big Hindu wedding with lots of singing, dancing and eating and I was their VIP guest. Let's not forget, with my constant supplies to them of Motorola phones, they had made *a lot* of money on the resales and as I was the source of that increased income they treated me with a huge amount of respect. I smiled as much I could, but in my heart, my soul and my mind all I could think about was my brother Bosco. I cried in secret throughout the entire four days.

When I finally got back to South Africa I asked my boss's approval to make a private trip to Nigeria to pay my last respects to Bosco. By the time my visa came through it was January 2006. Bosco had already been buried, so when I arrived in Lagos the first thing I did was to go straight to his grave. It was there that I completely broke down. My Nigerian brothers were all there to comfort me. We had all grieved in our own way. I will never ever forget my Nigerian brothers. The passing of Bosco made our bond stronger and to this day, even though I may not speak to them every day, these guys are my brothers for life.

Bosco was only 33 when he died. They say God takes his favourite children away at an early age because he misses them too much. Well, he is now with God. May his gentle soul forever rest in eternal peace.

INNOVATE TO ACCELERATE
nothing happens until you move!

CHAPTER 10

DUBAI BLING

After I returned from paying my respects to Bosco in Lagos I moved into fifth gear at work. I had to hustle my move to Dubai. I had actually done so well up until then in that I had created a new role for myself. I had the full support of my boss and if he didn't agree, he didn't get the numbers. That was the bottom line. I had figured these corporate guys by now.

By March 2006 I received final confirmation that Motorola would be moving my family and me to Dubai to head up the Africa and Middle East trader channels. In formal terms, I was to be the director of sales for the Middle East and Africa region. Not only would I continue to report into the African office, but now I also had to co-report to the Motorola Middle East management. I had been in that office a few times and it was very obvious that I was not wanted there. I was like an outsider encroaching on their treasured territory. I was disrupting their normal way of doing business, but they couldn't do shit about it because the approvals had come from way above. It goes to show that in the corporate world it's all about the numbers. Get the numbers and you call the shots. To a certain degree that is. Motorola had become too dependent on me and I was always the go-to guy when anyone needed the numbers topping up. It felt quite good to be in a position of some kind of power and, despite our regular fights and debates, not once did I consider moving to another brand. My heart was firmly entrenched and intertwined with Motorola. I loved the brand

and was passionate about what I was doing. I guess that's why I was so successful.

We finally moved to Dubai in June 2006 and Motorola offered me a package that was simply out of this world *ridiculous*. Just three years before I had been unemployed and now, within a short space of time, I had become their director of sales for the whole continent of Africa and the Middle East region. The package itself included full relocation for my family, a great housing allowance, car allowance, school fees and my wife even got a hardship allowance. Hardship in Dubai? Get the fuck outta here!

We settled into a beautiful Dubai marina apartment and as I had some cash, it wasn't long before I had secured a couple of nice cars for us and started mingling into the social scene. Dubai was in its heyday in 2006. The city was booming and the skylines were full of cranes. There was a lot going on and champagne-fuelled parties were the norm virtually every night. My orders were now flowing in regularly from my big Dubai buyers and I was also frequenting my travel across Africa.

My role in South Africa had become vacant and I suggested to my manager that my brother move over from the Motorola radio solutions division to the devices sector. It was funny because he was the one who had hooked me up in the first place and now there I was, hooking him up. We did the appropriate checks around conflicts of interest and the move was approved. My brother took over my African customers, while I focused on the Dubai channels. This raised eyebrows with certain people within Motorola – how can two brothers control the Dubai and Africa business?

Life in Dubai was amazing. It was like being in la-la land and everything was so smooth. I was in the zone, I was in the flow and I wanted to maximise the moment.

The bling bling is better with the ching ching

I got myself into the Dubai property market. It was a frenzy back then and I wanted in. It seemed everyone doing it was making some nice cash. I approached my bank into which my salary was deposited to check if I was eligible for a mortgage as I was now an official resident of Dubai. I was renting a nice apartment already that was paid for by Motorola's allowance, so I wanted to buy a separate property for investment purposes. The bank, knowing that I was employed by Motorola, a well-known and credible company, immediately offered me a mortgage with a 20% down payment only. That was all I had to put down to get a place. I showed the bank that I had the money and within a week I had a mortgage pre-approval document and off I went property hunting.

I had to get something that was ready and rentable as most of the Dubai developments at that time were just plans on paper. As a result, many developers were selling apartments that were going to be ready in two–three years' time, but this was not feasible for me because I needed rental income to cover my mortgage payments. I secured a two-bedroom apartment in the Greens district of Dubai, one that already had a tenant. It was so easy. The rental itself covered the mortgage and left me with some change. 'Not bad.' I thought. Now what else could I do?

Back in 2006 I figured out that Dubai did not even have a

credit bureau. There was no form of computer records as there were in the US or UK to allow people to check their credit history and current borrowings, so I decided to take a chance and cheekily approached another bank for a mortgage. I think my Motorola credentials and my business card really helped me and I was welcomed with open arms. Within two weeks I had *another* mortgage offer from another bank. I put down 20% once more and bought myself a second apartment, which was also tenanted.

These were not expensive places. No one is talking about Donald Trump's penthouse apartments here. These were simple one or two-bedroom small apartments in decent areas that were popular with the expatriate communities. None of the banks ever bothered to ask me if I had any other borrowings. They didn't ask, so I didn't tell.

In my first year in Dubai, by working with several different banks I had accumulated a total of seven apartments simply by going from one bank to another. Some of them even gave me 95% mortgages so my deposit amounts were not high. They all pushed me to deposit my Motorola salary into their bank accounts, but this was simply not feasible, so once I received my Motorola salary in my main account. I would simply transfer it between banks to show them incoming credits. I told them the money could not come direct from my employer as I was a special kind of employee, *blah, blah, blah*. It was all bullshit. Besides, these bank workers were not the smartest tools in the banking box. They were all on commission to sell mortgages, so in reality they needed me more than I needed them.

If ever they asked me too many questions, I would simply reply, "You want this or shall I take it to the bank next door?"

All the properties I bought were tenanted, which meant I had immediate rental income to cover my mortgages. I did not make rental profit on all of them as my aim was to simply ride each one out until the existing tenancy expired.

In Dubai, properties that were empty commanded a higher sales price than tenanted ones. Prospective buyers were willing to pay more for vacant properties as they were not obliged to keep the rental at the same amount as the previous tenants' agreement; they could either get new tenants at a higher rent or use the apartments for themselves. Whatever was the case, once my tenants vacated the place, I would put my property back on the market and within a few days a buyer would come through. This was how I offloaded the properties. Not only had the tenants' rent paid my mortgage but also, in most cases, when I sold the properties I would realise a minimum of 50% profit on what I had bought the same properties for. I would also get back my initial deposits, which I then used to buy new properties. Increasingly, I started putting down deposits on off-plan properties for which mortgages were not required. I would go to the Dubai property launches that were held every day, put my name down and pay a 5–10% deposit. A few weeks later I would flip the property; in other words, I would onward sell it as quickly as I could. Most developments had more demand than supply, so I used the right connections at the developer's office and they would always be able to tell me who they had on the 'waiting list'. I would approach the guys on that list and they would then buy the apartment from me at a higher price. I would get back my original deposit, as well as a higher valuation sales price.

I had amassed a few hundred thousand dollars through my

property exercise and on top of that I continued excelling at Motorola. Every three months I would also receive my sales commissions, which were, on average, the same amount as a month's salary. The beauty was that in Dubai there are no personal taxes on income. All in all, it was flowing. I turned 40 late in 2006 and never would I have thought that I would have ended up at 40 like this. I felt truly blessed. One of my biggest coups in Motorola was building my Dubai buyer's share of our business to an all-time high. With much manoeuvring and my phone ringing at all times of the day and night, I was fully engaged in work mode and loving every minute.

The biggest deal I did was to secure a $70,000,000 credit line for my buyer. This was one of the largest customers for Motorola besides the big MNO carrier groups. It had taken me six months of hard internal work to convince the finance department to avail this kind of open-insured trade credit lines to my customer. Their record of payment was impeccable. People had doubted the whole set up but the fact was – it was all 110% legit. With these additional massive credit lines, I was able to secure one of the single largest orders for Motorola ever – one million devices in one go.

My name had started spreading within Motorola all the way to HQ in Chicago and more than that, my name had started spreading across Africa. With the kind of quantities I was doing I had customers wishing to visit our factories. Everyone was curious to see where and how our phones were being made. Me too!

I wanted to know the whole supply chain and started flying out to Motorola factories in Singapore and Hong Kong/China. On factory visits I started learning how the supply chain and programme management worked. My aim was to keep fine-tuning the processes so that the minute I got an order, it had to become a priority for manufacturing. Fine-tuning meant that an average order lead time of say 45 days could, in essence, be reduced to 30 days if quick co-ordination between the teams was ensured and the communications refined. Having shorter lead times meant that my customers would always get their orders first, especially the new models, so that they could be the first to launch in the market and have an average one-month advantage over the competition.

The model that made Motorola in those days was the Motorola V3 RAZR. The company had spent millions on marketing this amazing product and there was pent-up demand. I managed to secure most of the allocations for the Middle East Africa region. I had to fight for these, but with a $70 million insured credit line, the aim was to get the majority of the stocks to my own guys. With that kind of credit line why would Motorola simply not supply as much as my buyers wanted? Just ship, ship, ship. The fine-tuned machine I had created was unstoppable ... or so I thought.

Motorola in early 2007 released a follow up to the RAZR – it was the K1 KRZR and HQ spent $150 million dollars on the marketing of this product. They wanted to ride the V3 wave, but for them it was a disaster in the making. The K1 never commanded the respect of the crowd and from the initial samples I had shown around, even my actual order forecasts were very low for this model. This then started arguments with management as I was insisting on continued supplies of the RAZR V3 and low-cost feature phones (dumbphones as they are known today). Even in my quest for high-margin driving sales like $700 RAZR V3s, I always kept a focus on the actual needs of the mass-market African consumers. They didn't have $700 to spend on any phone. They needed basic communication at very affordable price points. The only phones affordable for them were the feature phones. The one-million phone order I received was for feature phones, so even though it was a large order in terms of volume, the actual gross margins on this product were low. I had explained to Motorola several times that it was one thing getting market share, but another maintaining it.

My fights had also started when I began pushing for more business support for my African markets. By 2007, having delivered more than $500 million in revenues for the company, I had only managed to secure a three-man team. Yes, three people to run a business channel of this magnitude. The revenues and margins we delivered were very respectable and, naturally, I wanted to increase the number of people in my team. I wanted a certain portion of the margins we generated from Africa to be invested BACK into Africa. Every time I raised the point, I was met with deaf ears. I knew what was going on. I was being pushed constantly to bring in the business, but not enough was forthcoming to take the business to the next level. Meanwhile, some of my European counterparts and their European customers were doing much less in revenues but they were being given much bigger marketing and support budgets. It did not seem fair to me.

I began suspecting that there was an issue with Africa. I started to feel that, in all this, somehow Africa was getting short-changed. The guys in Motorola USA and Europe seemed to discount the value of the business generated out of Africa and this started to stir something inside me. I felt like a rebel and a revolutionary at the same time. The continent was making a lot of money for Motorola, but the proceeds were not coming back to Africa. Naturally, I had grown to love my continent and for me it was never about running Africa from some ivory tower – it was always about being on the ground. I grew up on the streets of London and the streets of Africa were no different. This was where I got my most valuable education. Sure, I could hang in the boardroom, but I was also very comfortable in the ghettos of Nairobi, Lagos and Johannesburg.

The fuck-ups with the K1 and the subsequent massive losses at Motorola led to one disaster after another. The then CEO, Ed Zander, decided to leave the company with a nice fat $20 million pay-out. Other heads were replaced, including regional managers. New guys came in, most of them the typical American swashbuckling types. I was regularly flying down to South Africa for team meetings and having to give presentations to the 'big boys'. This was something else that had started to piss me off. All my managers and co-workers would work to please their bosses when our real aim should have been to please our customers. Motorola's success had turned into a state of arrogance and complacency. They seriously thought that the V3 and K1 were enough to keep them with a number one market share. The V3 was a dead cow by now and, as we all know, you cannot get any more milk from a dead cow.

In the eyes of the customer everything was hunky dory. Motorola may have had internal issues, but to the external world all was great. Motorola spent a lot of money on their public relations. They also had an exclusive premier event that was held once every year called the Voyage of Discovery (VOD) and it was a trip that I had been trying to get on for two years. The VOD was a four-day cruise in the Mediterranean with all the top management, regional heads, key sales staff from Motorola and their top global customers. Everything was paid for by Motorola. Customers were flown with their partners in first or business class to where the ship was waiting. That year the boat was docked in Dubrovnik in Croatia and set to sail along the Adriatic Sea, with final disembarkation four days later in Venice. By 2007 I had managed to create enough visibility for myself and my customers to get an invitation. I was to be the official concierge to my set of customers – most of them Indian multimillionaire traders. My thoughts were to shine on the boat with my customers and, regardless of the nonsense going on behind the scenes, Motorola had to show a strong face and continue attracting the large orders by not only ensuring that our customers had the best time on the boa, but also by setting time aside for one-on-one meetings. This was one hell of an expensive PR exercise.

Once we were on the boat it didn't take long before I started getting a feeling that something was not quite right. Here I was, a solo hustler within a corporate environment. I had built a name around being a results-driven individual, but I was not known for my political correctness. I was brash and rebellious. One thing that had always amazed me when I worked at both Harris and Motorola was the amount of people who just kissed ass all day long. Schmoozing and manoeuvring was the way to get forward. Some guys got promoted because they were so clever at business politics. I wondered at times how the fuck some people kept their jobs or got promoted, because it seemed they did nothing but kiss ass all day.

Kissing ass had never been my forte. That simply was not my world. I wasn't clever enough to manipulate people. If you were to talk to me about smoke and mirrors, I wouldn't think about the level of deceit that goes on. Rather, I would be thinking of the discos I used to hang out in back in the day. The only way to become more visible that I knew was by doing the numbers.

On the boat there were a large number of Motorola executives who had no substance and it made me feel bitter about how we did all that business in Africa, yet we were not getting the real recognition we deserved. At times I felt like a highly paid slave. We had taken Motorola to number one market share in several countries, like Kenya, Zambia and DRC, but it seemed that no matter how hard we sold the case for Africa internally, some other region somewhere that was doing less than us would get more attention.

What was it about Africa that most corporates like Motorola just did not get? Did they not see that this was the last emerging market? A market of close to one billion people and 70% of the population was yet to be connected to mobile phones.

It seemed, though, that my performance had ruffled a lot of feathers internally. One of the companies that had an issue with me was a large USA-based distributor. They had grand ambitions to enter Africa and they had the blessing to do so of Motorola USA – the HQ. I was asked to see if I could get some of my distributors to buy from them instead and I found this strange. Why would our customers, who had been loyal to us up to now, have to be told to buy from a third party when they were so used to dealing directly with Motorola?

I was naturally protective of my patch. Rumours then floated that Alpesh was too close to his customers. How was I able to, quarter on quarter, bring in so much business? What tricks was I playing that the orders kept on coming in?

I realised that this was the first time in my life when I had achieved considerable 'corporate' success, but success, as they say, brings envy. I was never in the Motorola Dubai offices and rarely attended internal meetings. I simply was not built that way. I didn't see the need to watch PowerPoint presentation after presentation and I didn't have time for any bullshit talk.

On our last evening on the boat there was a black-tie gala dinner. The next day we were to all disembark at the port of Venice. My wife and I were dressed up to the nines and all the couples could have their photograph taken with the captain of the ship, after which we would be led into the main dining room of the boat. Huge chandeliers everywhere, an orchestra playing on the side and everyone looking as elegant as they possibly could. As I walked into the room I scanned the place to see where we would be seated. As my eyes ran across the room I caught the eye of our new Motorola global boss. I will never forget the look he gave me. His eyes pierced right through me. It was the look that said 'game over my friend'.

From that moment, my initial uneasy feelings were getting close to being confirmed. I was caught up in something much bigger than me. I suspected there and then that there were some knives out for me as the new management wanted to do things in their own new ways. I knew they wanted business from emerging markets to be controlled out of the USA via USA distributors.

We docked the next day and spent three further days in

Venice. I had never been to Venice, I was with my wife and it seemed the perfect time to enjoy ourselves in one of the most romantic places on the earth. However, to be honest with you, I couldn't relax because those eyes kept haunting me.

By November 2007, Motorola had become so toxic that it reminded me of the movie *Titanic*. Everyone was freaking out, running about everywhere in the dark. You knew the ship was going down, but you didn't know how long it would take. The pressure on all regions was becoming immense. Every region's numbers had dropped and this had led to the pressure on certain management to call it quits. Our South African office was also not spared and week by week people started walking. In that month of November I had decided that no matter how great my time had been, I knew that I was not wanted there anymore.

Motorola was finished. It tried to do so, but it never came back. Eventually, it was acquired by Google and then sold to a Chinese firm called Lenovo, who decided by 2016 to relaunch the Motorola brand – but in my opinion it had been dead since 2008. The great Motorola, the first phone manufacturer, had been brought down, not because of its products, but because of the quality of its management team. They simply did not have a fucking clue.

My time at Motorola taught me many things, more so than I learnt at Harris. It taught me how corporate companies work. I saw all the bullshit and the cloak-and-dagger games people would play just to get ahead. Everyone was in a rat race. Everyone wanted to be better than the person next to them and everyone wanted to be the boss.

*The problem with the rat race
is that even if you win, you are still a rat!*

I had just turned 42. I had now amassed two decades of experience from being a suitcase mobile phone trader, selling communications equipment to MNOs and being part of the biggest cell phone brand on the planet. At that point I was grateful to have had the chance to experience a 360-degree journey into the fast-paced mobile phone ecosystem.

When I left Motorola I didn't have a backup plan or another instant job offer waiting for me.

The next few chapters are longer than the previous ones – mainly because the memories are the freshest. At the age of 42, I was sitting on top of the world and I thought I knew it all. What I didn't realise was that I was about to embark on an eight-year education lesson, a hustle where I truly learnt about business, people and, above all, myself.

I decided to convert myself from a corporate intrapreneur to a standalone entrepreneur. I had decided to jump off a cliff and build a plane on the way down.

IN THE CORPORATE WORLD, THE BOTTOM LINE IS THE NUMBERS

Money talks and everything else walks. Do your numbers and the rest will take care of itself!

CHAPTER 11

MI FONE

C hristmas 2007 was spent in Cape Town, South Africa. I rented a large villa right on the water in Bantry Bay. I had the money and wanted to celebrate life with my family and my close friend Deji. It had been one month since I had departed from Motorola and as nothing much happens in Africa toward the year end, rather than rushing it, I decided to spend a good two weeks in Cape Town to prepare for whatever may come next.

A true friend, a brother and a mentor was what I saw in Deji. He had managed to sort himself out after our stay together in South Africa back in 1998. He had prepared his own plan on what he would do next. I wasn't part of it but I was fully supportive of what he was aiming to achieve. By 2007 Deji had created one of West Africa's largest quick-service restaurant chains. He had taken a Chicken Licken franchise from South Africa in 2001 and had set himself up in Nigeria.

A year later, by 2002, Deji had figured out that he was simply working to promote someone else's brand and paying them franchise royalties on his sales turnover. Meanwhile, he was the one who had to invest his time and money to set up in a difficult environment like Nigeria. The franchise holders did not invest a penny in Nigeria. Deji then decided that it was best to set up his own chicken brand and enjoy the fruits of his own labour. He created a new local brand called Chicken Republic. The South African Chicken Licken guys were pissed off, but, hey, Deji was right. He wanted to build something that belonged to him.

Chicken Republic was his first brand and very soon he opened offshoot brands in the bakery and ice-cream sectors. Together, the three brands were part of the Food Concepts group that Deji had formed with other shareholders. I had also invested in his company by taking up some shares. By the time I saw him in Cape Town in 2007, they were clocking $50 million in annual revenues. Deji had also conducted a very successful private placement, which was completely oversubscribed. That exercise led to Food Concepts raising approximately $30m as expansion capital to increase the pace of growth of the business. If there ever was a man of the moment, it was him. For me, he was a pure inspiration and I remembered the days we struggled in South Africa with the 'body condom' jackets, laptops and loaded guns pointed to our heads.

One morning we were having breakfast on the outdoor balcony of the villa overlooking the Atlantic Ocean. As always, we were talking about ideas about what to do next. I had started thinking quietly about how I could remain in the phone business, but have some control over the direction, considering what I had experienced at Motorola. I recall telling Deji, "I've been thinking of starting my own phone brand. I want to build something just like you did." I had even thought of a name.

As our conversation got more heated, with excitement I said to Deji, "What if I start a brand and called it simply 'I', then everyone would refer to it as 'I-Phone' and it can create some great momentum and piggyback off the increasing success of Apple's iPhone? The 'I' would stand for 'information' similar to the information sign you see at every airport."

"I don't know, bro," replied Deji. "Sounds a bit confusing and you may run into problems with Apple. Why don't you just call it My Phone instead? It's personal, it's a phone. Join the two and you have My Phone."

"WOW! My Phone ... I love it!" I said.

I now wonder what would have happened if I had gone with my initial gut feeling. Would there have been trouble with Apple or would I have benefited from them? We will never know. I twisted the name around a bit and after jotting some ideas on paper. I changed the My Phone to Mi Fone because I still wanted the 'I' in there somewhere.

In 2007 there were no second-tier brands in Africa. There were the big brands, but that was it. No other company had actually thought of creating a new device brand based on market segmentation. My thinking was simple; I had gained a great experience at Motorola, I had acquired immense knowledge at Harris and I was the original suitcase trader. Why not bring all these elements together and now offer the market in Africa products that the other big brands were not – low-cost feature phones to the MNOs and to my retail customer distributors.

Taking a note from Deji's page of progress, I also believed that I was ready to have my own brand and build something that truly belonged to me. Even if I could create a small portion of what I had generated at Motorola, I would be fine. Motorola had two devices priced sub $100, as did most of the other brands like Nokia, Samsung, Sony and LG, so how could I fill that gap?

I had been thinking about this for a while and by chatting with Deji my thoughts had progressed even further. That morning everything came together. It was as if each wave of the ocean hitting the shore was triggering a new idea in my head, showing me how to make this a reality. By the end of that day I had the plan mapped out in my head.

Build something that belongs to you

All I had to do was to execute in reality. I had heard somewhere that 'vision minus action is equal to daydreaming'. I was not prepared to daydream in sunny Cape Town. I needed to take this to the market and own the space.

The rest of the holiday was spent eating, drinking and laughing. I was content in in the knowledge of what I wanted to do next and that was a big weight off my shoulders. We headed back to Dubai the first week of January 2008 and then started the next steps of putting the business together. Most important to me was the fact that I had the funds to start this myself; hence I didn't need anyone's permission. I alone was going to do this.

I put my life savings into setting up Mi Fone. I put my own skin in the game. I was to be my own angel investor. I also managed to get some initial support from my best friends Deji and Doron. Every dollar counted. In 2008 there was no such talk about start-up funding, entrepreneurs and tech ecosystems. I was on my own on this one.

It started with the logo creation. How could I twist it? The word Mi is so generic, so I told my designer friend to come up with something that had an 'M' that was curved and an 'I' in the shape of a handset. I then instructed one of Africa's top law firms to start registering the trademark logo across several regions. It wasn't a cheap exercise, but it had to be done. I then worked on the product and the only thing I knew was that all the phones were made in China. I didn't want to go to my Motorola factory guys as they were just too big. I needed to find an easier and more flexible way of getting my products made. Now, who did I know in Hong Kong and China that could be off assistance …?

Alex Li!

He came to my mind. Just like that. Alex had been my first customer back in 1990. We had done a few deals together, but after I left Hong Kong I had lost touch with him. It had been 11 years since we last spoke and I didn't even know whether he was still alive. I had his old mobile phone number and as I dialled it I prayed the number was valid. It rang! I asked if it was Alex Li and as soon as I heard a man's voice I knew it was Alex. There was immediate joy on my face.

We exchanged pleasantries and spoke about the highlights since the last time we'd spoken. I told him about my family and my work at Motorola. I then told him I had an idea to make our own phone brand for Africa. Alex went on to explain that he had left Hong Kong many years previously and had moved across the border to Shenzhen, where he had fallen in love with a mainland Chinese woman. Staying in Shenzhen was also much cheaper than living in Hong Kong. Unfortunately, Alex had also been through some bad times just as I had. Over the past few years he had become familiar with all the mobile phone ecosystem players in the Shenzhen district. He told me he could help, but it would be best for me to go to see him so we could discuss my ideas further and look at the best options for us to move forward.

I immediately booked my flight to Hong Kong and Shenzhen and off I went in January 2008. I arrived in Shenzhen and was amazed by how the place had developed. I remembered Southern China from the early 1990s and recalled seeing grass everywhere. Now there were just tons and tons of concrete skyscrapers. There I was, a guy who was one of the first to sell phones into China and now they were going to sell the phones back to me. Their pace of progress never ceases to amaze me.

One thing for sure, I have always had immense respect for the Chinese and how they manage to sort their shit out. They didn't give two fucks about anyone except themselves and, rightly so; they have taken care of themselves. I have wished many times that Africa and Africans could have the same attitude; the continent would be far more advanced than the state it is in today.

Alex met me in Shenzhen and on our first night we had a very long and fruitful dinner meeting. We were both keen to do something together, but we had history and needed to set aside time to catch up. The next day Alex picked me up at my hotel and took me to meet a few of his various phone factory contacts. These factories were known as phone assembly plants and original design manufacturer (ODM) suppliers. They made phones for third-party brands. We started at a factory that was making a large quantity of phones for the Philippines market. Due to Alex's relationship, we managed to convince the factory to allow us to piggyback on the Philippines order production by adding a few thousand units to that production run *but* with *our* Mi Fone label. This way I could start with the lowest financial exposure possible.

Our first model was the Mi-100, a basic black-and-white feature phone. I placed my first trial order for 5,000 units. The Philippines order was for 100,000 phones, so the factory simply made 105,000 phones and I got the price as if I was buying 100,000 phones. All I had to do was pay a bit extra for our logo branding on the phone and our own box. I agreed there and then with the factory that we would move forward. In fact, I gave the factory my order whilst I was there.

I didn't have a market as yet, but knew that if we latched on to the Philippines production in January, the phones would be ready by early March 2008. I had no sales plan or blueprint as to how to take this new brand to the market, I just felt that if I had a product coming in March the time between January and March would enable me to pre-sell the stock as much as possible.

Whilst in Hong Kong I set up Mi Fone as a corporate entity. With some contacts, I managed to create a BVI offshore company based out of Hong Kong as our head office. I did this for a few reasons and, most importantly, I was loathe to open local entities in Africa, simply because I did not wish to get bogged down with the bureaucratic bullshit that happens there. It could take months to open companies in Africa. I didn't have that kind of time to waste.

Setting up in Hong Kong was relatively simple and bank accounts were also easy to open. I started with Standard Chartered Bank in Hong Kong as my main bankers. I had arranged a nice deal with Alex as well. He would act as my procurement agent and get a dollar fee per device he made for us. He would also provide his Hong Kong warehouse as our address and provide his staff and his China office facilities. He would take care of all my production, warehousing and logistics, all for a fixed fee per handset. Besides giving him a fee per phone made, in good faith I also offered Alex a 5%

equity stake in Mi Fone for free. This was a strategic move on my part to secure his long-term commitment to the business and, in return, he would provide his services for only Mi Fone and no one else. With the deal I had proposed and based on the business we aimed to do, Alex could make regular money to pay his overheads and have some upside a few years down the line as we grew the value of the business.

I also used this strategic share idea to attract other much-needed support partners. On the sales side I went straightway to my Kenyan contacts that were previously my Motorola distributors. There was an element of trust and goodwill already in place. My Kenyan partners had the largest chain of retail phone shops in Kenya; 104 retail stores to be exact. I was very familiar with their setup and with the dwindling sales on Motorola, I was hoping that Mi Fone could replace Motorola on the shelves. I really needed access to their primetime retail space. I offered them exclusivity on supply for Mi Fone into the Kenyan market. In return, they would have Mi Fone stocked in all their stores as their *de facto* in-house brand. Mi Fone was to be positioned next to brands like Nokia and Samsung in the top grade-A retail stores. This would add immediate credibility to an unknown brand. If I could cut similar deals with the other retailers and distributors I knew in Dubai and across Africa, I would have a pretty strong distribution network in place in no time. All sounds very smooth, right? In reality, it wasn't.

Little did I know that lobbying a brand that no one has heard of was not going to be the easiest task in the world. I went back to many of my old Motorola customers whom I thought were going to be supportive, but this was when I realised that people only want to deal with you only when they can make quick easy money (as was the case with Motorola). Here I was, asking them to take on a new unknown brand with no guarantee of sell through or market acceptance. Many thought I was mad and stupid to even think about entering the market with a new unknown local brand. How would I be able to take on the might of the big brands like Samsung and Nokia? In hindsight, maybe they were right in that to enter this industry one needed very deep pockets to be able to compete. I didn't have deep pockets, so how was I going to further my brand awareness? I had this passion burning inside me, so I never really took others' opinions to heart. I had already started and my first production run was already under way. I was doing this whether they liked it or not.

In the first few months, whilst waiting for the first Mi Fone stocks, I was confronted by many a naysayer. What I was doing had simply not been done before in Africa and just like my Hong Kong hustle, the Safebag hustle and Reign, it was all unknown territory. Was I again way ahead of my time?

In terms of my operational setup, I had Alex and the factory supplier in place and my first retail market was going to be Kenya. I did not employ any staff and I converted my spare bedroom in my Dubai apartment into a mini office. I didn't need fancy offices as I had Alex and his Hong Kong facilities and team as my backup. I also started to use Skype to make all my calls so that I could curtail my cell phone bill from heating up. In Dubai the call rates then were very high, but sometimes I had no choice. I had to make certain calls to start sharing the vision and getting the right partners on board. One of the first guys I called was Nicolas Regisford from my Motorola days. In my opinion, he was probably the best marketing guy on the African continent.

I told him straight. "I'm running a lean ship here. I don't have much money for you, but let's build this muzzerfuzzer."

Nic agreed immediately as he had seen what we had done with Motorola. Now with our own brand we could really go to town and activate all the marketing ideas we'd had before but had been seen to be too radical and rebellious for Motorola to agree to. Mi Fone needed to be different and it needed to be African. We had to maximise our brand message in the quickest and coolest manner possible. We were one of the first tech hardware start-ups in Africa – in fact, the word 'start-up' itself was not even known back in 2008.

In the early part of 2008 I had formulated the business and taken it from paper to reality. The rapid pace of getting the brand started was something unreal. We had our logos, we had our brand guidelines, we had our initial products being made. We had our vision in place. Now it was time to take it to the market. In order to get immediate brand awareness we needed to do some launches. Nic's expertise lay in event management and as per our Motorola days we knew how to throw a party, although I was fully aware that we wouldn't be seeing an immediate return on our launch investment. Plans were set in place to hold our first public launch in Kenya for some time in April 2008.

In the meantime, I needed to figure out how to bring in orders. Most of the Motorola customer contacts were not keen to take on a new unknown brand, so I had no choice but to call round looking for other potential customers. I cold called and sent introductory emails to as many people as I could – both MNOs and mobile phone distributors. Luckily, one of the positive replies I received was from a Ghanaian MNO. They were looking to have 5,000 branded phones for their network and, without even checking on us, they sent the request for proposal. I called them to introduce myself and get some clarifications.

The MNO guy told me straight. "You don't have much chance. No one has ever heard of Mi Fone and you are up against some pretty big brands like Nokia and Huawei. Unless you wow us with something special and something different you are not going to get far."

I knew exactly what needed to be done. Big brands have *big ass egos* and I knew from my days at Motorola that in their eyes they are first and everyone else is second. What I had to do was to *innovate*, get creative and do something with my offering that the others simply could not and would not do because of their internal policies. Big brands, for example, would *never* put someone else's brand on their phones. They didn't have to. This was my edge. I then immediately instructed my outsourced design team to put together the phone design proposal for which we would co-brand the offering.

We came up with Mi-X (for confidentiality reasons I don't want to mention the name of the customer we collaborated with, but they were a growing pan-African MNO). We then took their corporate colours and created the outer packaging tuned into these colours. After adding both their logo and ours to the front screen, we then worked on the battery door, which we made with their corporate colours and our logo at the top and theirs at the bottom. Going further, we took some images they had supplied, together with their promotional ringtones, and we created the phone software wallpaper, power-on graphics and power-on sound. The design was totally based on their brand but with a big fat Mi logo everywhere.

Apple always printed on its box 'Designed in California and assembled in China' so I emulated them, but used 'Designed in Africa. Assembled in China'. Our co-branding proposal had to be backed up by a good price point and we had to be competitive. From the Motorola days, I knew about the bill of materials (BOM) costs, as, from my Motorola factory trips, I knew how much phones cost to produce. I also knew the average margins that the big brands worked on. I didn't need those large margins, I just wanted to secure an order and get started. For me, it wasn't about making money from day one. We then duly submitted our bid. Two weeks later I got a call.

"Alpesh, we have decided to shortlist you. We like your offer as this is exactly what we wanted and it seems none of the other brands are proposing what you have proposed to us. However, we are not going to simply go ahead without knowing more about you. Can you please come to Ghana and meet with us?"

I couldn't believe that there was an opening for me. I had not even officially started Mi Fone.

We had planned to launch on 1st April 2008 (April Fool's Day but this was not a joke!). I quickly had to make the plan. In a matter of one week, with some intensive hours spent working, Nicolas and I had put together the plan for March and April. I would be receiving my first stocks from the factory by mid-March. We would then use part of the stocks as samples and I would convince Alex to arrange some other phone models with our logo on them to use for our launch event. We would go to Kenya first, do the brand launch followed by another one in Uganda. Then we would head straight to Ghana to meet the potential customer, but while we were there, we might as well do an event too. This way the Ghana MNO would also see us in the press and it would further confirm that we were a serious contender. I let Nicolas handle the marketing side of the launch events and, with our combined industry contacts, it was pretty straightforward to get this done.

Our Kenya launch was a great success. We had managed to bag the confirmed attendance and a keynote speech from the then Permanent Secretary of the Kenya Telecoms Ministry. The press had also turned up in full force. An African device brand was simply unheard of. Naturally there were numerous questions and much negativity, but at the same time, also much interest and curiosity.

Who were we?

Why did we think we could take on the big boys with all their muscle?

Never frightened of taking on a challenge, I handled the press pretty well, but it was a challenge. Traditionally, and even until today, the majority of Africans were known for not supporting local brands. Besides showcasing our range of low-cost devices, we had to also convince the market that we were serious about what we were doing. We did the launches in Kenya and Uganda and then arrived in Ghana. We had decided to do the press launch first and we invited some of the MNO staff to attend so they could see who we were. The next day we arranged to meet them again at their offices. The MNO chief executive officer (CEO) himself came to meet us at the reception area – this was not because we were special, but because he was as curious as everyone else to see who the fuck were we.

He looked at me up and down. I don't think he had

expected someone like me, but nonetheless he was extremely polite and led me into the boardroom where five others were sitting. I had met a couple of the folks earlier at the launch, so I knew they had already told their colleagues about what they had witnessed. I knew I was going to get a grilling from them, but we kept our cool. The questions started coming left right and centre.

"How will you support the product?"

"What happens if you are late in supply?"

"Why should we pay a deposit?"

"Who are you?"

"What have you done before?"

We were bombarded from all sides. I guess I had all the answers, because I simply referred to the fact that I had been with a big brand in the past and I knew what the big brands could and could not give them. I further explained that it was for this very reason that we had decided to set up our own African brand, so that we could cater more for local tastes. After two hours we had agreed on all the terms and conditions of the deal.

"Alpesh, come back tomorrow to get your purchase order."

Even before we had officially launched as a company, we had received our first purchase order for a whopping 5,000 units at $20 each; a total order value of $100,000. The order was placed into immediate production with our factory in China. For them, it was a first to receive an MNO order from an African brand.

By 1st April 2008 we were in business. NO JOKE! We had received our first purchase order and technically we were revenue generating from day one. Our first year was nothing short of awesome. I ensured by hook or by crook that we executed the Ghana MNO purchase order exceptionally well and delivered the product on time. The pilot project of 5,000 units sold out pretty quickly and very soon we received a repeat order. The MNO customer then introduced me to one of their sister companies in Senegal and without them even getting a sample, we received an order for 10,000 phones from Senegal. Same specification and build as the one we had done in Ghana, but this time with local Senegalese ringtones and the box in English and French. This was the level of detail we went into in order to provide a localised solution. As we kept getting the MNO orders, the word continued to spread amongst the MNO's group of African companies that we were the chosen supplier for their co-branded devices.

Many people commented on how it was possible for us to get these orders so quickly. In Africa, everyone assumes you *have* to pay bribes to get business. Some people do, but in our whole history not once did we have to pay off anyone or pay a bribe to buy someone's business. Our first set of orders was purely received on merit. We performed well and therefore got the repeat orders. The MNO operator group was the first in Africa to offer branded devices and it was a novelty for sure. In our first year, we ended up supplying to their operations in Ghana, Senegal and Tanzania. This was where we got our volume orders from, but in parallel I also had to build the brand via retail. This proved to be far more difficult. We simply did not have the marketing muscle that the big brands had to complement our sales efforts.

We applied to exhibit at the famous AfricaCom show. AfricaCom was the annual industry gathering that took place once a year in Cape Town and it was our first foray into building our brand awareness within the mobile phone industry in Africa. I had wanted to do something different and knew first-hand how boring the industry had become. We wanted to change that by bringing the 'sexy' back to the industry. In order to grab the attention of the visitors we went all-out sexy. Yes, we had to make some noise. We had positioned ourselves as the hip-hop brand of the telecoms industry. Our booth designs were vibrant and colourful and we employed three of the hottest local female models to represent Mi Fone at our booth. On our first day the booth was overcrowded, not only because of the products, but more so because of our female models. The visitors (mostly middle-aged corporate types) were attracted to the booth, then once they got there, they saw the girls but they also saw our brand and our phone offerings. It wasn't as if we were inundated with immediate orders for phones, but that wasn't the point. It was rather that we wanted them to remember they had gone into to the Mi Fone booth; they would then somehow remember our brand.

We had the colour, the music and the girls. This was when we knew that Mi Fone was not simply a device brand; it had to become a lifestyle brand. We received many complaints from fellow exhibitors for hogging the limelight, but our immediate neighbours loved it as the crowd at our booth waiting to see us would then also see what they were offering. For me, any talk, good or bad, was free publicity. We threw our first evening party event at Asoka, a famous Cape Town bar. I encouraged people to be themselves and, in such a stiff industry, we wanted people to let their hair down and enjoy themselves. None of the guests were immediate Mi Fone customers, but for sure they would never forget the brand and that's what it was all about. If we wanted to be remembered, it was up to us to make sure that happened.

In the nine months of our first financial calendar year we managed to close off our books with a nice $1.2 million in revenues. Looking back, even though that was a pretty small number, it wasn't for us, especially in only nine months of operation. Compared to most start-ups, I think we got off to a great start. Most start-ups in the USA don't even make a dime in revenue, let alone profit, for the first five years, but in Africa we didn't have that ecosystem. We were on our own. Quite simply, if we didn't generate revenue and profits we couldn't pay our bills.

For most African consumers Apple was 'aspiration beyond reach' and Mi Fone was aspiration within reach
... you can actually have it!

In 2008, we had laid a basic foundation for the introduction of the brand. By November I had already started thinking about how, in 2009, we could elevate Mi Fone further. November 2008 was a historical month for the whole world. The USA the most powerful country in the world had just elected its first ever black president Barack Hussein Obama. He was to be inaugurated in January of 2009 and he happened to be half-American and half-Kenyan. Did you say Kenyan?

It was only a matter of days before we came up with a great idea. Call it a hunch, call it whatever you like. All we kept seeing in the press and on the internet, was Obama mania in the USA during the run up to and after the election, so we put two and two together. I figured that if someone could put Obama's face on a t-shirt or a coffee mug, then why could we not put his face on a phone? Why could we not do an Obama-branded device and launch it as a memento for Kenyans only? What was stopping us from doing this? Absolutely nothing!

I mobilised my design team. We took the experience we had gained with our Ghana MNO customer and together we assembled the colours of the USA flag, the blue colours of the USA democratic party and as many Obama royalty-free images as we could gather.

We came up with the Mi OBAMA mobile phone.

We even printed the words *YES WE CAN* on the back battery door and images of Obama would be used as wallpapers on the phone screen. We placed an order with our China factory for 10,000 units. It was a gamble that I had decided we must take. The day came for Obama to be the official president of the USA and we launched our Mi Obama phone in Kenya via our retail partners. Very soon, within a matter of two weeks, we had sold out.

We didn't make much money, but again that was not the point. The point was we needed to get press coverage. For us this was a boon from above. *Everyone* and their mothers wrote about the Mi Obama phone.

'African company launches an Obama branded handset.'

We received thousands of mentions on syndicated websites and had enquiries from all kinds of press. There was nothing special here. Mi Fone wasn't known, but Obama was the hottest name on the planet. We had simply piggybacked on the momentum he had created.

I had some people tell me, "Oh, Alpesh, you are going to get into so much trouble. Are you sure you are allowed to use Obama's name and his image?"

"Well that's a problem I want to have," was my standard reply.

I wanted that call from the White House to either embrace us or tell us off. Neither happened, but the fact is we did what we had to do. I had needed no permission to do Mi Obama. The freedom of making a decision like that without asking anyone and making it a success is a superb moment in any entrepreneur's journey.

We continued throughout 2009 with increased business. We also increased our presence at AfricaCom 2009. 'Bigger and better' was the motto. By the calendar year end of 2009, our full first year of business, we had clocked another $2.4 million in revenues.

We had doubled our revenues in 12 months.

SEIZE THE DAY!

When you have an innovative idea, you must bring it into reality. Otherwise someone else will seize your day

CHAPTER 12

THE DOUBLE Gs

B y early 2010 we had started to create some noise in the industry. Mi Fone was starting to be known as the only local African-owned mobile device brand. We were definitely not a tier one brand similar to Samsung, Nokia, Huawei, LG, Sony and Apple, but we were considered a tier-two or tier-three brand. Our work was definitely cut out for us just trying to make some noise in the industry compared to the immense amount of marketing that the tie- one brands were doing. By this time the majority of our distribution was still focused on delivering our handsets directly to the MNOs. The balance was then delivered to our in-country retail partners, who sold the handsets to the end users via their retail shops. Even though both channels were very different, they were both distributing our products.

We were receiving regular rolling orders from our first MNO group customers in Ghana, Senegal and Tanzania. On the retail side, we faced many challenges with our partners, one of them being the fact that we simply did not have the money that the tier-one brands were pouring into the market. They had enough money to command the retail shelf space and they also had deep pockets when it came to newspaper advertising to help drive customer traffic to the shop counters for eventual purchase.

We also faced obstacles from the Indian traders. As mentioned, the majority of the East African cell phone distribution business was controlled by the Indian traders based out of Dubai. On the West African side, it was more the Lebanese business groups controlling the action. Both were used to selling fast-moving brands. They were not pioneers in the development of the mobile device business, but, more, they were a conduit for brands to distribute their goods. For these traders only one thing mattered – how much money they could make

The tier-one brands did not help our case and these guys simply could not be ignored. They were already established, successful, had a lot of resources at their disposal and were used to making big bucks. I knew from my Motorola days how owning the retail shelf and branding space was of prime importance to the big brands. To be as prominent as possible, they had to pour money into these channels. We had our backs against the wall. We needed the retail space exposure too, but we couldn't match the capital of the big brands.

The only way I thought it could be possible was if we were to offer extended credit terms to our retail partners. Their retail shops were the last link to the end user, so it was crucially important to embrace this powerful channel. The whole business basically ran on credit, with the exception of Apple, which had people queuing up to buy their product. We had to make it as easy as possible for our retail partners to buy our products. A classic example was to offer longer payment terms, such as 45 or 60 days, from the issuing of our invoice. They would place our products on their shelves and the quicker the sale, the better because the retailers would collect immediate payment from the end customer at the shopping till (point of sale). However, the retailer would not have to pay us until the due date, so in no uncertain terms we were, therefore, a *de facto* bank. Why would a retailer need to borrow money at high interest rates from their banks when they could simply use their supplier's money for 60 days *interest free* before settling their supplier invoices?

It bothered me that this was the only way forward in expanding our retail sales, but there was no other option. I realised that Mi Fone as a phone supplier would not be able to generate general market awareness in retail channels if we did not start taking more risks. Consequently, the year 2010 became a risky one … .

To push our brand further, besides offering credit terms to our retail partners, we also had to do what we could with what little we had when it came to our marketing spend, otherwise the phones would just lie on the shelves gathering dust. We had to come up with something to help push the customers into the stores to ask for a Mi Fone.

We decided to become more provocative and created a set of photographic adverts poking harmless and cheeky fun at the big tier-one brands. We targeted Apple, Samsung, Nokia and LG and assembled an amazing photographer and designer to come up with images that reflected our brand; cheeky, sexy and fun. We were careful to never print these images on billboards or in the press; they were purely used on Facebook and via our own database. I passed these images by our lawyers who told me not to even try to go public with them because we could face major legal challenges. My gut was telling me to go all out but I restrained my urge. Anyway, I didn't have any cash lying around to pay lawyers for any potential litigation cases.

That year took a lot out of me in terms of travel. Every other week I was either in an African country or in China planning new products. Everything was flowing well. Yes, we had issues with payments and product-quality issues but nonetheless the business was still moving. The cash I had put into Mi Fone was circulating well between receiving purchase orders and payments.

I was still working from my home in Dubai and by now I had taken on an assistant manager to help me out. All other services were simply outsourced. I decided to start employing some local staff in markets like Kenya, because that was where we had the strongest retail presence via our retail partner who owned 104 stores across the country. Having local staff would ensure that there would be immediate support in that area to the retail partner, as well as for the end customer buying our brand. I didn't think about going to recruitment companies; I simply relied on recommendations from people I knew. I had learnt my lesson on this one.

I was making decisions based on my emotions, so if a potential candidate was recommended to me and I liked his or her face and mannerisms, I would hire them there and then. There were no industry standards for wages, so we kept it simple by offering freelance full-time contracts. This was a big mistake on my part and something that I kept repeating over and over again for many years, only to realise that I had fucked up badly when it came to getting the right people. I have always been someone who trusts too easily and someone who is always ready to help anyone, regardless of their age or background. What I didn't realise was that the remote freelance contractors were operating on their own and we could not monitor what they were doing at all times of the day. I simply trusted that they would deliver on what they had promised. At times, it felt as though the contractors were just collecting the monthly fee from us until something better came along.

Regardless of the slow pace of work from some of our freelance contractors, my assistant and I and the Hong Kong/ China team worked very fast. We were putting in 18 to 20 hours a day and due to time-zone differences, it was norm for me to be on a call to Hong Kong at 5am Dubai time when it was 9am in Hong Kong. By my afternoon in Dubai (Hong Kong evening time) we would compare notes and tick off all the action items we had completed that day. Somehow the machine was running pretty smoothly.

Our brand name was also quickly gaining increased awareness. Then, we were approached by someone at Western Union USA (WU) who wanted us to make a customised mobile phone for them in yellow, their corporate colour. I immediately jumped at the opportunity – it was a potential $250,000 order for us and all we had to do was to put the product together. WU's aim was to launch 10,000 phones with their mobile wallet system embedded. They planned to introduce this innovative phone via an MNO they had partnered with in East Africa. I guessed they would use the MNO's distribution network to get the phones out to the consumers. The overall project size was a whopping one million units but they had to run a pilot phase first to provide proof of concept. We were all very excited and started having several calls with the WU team who were based in Denver, USA, about 12 hours behind Dubai time. So now not only did we have 5am calls with Hong Kong, but we also had 11pm late evening calls with USA. All in all, there was very little sleep.

The team at WU USA were some of the nicest people I

had ever dealt with. Their whole manner and attitude to the business was so different from what we were used to in Africa. They were the buyer but they acted as if we were doing them a really big favour.

We processed their order very efficiently and within six weeks we had all the phones delivered to their nominated address in East Africa. WU's aim was to immediately release the phones into the market. I, too, was keen for this, as the sooner we got feedback – hopefully, positive – the sooner we could kick off repeat orders. After a few weeks of going to and fro, we found out that WU were somehow themselves in the dark as to what was happening with their own phones. Apparently four weeks after delivery, the phones were still lying in a warehouse.

What the fuck was going on?

I had then coined a phrase known as the 'Double G Phenomenon'. The Gs stood for the 'gatekeepers' and those on the 'gravy train'.

Some may not say it, but I will …

In doing business in Africa we often come across the gatekeepers – those who will block your progress until you simply give up, tired of waiting. An example of a gatekeeper would be someone asking for terms and conditions they know you, as a small company, could never meet. An example of someone on the gravy train would be a person who asks for some kind of monetary rewards in exchange for certain favours. The problem is once you start paying, you never stop.

I started suspecting that something was not right in the relationship between WU and their MNO partner. I don't have any exact details but we knew that WU had signed an agreement with the MNO partner to promote their phone with the WU money transfer software that we had embedded into the phone. Something had happened in that relationship. I never found out in full but I kept asking myself, 'Why did it take such a lot of time to distribute the initial 10,000 phones?'

Someone somewhere was acting like a gatekeeper in order to delay any of this from moving forward. As we were close to WU we could hear the tension and the desperation in their voices and I genuinely felt sorry for them. They were such nice people who had probably witnessed first-hand the difficulties of getting things done on time in Africa. Someone had stalled their deal and they were frustrated. It was a classic example of how a gatekeeper acts.

We, though, had completed our end of the deal and, thankfully, WU did not make their problem our problem. They were probably the fastest payers we ever had. Within a couple of weeks of our delivery they had transferred the full amount due over to us. We tried to explore other markets with WU, while their original market deal had stalled, but it seemed that wherever they were going in Africa, they were faced with one challenge after another. This was WU, the largest and most famous remittance company in the world. I imagine they also felt the pain of doing business in Africa, even with all the money they had.

Unfortunately, the one million phone unit order with WU never materialised. I kept hounding WU over it but I knew they could not give me any clarity. They themselves seemed demoralised from what had happened in East Africa to the point that the whole phone project was shelved. I wish they had pursued it further and not simply given up at the first hurdle because they had the means and resources to keep going. The

Mi Fone–WU phone partnership was a game changer. It was 2010 and this would have been the first phone in Africa that addressed some form of financial inclusion for the masses. WU was ideally placed to own the mobile money space in Africa as the majority of the African diaspora used their service to remit funds back to their families on the continent on a very regular basis. Hats off to WU as they really supported us. Here was a US corporate giant that had acknowledged and embraced working with a small African brand. Why couldn't our own African corporates treat us in the same way?

After the WU episode, we went direct to their initial MNO partner and asked how we could position ourselves as potential supplier to their network seeing as we had already supplied them via WU. After lots of going back and forth, we were referred to their head office for meetings. I think they met me out of politeness. The way most MNOs in Africa conducted their procurement exercises was via official tenders and official requests for quotations (RFQs). These MNOs were big groups with solid corporate structures in place, including upholding utmost transparency and governance. In order to ensure they were always getting the best procurement deals, they had to regularly update their supplier database to see what else was out there.

It was amazing in some instances to receive an RFQ from a particular MNO requesting a quotation to submit a response to a very detailed technical and commercial set of specifications. Sometimes it was so obvious that the RFQ specifications had been written around a specific model from a specific mobile device brand, that even if another supplier like us did respond, we could never have matched their requested specification point for point. They had already chosen their preferred supplier and had prepared their documentation in such a way so that it would pass their internal governance processes. This always raised an eyebrow with me, because I knew that even if we did spend time and energy submitting a bid we would never win it as the winner had been chosen a long time ago. Another classic example of a gatekeeper practice.

A meeting was set up for me to meet with the heads of procurement at the new MNO, but I wasn't exactly welcomed in with much fanfare. In fact, it was quite the opposite. The minute I saw these two guys, I knew I had to be ready for a negative meeting. Out of formality, I explained our references and successes in delivering customised device solutions to other MNOs and specifically the work we had done indirectly with them via the WU deal. I asked the MNO to give us a chance to directly supply them, since the WU deal had gone quiet. We discussed another small pilot project and everyone round the table began nodding their heads, but in a we-hear-you-but-can you please-fuck-off kind of manner. They were rushing the meeting as much as they could so they could get it over and done with.

I knew that these guys already had their preferred suppliers in place. I had no proof so I could not make any claims, but let's look at this very objectively. We had customised the WU phone product, which had then been distributed via the MNO's channels. Our prices were competitive enough to have won the order with WU in the first place and we had also performed well on the product quality and the delivery. We had developed a proven track record since 2008 for good quality supply to the other MNOs in Africa *and* we were the only African brand.

Therefore, what genuine excuse would this MNO have to not give us a chance to do a small pilot project with them? What was stopping these procurement and product guys from giving us a chance? Why would an African MNO brand not have an African mobile device brand as part of their product portfolio?

This was when I suspected that the Double G phenomenon was at work again. Within large businesses in Africa some people are busy running their own side hustles. For example, someone in a procurement department of an organisation may want you to supply them via a very specific third party run by perhaps a family member or a best friend. The products would then have a local profit margin added and then onward sale to the organisation itself. All the profits generated from these types of transactions would then be shared between certain members of the organisation and the third parties who were mandated to supply them. Another example of the Double G Phenomenon could be when a head of a particular department within the buying organisation asks in a very shady way that if you want your product listed you need to somehow pay some kind of listing fee. However, as nowhere in the organisation did it state that there was an official listing fee, one could only assume that this was a private fee to be paid to the asker to gain his cooperation in getting your products listed. Normally, this fee would be paid in the form of a fat brown envelope stuffed with cash. This I would term as someone on the gravy train.

I'm happy to say that we in Mi Fone *never* entertained and *would never* entertain anyone asking us for brown envelopes. Any time I met someone I suspected of being on the gravy train, I would simply steer their thoughts to the merits of our product and pricing. We simply did not see the need to basically *buy* someone's business. By 'buying a business' I mean if we'd had pots of cash and no conscience it would have been much easier for Mi Fone to grow in leaps and bounds by dangling lucrative carrots to particular individuals working within certain organisations. I know of many companies that became very successful in Africa very quickly with standard product offerings – except that there was nothing spectacular about these offerings. I guess they simply worked *with* the Double Gs rather than *against* them. This is just the way some things progress in Africa. You either embrace it or walk away from it. If you walk away you will always be on the tougher path.

By 2010 we used the WU experience to our advantage and started contacting the banks because I knew mobile money was going to take off. Now in 2017, every bank in Africa is going on about mobile money. We started speaking to them in 2010 and they didn't get it back then. Again, were we too early for the market?

We managed to get a small deal with Banc ABC, which is now part of the Atlas Mara group. We supplied customised devices to their operations in Zambia and Mozambique with assurances that further orders would be forthcoming. They never came. I wondered why we were always a one-hit wonder with some of these customers. We never had any product returns, complaints or delays in the deliveries, but despite this, we simply would not hear from them again. Maybe we weren't charming enough.

By 2010 we had multiple opportunities to really take advantage of the scenario. As I already stated, Mi Fone would have been a much larger company in terms of sales *if* we had done things in certain ways. These ways included us embracing the Double Gs and we could have bought our own market share by simply selling our phones at below cost price just to shift more volumes and, in the eyes of the industry, increase our market share. We could have paid off many a guy here and there to 'grease the wheels', but all of this at what cost? I didn't want this shit following me around for the rest of my life like a shadow. We knew the path we had chosen was tougher, even though it was the right thing to do. We had to continue to keep getting orders on merit and not through what we had in our pockets. Mind you, there was nothing in our pockets in the first place.

Despite the initial success with WU and how we faced one obstacle after another in growing our business with the large organisations, we still somehow managed to end 2010 on a high note as we again doubled our revenues to $4.2 million. We had clocked nearly $8m in revenues in just 33 months in operation, but I wanted to go bigger and better, which meant I had to step it up for 2011. Our growth plans were causing pain. In order to do the $4.2m in 2010 we'd had to force some of our Chinese factories to start giving us some credit terms. We were giving them constant orders and now they needed to help us. I had also started borrowing private money at ridiculous rates like 35% interest per annum. We were collecting payments from customers and then paying factories to release more stocks for other customers. It was like taking money from Peter to pay Paul.

I had become a master circus juggler of cash.

EMERGING MARKETS

if you don't know the rules you can't play.
Don't hate the player, hate the game!

CHAPTER 13

THE 'JUNGLE'

F rom the outset we had vowed to carry on building the brand and increasing our sales volumes. We were also making sure that we kept our creativity going no matter what. We had to try to figure out what else we could sell to our MNO customers that they couldn't easily find elsewhere.

During this time, the African cell phone market was beginning to boom with the influx of cheaper handsets coming out of China and by now others had caught on to the white label bandwagon. We were starting to feel the heat from the competition, which most definitely had deeper pockets.

One thing that continued to set us apart, though, was our marketing and consumer communications. At the beginning of each year we would always send out a Mi Fone newsletter to the whole database of our contacts. The newsletter was basically highlighting the successes we'd had in the previous year and promoting some of the new things we would be doing in the following one, whether it might be a new product, a new market entry or a new marketing campaign. We let the industry know that Mi Fone would be the first device brand to ship low-cost smartphones to Africa. The added twist was that all our Android smartphones would be dual-sim enabled – that is, each phone could carry two sim cards. Dual-sim smartphones had not been done before in Africa in early 2011.

Our first shipment was in mid-2011 when we received a massive 5,000 phone unit order worth $750,000 from the same MNO that had given us our first order in 2008. We were extremely excited to receive a large smartphone order from a credible MNO. It could only mean bigger and better things for us, even though I was so cash-strapped. In hindsight, I regret accepting this order. The problem was that as much as we were in a hurry to introduce dual-sim smartphones into Africa, our factory and chipset processor partners were simply not ready to support the realities on the ground.

The mobile device industry was in full swing in 2011. Many companies had started targeting Africa. It seemed that even the big chipset producers had started to take an interest in the last emerging market. I would meet them on a regular basis when they invited me to their events and conferences. All I can say is that there was too much talk and not enough action in their words. I regretted our MNO smartphone order because I allowed myself to be seduced by the power of the big companies who had assured me that they would support my business on the continent of Africa. In reality, the muzzerfuzzers did not do shit! I am coming back to this major turning point in our journey at a later stage so you can see how the pieces all fit into the Mi Fone jigsaw puzzle.

In 2011, I was operating with three full-time staff and, besides my immediate assistant manager; I also took on a service head based in Mauritius, because it was important for us to have a dedicated service manager. We were in the phone business, one of the quickest supply chain businesses on the planet. With that speed, you can bet your bottom dollar that not every product is going to be perfect. As we were an unknown brand, we had to ensure our quality control (QC) at the factory level was several times higher than the norm. I knew that if our products failed the customer would be very quick to label our phones as cheap Chinese knock-offs.

Despite our three-stepped QC process some of our customers would always find a reason to complain by trying to see how far they could push us for further price discounts or an extension on their payment terms. We always had our intelligence on the ground and a few times we would send anonymous people into the retail stores as potential customers to check up on Mi Fone. In some cases, they would find our products were sold out. I learnt that this was a classic trick played by many resellers. They would tell us that the stock was not moving due to quality or price issues, that they needed more time to pay or they needed further price reductions so they could clear the stocks. The reality, however, was that they had sold our stocks and were using our money to pay other suppliers. This was how it worked in Africa, so even though we continued to receive orders, our payment cycles kept getting longer and longer.

One of our retail customers in Africa was also used to placing very small orders as he was on a 30-day-from-invoice payment term. He had credit for one month before he had to pay our invoice. He did not want to be in the position of finding himself with a large amount of Mi Fone stock so that when it came to payment after 30 days he was stuck to pay us. In order to curtail the risk, he bought in smaller quantities, so he knew he would be able to pay the invoice at the end of the 30 days. It was a good sales channel for us and I was very eager to expand it. The only way I could do this was to take some chances, so I offered them a consignment deal.

We would supply the stocks and the customer would sell. Only once they had sold the goods would they then pay us. This was the definition of a consignment deal; basically 'pay as you sell'.

Funnily enough, the minute I agreed to do this deal with our African retailer his first order increased to three times the original amount. It was a great deal for him. He was not required to put up his own money to move our stocks and he was not liable for anything. He would simply sell our products and then pay us back on time. The problem was he never did. This customer had now taken on more stocks but, due to the lack of marketing, our products were not exactly flying off the shelves. We had to conduct various exercises, like events and activations, to drive consumer traffic to the retail partner stores to get our products to move. All of this took time and hence we found we were waiting longer and longer for our money.

In one instance, our same African customer told us that some product models were still lying in their warehouse, but via our local intelligence and the store front staff, we discovered that the stocks were sold out. If the stocks had sold out what were they still doing in the customer's warehouse? Quite simply, they did not want to pay us at the due time. Our money was free to them, after all, because we were not charging any interest. These were some of the tricks that we were up against.

In 2011, we opened our first office in Dubai. Our sales were good, which meant I couldn't keep working from my spare room any more. It was my first time setting up a company in Dubai, so I didn't know what I was in for, but let me tell you straight, I have never run around like I did in Dubai just to open a simple trading company. Don't let anyone fool you. Contrary to popular belief Dubai was not an easy or cheap place for entrepreneurs to set up back in 2011. There was too much red tape in getting the trade licences, staff visas and office space. We had set up in the TECOM, part of the Dubai Internet City Freezone area, and we could only rent an office that was approved by the authorities – most of them were very expensive spaces. There was one building called Concord Tower that was in the middle of TECOM. It was owned by a sheikh from one of the Emirate states and seemed to be the cheapest place for us to move into and for that to happen we had to get permission from all sorts of people. Much time was wasted in setting up in Dubai but meanwhile during every step in the process we were constantly paying for different charges. This is how the Freezone guys make their money. Everyone thinks Dubai is great because it's tax-free – yes, it's tax-free on personal income, but they will get your money in one way or another.

I was doing all of this to make Mi Fone more officially recognised. If we wanted to grow we had to show that we had a presence. I started thinking about funding and everything needed to be in order. One thing I always did from day one was to ensure I had a proper set of books. We had audited accounts for every year and this came in handy when putting together the financials in order to raise funding. I tried with more than five different sets of people to see if we could raise some money, either by selling shares or raising cheaper loans. All of these five sets of people claimed to be heavily connected with lending banks, but what a fucking waste of time that was. All these guys gave us the run around. They came and pitched to me, encouraging me to sign them as advisors on the premise that they believed 100% they could help us raise money. They all worked on retainers. I happily paid some of them as their services were sold to me so well, but ultimately none of them performed and some even had the nerve to keep asking me for more money to retain them while they 'found us the money'. I had to quickly shut them down.

This started my annoyance with the so-called 'advisors' out there. Nowadays, I tell every entrepreneur that they need to be careful when dealing with so called 'advisors' or 'consultants', because at the end of the day all they want is your money. The first questions to ask any of them are, 'have you built anything yourself?' 'do you know what it takes to build a business?' Most of them will answer no. It's like meeting a food critic who recommends a restaurant for you to dine at but they themselves have not even eaten there.

My emotions always got the better of me. You would have thought that after all my years of hustling I would have become a bit harder! No. Not me. I was always seduced by the smoothness and the promise of funding. With the advisors on board I thought I could then focus on the daily business while they helped me raise money, but in the end the Dubai fundraising plan didn't work out for me. I went from one meeting to another to meet flashy guys who, in reality, were just time-wasters. They all wanted to know the story and they all got excited, but when it came to delivering, they just didn't perform. Dubai is like that. Even though there are guys with genuine businesses, Dubai also has its fair share of dodgy dudes hustling their way from one deal to the next.

By 2007 Dubai had become the biggest washing machine on the planet. There was Iranian, Russian, Pakistani, Indian, African and European money flowing through the city's veins and the banks didn't care where the funds were coming from.

My personal opinion is that the whole Dubai property boom was due to a massive influx of money coming in from other countries. Much of this money was undeclared income or gained via illicit means. Take an Indian from India ... Why would he pay tax in India if he could find a way to get his cash to Dubai, buy a property and simply sit on it for a few years, then flip it and make some money in the process? What bearing does this have on me? Well, why would someone invest in an African hardware start-up like Mi Fone when there were easier ways to make money?

Dubai also did not really understand Africa. It was a trading hub and traders came to Dubai to buy goods and take them back to Africa. Besides that, there was no formal business investment from the UAE to Africa. One notable group was Mubadala, which started expanding into Nigeria, but I can't think of anyone else that looked at Africa as a long-term opportunity. It's changed now as a few associations have been set up to foster Arab–Africa trade. As difficult as Africa is, you simply cannot ignore the opportunities.

We always met up with one person or another in Dubai. One prominent guy introduced us to a group owned by one of the members of the Abu Dhabi royal family. I had proposed that as the UAE was our base, would it not be good to explore the idea of building a world-class mobile phone assembly plant in the UAE? The idea was very well received. It was actually a no brainer. Setting up a local assembly plant coupled with the UAE's excellent location and logistics would then enable us to supply phones, not only into Africa, but the whole of the Middle East and the CIS countries as well.

After six months of meetings and negotiations, we believed that we had convinced this group to invest in the setup of a local plant, but at the last minute someone somewhere shut the deal down. I think they made a mistake because if at that time we had moved forward – coupled with the pace of technological development in the UAE – now, in 2017, we would have had a world-class mobile phone plant catering for the whole region and as a consequence generated thousands of jobs. It is evidently clear that there has been a massive increase in smartphone usage since 2011 within the overall region.

With the lack of funding from Dubai and the disappointment of having the assembly plant idea shut down, I lost faith in my presence in the UAE. I had to look outside Dubai for funding and by mid-2011 I started making several trips to London to see if I could raise any money there. I met with a few contacts and referrals that then led to other referrals and very soon we had some interested parties who wished to speak to us. One thing that did help us with our cash flow was the fact that the Chinese factories had also started giving us 60-day credit with the risk insured with SinoSure, the China export credit guarantee department. I had breathed a huge sigh of relief as I was not pressed to always come up with cash to pay for goods when they were ready. This arrangement really helped with our cash flow and in a way the business continued as we kept juggling orders and cash to keep afloat while still paying our bills.

It was also the first time I started to draw an official salary. For the first three years I had relied on savings that I had made at Motorola to keep me going. All my expenses, like rent, my children's school fees, food and travel were covered by Mi Fone. The deal I had made with myself was that I would work for free, but my expenses would be covered by the company. Besides the small investment that Deji and Doron had made into Mi Fone, I was the only one who had put the majority of the money into the company, so I was not prepared to screw the company over. Mi Fone was my baby, my third child and I had to make sure it could feed itself as much as possible

Unfortunately, my early efforts in London were not paying off as well as I had hoped. The action was on and off like a hot water switch. I had to keep an eye on the customer orders and at the same time look for funding, plus all the other tasks involved in running a business. I always had high hopes and constantly felt that everyone I met could be a potential saviour, but in most instances, that was not the case. I had spent a lot of my life living simply on hope – it's still the only thing that keeps me going today.

Hope

I made a trip to Kenya in September 2011 during which I was introduced to a local private equity (PE) fund. I thought they would understand our business, because they, too, were local. They had perused our business case, invited us to meet with them and Nicolas and I turned up at their offices to do our pitch. Upon arrival, we were greeted by three members of the PE fund; a lady, a local Kenyan and the boss, a Kenyan of British origin. I will never forget the manner in which they asked us questions. We had taken along a lot of our history, including past and current customer purchase orders to show them that we had a genuine business. We even showed them our bank statements so they could see the amount of cash moving in and out of our account every day, but they questioned everything. At one point the British guy even told his assistant to call one of the MNOs who had given us the order to see if the order was real or fake. Nic and I sat there speechless. This guy was convinced that we were lying about *everything*. What a wanker!

"Why are you questioning our orders? Do you think we came here to steal your money? Do you think we are a bunch of fraudsters?" These were the words I wanted to say, but I just kept quiet. I felt utter disdain for the guy and told him he could call whomever he wanted as we had nothing to hide. We simply packed our documents and walked out of the meeting.

I went through several episodes of similar nature when people just would not believe that we were a genuine firm. I asked myself at times, 'why?' There we were, a business that had generated more than $10 million in sales and one that was now shipping to 14+ countries across the continent. Why were people still doubting us? Would we have experienced the same reaction had we been a couple of suited Americans or Europeans with the *exact* same business, the *exact* same set of numbers and the *exact* same vision? Would we have been treated any differently? My guess is most certainly, yes.

I do believe there is something called 'white privilege' in the funding game; even more so in Africa. Some would say it's taboo for me to say that we couldn't raise money because of the colour of our skin. Some may say it's an excuse I am using for my own shortcomings, but the fact remains that most companies that get funded in Africa have a large element of white ownership or are backed by Europeans or Americans.

I faced these questions all the time about our existence and each time I would get more and more worked up. This was what was burning me all the time. I felt that either people simply did not like what we stood for or they did not understand the business. In other markets, local brands, such as MicroMax in India, were getting funded. Many had figured that the big tier one brands were losing their momentum in the mass market consumer sector and that this momentum was well addressed by the local brands. There was evidence of this everywhere; for example, the fact that Motorola had disappeared and Blackberry was on its knees.

My argument to the financiers was always this. "Imagine how our numbers would look if we could raise money at cheaper interest rates to fund the business instead of paying private lenders 30% in interest."

"Oh, your net profit is too low," was the standard reply.

"Yes, we know and that is because, as you can see, most of our expenses are spent on heavy current finance costs. If we could have borrowed funds at cheaper rates then naturally our net profits would have been higher and hence our valuations would have been higher."

They never seemed to get this for some reason and they were not stupid so it just baffled me all the time.

Many people were interested in our story. They were curious to know more about us and how we managed to survive and create so much noise. All the investors we met wanted to be part of the 'African Dream', but it seemed none of them were willing to go through the African pain first – and there was major pain in building a brand in Africa.

By October 2011 we were making some serious inroads with the brand and the big annual AfricaCom show was coming up, which I wanted to be our biggest and best to date. Luckily for us, we were invited by Google Africa to showcase Mi Fone next to Huawei and Samsung at the big Google event. It was such an honour for us. We had verified our presence at this Google event as it was widely known that Mi Fone was one of the first to introduce low-cost smartphones into the African continent.

Our dual-sim smartphone strategy was quite a neat one. We would approach tier-two and tier-three MNO carriers only. Tier-one carriers were the big pan-African MNOs owned by European or South African parent companies. Tier two and three were slightly newer entrants into the market and had a minority market share. I also wanted to fight the tier-one carriers who had shut the door in our faces

We did something with our dual-sim smartphones that would assist the tier two/three MNO customers to win in the marketplace. Inside the phone the 'sim 1' slot was locked to our MNO customer for both voice/data and the 'sim 2' would be open for any *other* MNO carrier, but for voice services only. The aim here was to entice existing subscribers from a tier one MNO to get a low-cost smartphone from a tier two/three MNO. The hook was that they could still keep their original number in the 'sim 2' slot. We knew that once this happened, psychologically the user would end up using more of 'sim 1' due to having data internet access and voice, so in a way over time their 'sim 2' original number would be more of a redundant number for incoming calls only (on which a tier one MNO makes little or no money).

Our plan was accepted by our MNO customers and we started shipping smartphones.

You remember earlier I spoke about the 5,000-unit smartphone order that I regret taking? Well let's revisit that.

We proposed this strategy to the MNO customer who then

gave us the order. After we had delivered the 5,000 units we started to receive complaints a few months later from the customer. Our smartphones had started to fail. The word internally in the MNO group then spread to its other operations across Africa and our sales efforts in those markets came to a standstill due to the complaints we had started receiving. We looked into the matter. It was a product issue and specifically a chipset issue. The chipset in those phones was not aligning well with the carrier's network, so in certain areas the phone simply could not pick up any signal. The MNO could not care less whose fault it was. As far as they were concerned, they had given Mi Fone the order and it was our mess to fix. We sent our service guys twice to that country and did all the field tests and our findings were correct. The phones would not pick up any signal in certain areas.

We complained to the factory, who then laid the complaint squarely at the feet of the chipset manufacturer, a large USA company. The chipset is the phone processor chip; it is the power, the heartbeat and the brains of the phone. Our complaint did the rounds with the chipset company and after a series of never-ending emails it seemed everyone in that company was simply passing the buck. None of them wanted to accept responsibility for their own product's shortcomings. They simply could not be bothered to fix the problem as it would have meant sending one of their engineers to West Africa to do the fieldwork. The volume of 5,000 units we had sold was in their opinion "not worth our while". However, in parallel, their sales teams would keep pushing us to see how we could increase orders for their chipsets with our factories.

Mi Fone had been used as a guinea pig to test untested

software and this had got me into serious trouble with our carrier customers. We had been let down by the chipset partners and the factory. This was the beginning of the end of our time with this particular MNO customer.

Everyone wanted the African dream,
but no one wanted the African pain

The fuck up with the first smartphones meant we took a big hit. It was our first major smartphone order from the same MNO customer in Ghana, our first Mi Fone customer. They never ordered stock with us again and stopped doing business with us after four years.

The phones were made at a third-party Chinese factory, the chipset was a USA product but the name on the phone was Mi Fone. If the phone didn't work, the end user didn't care about the chipset. All he saw was the word Mi Fone and the MNO that had supplied it. It wasn't good for our reputation when a phone failed. But then it got even worse …

Due to this expensive mistake on their part, the MNO's whole group decided to create a policy of consignment deals only. The exposure for the 5,000 order had been high, but it had backfired due to customer complaints. Now, the whole group policy had changed and they would no longer issue purchase orders for handsets; instead, they would only deal with stocks under a consignment deal agreement. In other words, they would only pay when the goods were sold. This was a risk I simply could not take. I could not make 20,000 phones for an MNO with our brand and their brand and then wait for sales to occur. What if they didn't sell?

This was when I knew that I must start focusing more on brand building in the retail and independent channels. For far too long I had put our eggs in the MNO basket. Now we had to branch out.

Returning to the AfricaCom event, we knew that the big brands were coming in with even deeper pockets and we were losing our momentum with the MNOs. We had to go all out to develop our other channels. By late 2011 we started aggressively pursuing retailers and independent distributors for our product. With the MNOs, we had been selling either feature phones or a single model of a low-cost smartphone and yet we had such a nice range of other products. It was then that we decided to move towards the open market with a larger range of product offerings, plus there were also greater profit margins to be made from independent retail chains and wholesalers.

I told my team that AfricaCom 2011 in Cape Town was where we needed to make the most noise we could. I told them to go all out and put the plan together to get this done. We also ensured that we documented everything and created a 15-minute reality type documentary of what it took to create maximum impact in the mobile phone space in Africa.

Besides the Google event, the highlight of our AfricaCom show was our own exclusive event held at the Grand Daddy Hotel rooftop. No expense was spared in getting the hottest DJs, dancers, models and staging. It was a truly amazing experience to witness 500 people attending a Mi Fone party and leaving with smiles on their faces.

At this point I believed with all my heart that we were going to go big regardless of the funding issues and the problems with the MNOs. We had shipped close to two million devices since we had started.

Little did I know that AfricaCom 2011 was going to be our last Africa Com, the reason being I had got into an argument with the organisers for lying to me about the place being fully booked. The organisers were billing everyone in euros and we paid a massive €16,000 for a two-day exhibiting space in Cape Town. They were paying for the space in the local South African rand but billing everyone in euros, which meant the organisers were making massive margins on the sales of the space, plus I'm sure they were taking a nice packet through the foreign exchange rates as well. They pushed us to buy the space by telling us that the show was fully sold out, only for us to discover that the booths around us were empty. It showed me how blatantly people get ripped off in Africa by the large organisations. Who were we going to complain to? There is no consumer complaints council in Africa.

I needed to think about 2012 and beyond.

Despite putting on a strong front, there was pain behind the scenes and it was showing through the cracks. There was the simple lack of funding, but I also needed management help. It was getting too much for me to handle everything on my own, so I settled on a guy called PN with whom I had been in regular touch over social media for a few years. He was a Gujarati living in the US and he had kept in touch with the brand, seemingly genuinely interested in Mi Fone and wanting to work with us. He had *zero* experience of phones or Africa but I could see he was very keen to help, so I invited him over to Cape Town for AfricaCom to meet the Mi Fone team. It would give him chance to live, breath and *feel* the brand.

I was desperate for a right-hand man, a daily go-to guy, which would then allow me to focus on fundraising and developing business strategies that could generate new revenue streams. I thought with someone like PN to manage the daily runs I would be free to go after the big fish. I mean I couldn't have multimillion-dollar fundraising issues and at the same time have a customer calling me shouting, "Alpesh, where the hell are my two samples?"

I took PN on. Initially he worked from his base in the USA but eventually I was going to have to move him and his family out to Africa to be closer to the business. It was yet another gamble. You're probably thinking why would I employ someone I didn't really know, with little experience of the product or territory? The answer is, I don't know. Maybe it was my emotions kicking in again, enthusiastic about helping someone who wanted to make a difference. PN showed me a passion and eagerness that could really help Mi Fone. In hindsight, knowing that my people-hiring skills were weak, I should have left it to the HR experts. They would have found me the right candidate for the Chief Operations Officer (COO) role of a multimillion-dollar business, in contrast to me simply hiring someone just because I felt good in my heart about that person. Operating from the heart had gotten me into trouble before, but 2012 was when I thought things would be different. We finished 2011 with close to $8 million in annual revenues, another year of amazing growth. If I could beef my team with the right folks, then we would have a great 2012 ahead of us. Or so I thought.

In early 2012, through an associate, we discovered that hip-hop star 50 Cent had heard about Mi Fone and was keen to look at how he could help us. Naturally we were very excited.

Why was collaborating with 50 Cent such a big deal?

Here is a little bit of background just in case you don't know. In 2007 Curtis Jackson (50 Cent) was named the second wealthiest artist in the American hip-hop industry, beaten only by Jay-Z. He made his multimillions from music and celebrity endorsements, but also through investing in a wide variety of industries including artists, records, television, film production, footwear, apparel, liquor, video games, mobile apps, book publishing, headphones, health drinks and dietary supplements, financial market investments, mining, boxing promotion, vodka, fragrances, consumer electronics and fashion. By 2015 he had become the fifth richest hip-hop artist with an estimated net worth of $155 million.

A collaboration with 50 Cent would have taken our brand to the next level and would have bridged that elusive gap between Africa and America. It was a potential lottery ticket for sure. With 50 Cent on board it could mean serious *global* brand awareness! We had already seen what he had done with Vitamin Water and some of his other investments. After some quick phone calls in early 2012, we were invited to attend a meeting with him and his team at his New York City offices. I travelled there with Nic Regisford and asked our new soon-to-be manager PN to join us. The three of us would show a good credible foundation in front of 50 and his team.

The night before our meeting we were in the business centre of our New York hotel going over and over our presentation to him. This was the biggest opportunity that had happened to us so far and preparation was key. We knew that he was interested, but that was not going to be enough. The next day we entered his office next to the *New York Times* building. It was a cool office with awards everywhere and all the products he was endorsing at the time were clearly showcased. We were seated at the open boardroom table with 50's manager, Chris Lighty, his PA and his accountant.

"Let's get started," both men said.

I was surprised. I hadn't come all this way to meet his managers only.

Fortunately, as soon as they spoke 50's PA firmly replied, "No. He *wants* to be in this one. Please wait for him."

I breathed a sigh of relief.

I saw 50 enter, dressed in his trademark jogging suit and baseball cap. He was extremely polite, shook our hands and sat down. After the initial introductions, I went on to explain who we were and, more so, why we were operating in Africa. The meeting went on for two hours and every few minutes 50 would ask a question. He seemed genuinely interested in what we had to say. We then came to what we were offering and it was a very simple proposition. We wanted 50 Cent to own 20% equity of Mi Fone for free and in return he would provide us with the brand endorsement that would lift our brand to new heights not only in Africa but also globally. No other US celebrity had done this before and he was very well-known on the African continent. An initial customised top-of-the-line Mi-50 handset, endorsed by him, would help us increase our sales and fast-track our brand awareness.

After lots of talking, we closed the meeting and left. I could see that there was something there. Our associate called me an hour later as I was rushing through the traffic trying to get back to JFK to connect with my flight back to Dubai.

"Bro, he is down. He is keen. We need to move to the next phase."

When I heard these words, I couldn't have been more excited. Imagine having 50 Cent as our shareholder and brand ambassador! He had expressed his interest but was then leaving all the negotiations to his team. Naturally, they wanted the best deal for him but from the outset we were very clear that we were happy to give him free shares in the company in exchange for his services. Unfortunately, 50's team had a different agenda. They were responsible for 50's brand and were being approached by companies all the time asking for endorsements so, as you might expect, endorsements came at a price.

A couple of weeks after I returned from the meeting we received an email from 50's office. His team were asking for a $1 million upfront fee. This shocked me, as this was clearly not what we had discussed around the New York office boardroom. I had offered *shares* in exchange for brand endorsement but they were now asking me to pay a fee *and* they still wanted the shares. I simply could not do it. I didn't have $1m lying around.

Negotiations then started to stall. His team wanted the best deal for themselves, while I simply couldn't pay and kept insisting that we stick to the original premise as offered in our face-to-face meeting in New York. Things became tricky. Not only did I have to raise funding for Mi Fone operations, but, in addition, I now also had to look for money to pay 50 Cent a minimum fee to join us. I included this in our business plan. If I could show investors that I had a superstar ready to come on board maybe my overall fundraising would be easier. I then had to reconnect with my London contacts. Surely, with a name like 50 Cent I would be able to open some doors and justify asking for more money?

I then took on a part-time CFO called DS who was introduced to me by a wonderful lady based out of London. We needed some expertise on how to put the whole business plan and financial model together. He was a South African guy and, to this day, one of the most genuine and down-to-earth guys I have ever come across. DS was one of the few guys who actually had my interests at heart; not like the multitude of scavengers that just wanted to take money from me.

I cut a deal with DS through which, for a small retainer, he would help me put together a solid set of financials and act as the official CFO for Mi Fone. With several phone calls to London, I had managed to put together a series of meetings with a number of different PE and venture capitalist (VC) firms. DS and I had to go to London to meet all of them one by one. My focus from the outset was to ensure we started getting our name known in financial circles so we could get some funding. In addition to my own funding to the business, we had also received credit lines from the Chinese factories, which meant that we could assist our cash flows because we did not have to pay the Chinese factories immediately. Nonetheless, we still needed to keep borrowing from private lenders at ridiculous loan-shark rates.

We managed to open invoice discounting lines with an African bank, but the deal was not in my favour. I had started talks with them in 2010 and it took until 2012 for them to finally agree. I don't think they knew what they were doing. How could it take them two years to come up with a solution? Some of these African banks never ceased to amaze me in their modus operandi. The bank finally gave me a line based on MNO purchase orders, but in local currencies for which the interest rates were close to 20%.

"How I can I pay 30% to a lender and 20% to banks?"

I knew we were getting ripped off; however, I had no choice but to accept as there simply was no easy access to cheaper funding elsewhere. Trust me, I tried.

When you show your eagerness,
people will take advantage of the situation

By March 2012 our new manager PN was on board and we had a team of five full-time staff and a nice outsourced bunch of people. I quickly had to train PN on how things were done and I took him everywhere with me; all over the world in fact. This was my investment in him to ensure he learned about our brand, our customers and, more so, how to keep things going. He was a 'yes' man and I believed him. We had lots going on at the same time. It was a year of multiple tasks on multiple fronts. I don't want to bore you with the details, but I do need to let you know the key points.

Sometime in April 2012 I refocused my efforts on trying to get the funding going. With a full-time team and DS by my side we had prepared a pretty in-depth business plan. I reached out to the UK contacts and we managed to get introductions to some advisors, who told us they liked our case and would certainly put it forward to some of the PE/VC houses that they knew. A set of meetings was arranged in London for September 2012, but before that there was a pending problem I needed to fix.

Dubai was simply not working for me as an entrepreneur.

I had to think about where best I should locate myself next to take advantage of our pan-African operations. We needed a cost-effective central base. In Dubai, I was not making progress with the local finance crowd and there were major miscommunications in understanding our African vision. I was at a Dubai party once and overhead people.

"The rich folks in Dubai don't respect you if you work hard. Making money is something that's meant to be easy."

I felt that some of the rich folks I bumped into were mostly interested in partying – they never seemed to do anything. Maybe a property deal here or there, but many of them had derived their wealth from unknown sources or had massive family wealth. One very lucrative source was the amazing VAT carousel fraud that was going on in Europe. The Indians used to call it *chakkar* (taking a walk back and forth). The VAT fraud was a key reason how some people were able to set up in Dubai in the first place.

I also understood then why there used to be lines of traders wanting to meet with me at events and conferences during my Motorola days in Dubai. They all wanted allocation of stocks so they could do the carousel rounds and get the money back without actually focusing on selling the goods into the proper markets.

I didn't want to be in an environment that was trapping my vision, so by mid-2012 I had to decide where we move to next. In hindsight, it should have been London, my home and the centre of international capital. At the time, I had a firm belief that I needed to be closer to Africa and in a place that could address all my pan-African operations. The only choice at the time was Mauritius, an idyllic tropical paradise dubbed the 'Switzerland of Africa' because of its reputation as an offshore centre and for the ease of doing business from there.

OPPORTUNITY
*does not waste time
with those that are unprepared*

Idowu Koyenikan

CHAPTER 14

MI CARD

Many folks were shocked when I said we were moving to Mauritius – a speck of land in the middle of the Indian Ocean miles from anywhere …

"Are you sure you are ready for the Robinson Crusoe lifestyle?"

My justification was that by setting up in Mauritius I had a jurisdiction close to Africa but would also be able to address our pan-African business. It also had much lower operating costs than Dubai – and I was desperately in need of cutting my operating costs. I had no choice but to keep paying the extortionate rates on my finance borrowings so other areas needed to be cut. Closing my Dubai office and saving Mi Fone's money by spending less on rentals, cars, school fees, and other high expenses associated with Dubai would be my only recourse.

It was a big change for us – we moved from the high-profile glitz, bling and glam of Dubai to a tropical paradise island with virtually no nightlife, very little social activity, fucked up roads and fucked up cars. With Mi Fone operating out of Hong Kong, we had now set up a parent group company called Mi Group International in Mauritius. The aim here was to create a holding structure so that Mi Group could start doing new things outside the core Mi Fone handset business.

Mauritius was the ideal place to set up the Mi Group. One of the reasons was the development of a concept I had imagined a few months earlier – a concept called Mi Card. I had visualised that in order to increase the sales of Mi Fone I needed to come up with a hook that not only garnered attention but also provided functionality to the users.

"Imagine every smartphone we sold came with a *free debit card*," I said to myself.

This would be a card for the mass-market African consumers. I saw the youth following the hip-hop lifestyle and they knew about the Amex Black card but obviously it was simply, again, what we call 'aspiration beyond reach'. With a similar looking product, we could change this to 'aspiration within reach'. It worked very well with our brand message, allowing African youth to have a luxury card in their pocket with the convenience that goes with it.

We had the retail points by now, especially in Kenya. To see if this would work and after some research, we figured that we needed to expand our revenues beyond only phone devices. Selling a device made us a profit margin only once, but what I needed was to find out was *how* I could make recurring revenues after we had sold that handset and, more so, *how* we could start capturing the phone user's internet browsing habits and spending patterns.

In 2012, nobody had figured out the way to gather, compartmentalise and monetise from the huge data generated from smartphone usage in Africa. With a free Mi Card given out with every smartphone, coupled with the right applications in the phone, we would be able to see where the consumers were spending a) their time and b) their mobile wallet money. From these additional features Mi Group could potentially derive a nice recurring revenue stream per user per month. Introducing a financial product like Mi Card into the business in Africa was not as easy as it would have been in the UK or USA. The first thing about getting a card issued was that each country in Africa had its own central bank rules to follow. We picked Kenya to start with, because that was the market where we had access to the largest retail footprint. I had managed to convince our local retail partners to join us in this quest. They were Mi Group shareholders so why would they say no to helping the brand grow?

I approached a few banks on my own. One was interested because they had a pan-African presence. The problem was that this bank, like most others, didn't have a handle on the smartphone banking revolution that was to come. They were still thinking about building retail branches when we kept telling them that the new retail bank was actually the mobile smartphone screen.

"This is where the average African consumer is going to run his or her life from. You need to embrace this now! To an average African consumer, the world is not round, it's actually a five-inch phone screen." That was my pitch whilst holding up my phone.

The banks welcomed a meeting with us. They were keen to know our plans and I presented to one of the pan-African banks that had initially given Mi Fone its first discounting facility. I went to them first out of respect and goodwill. I remember their head of digital banking was very excited about the project, especially after I told him we would give the card for free with every Mi Fone sold. This initiative would help Mi Fone sales and help the brand diversify into financial arenas, which would increase the brand's overall credibility. To top that, via the Mi Fone device, the bank would get a customer it never had. They loved the idea, but their arrogance showed very quickly. They wanted to treat it as their own project. For them it was a case of us giving them the idea for them to repackage as if they had come up with the concept themselves. Their approach was to simply pay us a one-off commission fee for every new customer we acquired for them.

In no uncertain terms, I told them to fuck off. Why would they think we were commission agents, especially when we had laid out all our plans? We were the ones bringing them the idea and additional access to well over 100+ retail customer points at no cost to them. All they had to do was issue us with the card and share the revenues on all transactions done on that card and on that phone. How difficult was that for them to understand?

This was, and continues to be, the problem with Africa. Had someone from the US or UK approached them with this proposition then the discussion would have been completely different, but when local companies like ours propose ideas, they would act as if they are doing us a favour by meeting us. You recall the MNOs I have mentioned before. Well, the banks were not that different. They had their own gatekeepers.

My sole aim was so share a percentage of *all* transaction revenues, such as cash withdrawal, POS, cash deposit and bill payments so that every month Mi Card would invoice the bank to pay us our share of all the fees generated. I wasn't there to be a commission agent!

We shut down talks with that bank and went to another in Kenya. This bank was known for being a bit more aggressive and flexible but at the same time they had quite a few card schemes out already. I had no choice. Fortunately, they seemed to be keen as they realised the value of our retail footprint and our hook of free cards with every Mi Fone phone sold. Through them I was introduced to Visa and MasterCard separately because we needed to have the support from one of these card-processing companies. At the time, my heart was set on Visa, because they had the most widely available acceptance points in Kenya. Visa was better-known too and, with their deep pockets, I had already prepared some great marketing strategies that would promote them and us.

Both Visa and MasterCard's regional head offices were in Dubai. Most of the large organisations from USA had their regional head offices in Dubai and from there they would manage their Middle East and Africa businesses. So, it was back to Dubai that I started going to present my case to both Visa and MasterCard. It was pretty straightforward. I knew my business and I could clearly showcase my ideas. I was a storyteller at the end of the day. I made them see my vision. I made them see the future that did not exist at that time.

Both companies loved the idea we presented and were keen to engage. I knew then that I was in over my head getting into the card game – I didn't know shit. The card business was a complex one with so many different line items to consider and by this time I was physically and mentally all over the place. I had my five-man team taking care of the Mi Fone business and I was keen to expand our business lines. I needed a hook to make our revenues higher by selling more handsets but we still could not afford million-dollar advertising campaigns. Mi Card was the perfect hook. Imagine a smartphone with a Mi Card mobile money app inbuilt. This app allowed you load your account and send money over the air and pay online bills and at same time you could present the card at any grocery store, bar or restaurant. It was the virtual and physical solution that was missing in Africa.

MPESA was a very popular money transfer system introduced in Kenya, funnily enough, by Michael Joseph, the same guy who had given me the 100,000-phone unit order back in Motorola days. MPESA was, and still is, the leader when it comes to mobile payments in Kenya. The only difference with our offering was that we had proposed a physical card to embrace all MNO money wallets under one umbrella app. When a customer used their phone to send money to another customer's phone, they didn't have to go to an agent, such as MPESA or Airtel Money to get cash, the app would simply update the card in real time. Customers could spend on their phone and also on their card. There were multiple revenue streams in place for us.

I was then introduced to a guy called TS through one of my contacts at Visa Dubai. I wish I had never met him. TS was the ex-CEO of a large global card-processing company. He was a seasoned older English gentleman and we didn't have much in common other than the strange fact that both of us had attended the University of Hull!

TS had left the card business to head up a regional travel company. He was bored and was looking for a new challenge. He had been briefed on Mi Card by my Visa contacts and he pushed to meet with me. I was too busy to even think about TS but he kept hounding me for a face-to-face meeting. I agreed finally and we met at the Sheraton Hotel at Jumeirah Beach Residence in Dubai. I remember seeing him for the first time. Bald and bespectacled. He had agreed to buy me a coffee. From the outset, he was very clear.

"Alpesh, I heard about this from the Visa guys and I absolutely love this idea of yours and I want to be part of it. It would be an honour for you to consider me becoming the CEO of Mi Card. I have a lot of experience and know this space very well."

He was an ex-card guy and I knew he wouldn't come cheap so I was also very upfront with him.

"This is a start-up. I have not raised any funding for this business so I cannot afford any salaries now, but if you are that keen then I would welcome you on board. I'd suggest you take some shares in the company and then we try to raise some funding for this."

He agreed right there and then on the spot. We shook hands. With a guy like TS, a seasoned British corporate guy, I would be able to have him push the Mi Card agenda further than I could. Or so I thought.

A few weeks went by and things were moving along well. I took TS on his first ever trip to Kenya to meet with the proposed bank partner. This was his first time in Africa. The banks were clamouring over him (they treated him with much more respect than they had treated me). Yes, TS was my 'great white hope'. He was an older British guy with a pretty decent CV and spoke the corporate language well. Besides, most Africans, especially in business, always loved the Anglo-Saxon guys. They looked up to them. Many African corporates had this colonial style mentality. Some still do.

TS kept hammering on that he needed to bring in a couple of his ex-card company mates for him to really do a great job; one as our chief technical officer (CTO) and one as our chief operations officer (COO). I had questioned why we needed three senior people when we had not even started.

'A case of too many chiefs and not enough Indians' … except me.

I wasn't paying these guys any salaries so in the end I just let it slide. They all wanted to be in Kenya and they paid their own way. What the fuck did I care, the more seasoned corporate types I had on board, the better the business case. I let them do what they had to do in terms of negotiating each and every clause with the bank. This process took us a good six months. By the end of 2012 we had set up Mi Card as a separate entity and TS and his mates were allocated 30% of the equity. Mi Group owned the remaining 70%. I was still the majority shareholder but now I had the three guys running the show.

I was happy with this arrangement because it was our idea and we were making the initial push with the banks to get it all going. TS, however, kept saying he couldn't work indefinitely without a salary. I asked him to issue me with the financials, so I could then add them into the Mi Group business plan. This would then greatly help me in securing funding – and let's not forget the addition of a potential partnership with 50 Cent. If 50 Cent joined our group we could even bring out a 50 Cent-powered debit card. How cool would that have been?

The Mi Card project began well. TS and his two mates had agreed to roll out the project with no pay. Fortunately for TS, he had some good connections in the Middle East and Europe and within a matter of a couple of months he had secured $1 million in funding without Mi Card generating one dollar in revenue. I was amazed how he had done this when I had been trying for so long with no luck to get funding for a revenue-generating business like Mi Fone. TS raised money with my idea where I hadn't been able to with the very same one.

We then had to carve up the company to make more space for the new investors. One of the investors was a rich Bahraini guy and the other was a venture capital fund that TS had known for a while. He had sold them on the premise that the idea was a strong one and, with his industry experience, it was actually going to be quite easy to get thousands of cards out in circulation.

I spent several weeks travelling between Dubai and Mauritius to represent the business with TS. Once we raised the money, TS started to forget the initial premise of the concept and began insisting that, since he raised the money, he should be more in control of the business and that I should relegate myself to becoming a non-executive director of the company. He merely looked at me as the guy who came up with the ideas and nothing else. This was when tensions started between us.

TS had never lived in Kenya before so he decided immediately that, once the funds were raised, he and his two lieutenants would base themselves in Nairobi to set up the operation. I gladly agreed as I knew there was nothing like being on the ground, but TS quickly made his own plans on how to approach the market. I introduced him to our Mi Fone retail partners – a crucial element in our card-distribution strategy. TS completely fucked up the first meeting with his colonial attitude. My partners called me that very same night and asked me what kind of guy I had sent? They were very concerned how someone with no experience on local conditions could suddenly decide how to run the show.

Further fuck-ups started to happen when TS changed the whole business plan to move away from free cards with phones to a stand-alone card distribution. This was like walking on fire. There was a plethora of cards out in the market and the only differentiating hook we had was the free card via the Mi Fone device and nothing else. TS was insistent and started dictating to our retail partners on how things should be done. This approach pissed off my retail partners big time. You don't order older seasoned Indian traders around, telling them how to run their businesses on their own home patch. That's like giving someone a slap in public. TS went into meetings with all guns blasting and dictated how things were to be done. Inevitably, an immediate clash of egos emerged between the local Mi Fone retail partners and TS. I intended to introduce them to work together but ended up being the solitary intermediary whose job it was to soothe out the issues.

TS and his mates then decided that they would introduce other ways to bring Mi Card to the market. This was a no-go because it would mean a severe dilution of our initial selling proposition. His true colours started showing when he began talking down to me as if I was his errand boy to run around as he ordered. He had lived in the Middle East for 15 years and perhaps he was used to ordering brown guys around, but that shit was not going to work with me. I wasn't his 'coolie'.

We started arguing and fighting and yet he continued to keep providing fancy weekly reports to the board showing how much great progress he and his team were making. In reality, however, there was very little progress. They had completely ignored the premise of the card project. We had a few thousand cards in circulation, but the cracks began to show when, out of the $1million we had raised, TS used $800,000 on salaries and expenses for himself and his two mates. He had brought his corporate way of doing things into a small African start-up.

Don't get side-tracked. Stick to your plan

It got worse when the three of them started making false promises to the investors of new pending contracts so they could raise even more money. Again, I don't know how he swung it, but TS managed to raise another $400,000 from the very same investors who had seen no performance on the ground. I was just baffled. There I was, having battled day in, day out to sell phones since 2008, with little luck on the funding side, and yet this guy was managing to raise money for a business that had generated next to nothing in revenues.

Accusations then started flying back and forth and I began to get very angry. How could Mi Card have raised $1m on the basis of our initial sales plan and then have completely diverted from that plan to take on another one that simply had no momentum in the marketplace? Had the same funds been invested in actual business development and marketing we would have had many more subscribers on board, but to spend 75% of the funds on personal salaries and expenses just pissed me off. These guys were not entrepreneurs; they were a bunch of seasoned corporate shysters who had taken advantage of an incredible African initiative.

Due to the internal fighting and the fact that all monies raised quickly dried up with no major customer contracts in place, we lost momentum with Mi Card. The investors were upset, but I told them it was because the original premise was never followed. They bought into the charm of TS and allowed him to do what he pleased without any checks or balances. They lost money. I lost a great idea and, more so, time.

Whilst all of this was going on I was also busy trying to sort out funding for Mi Fone. In one particular week, we met with six PE and VC funds in London – one of them being Bob Geldof's fund 8Mile. We knew from our contacts that all these funds had money to allocate to Africa. Most of the meetings went on for two hours or so and there seemed to be considerable interest in our business (otherwise we would not have been invited to meet in person). They had our plans, our numbers and wanted to meet us. They had done their research and all their questions were properly answered.

We were rejected by all of them. I don't know why or how they could do that after showing so much interest, but by the end of 2012 I was distraught in that I still could not raise any funds. All in all, we had met with about 50 funding firms, some large, some small, some VC, some family funds, some PE and some angel-type investors. All of them had shut us down. Mi Fone had started in 2008 with nothing and we had made some decent revenues in our four years, yet we found it next to impossible to raise funds. Then a guy like TS rolls up and raises a cool $1.4m just like that. Gaddddddddamm!

My business pressures were also growing. For year end 2012 our revenues dropped for the first time in our history. We should have been increasing revenues not decreasing them. We had a team in place and were shipping to more than 14 countries in Africa.

Something in my heart started telling me that I was on a downhill slide.

My family had settled into Mauritius but besides the business set up I was never keen on the island itself. I could not fathom walking around in shorts, wearing flip-flops and hanging out at the beach every weekend. I was not at retiring age and, despite being off the island two weeks out of every month, I would only return to see my family and the staff based out of the Mauritius office we had set up. Our Mauritius office was now running our Africa business and even though we had a team in place I still did not feel that I could hand over the complete responsibility for Mi Fone over to them. I had to keep an eye on the goings on. PN, our manager, was now travelling extensively to Africa so he certainly took a lot of burden from my shoulders by talking with our customers and making new inroads.

Mauritius did give us a nice lifestyle. We had hilltop home in a sugar cane plantation with views to die for. On the surface, we were living the dream. One Sunday afternoon my family and I were enjoying a fantastic Sunday lunch at the prestigious Royal Palm hotel in Grand Baie. As we were eating I saw a bald guy with a bunch of books in his hand enter the outdoor dining area. I immediately recognised him as Robin Sharma, author of the great book *The Monk Who Sold His Ferrari*.

I was not one to walk up to someone, but when I saw him I immediately remembered the summer of 2012 a few weeks earlier. We had taken a short vacation in the south of France and whilst dining one night at Villa Romana in St Tropez, we spotted the billionaire Indian tycoon Lakshmi Mittal sitting at the table right next to us. As we stood up to leave the restaurant he smiled ever so nicely at me (he must have known I was a fellow Indian). I responded with a smile only, when what I should have done was go up to him, greet him and pay my respects. Some of the best associations are met when people see each other in non-threatening, non-business environments. I had regretted not greeting one of the most prominent Indian businessmen on the planet and I was not going to make that mistake again. After the lunch, I saw Robin sitting on his own and thought I must say hi to him, so I walked up to his table

"Hi, Robin. I'm a big fan of yours and loved your book."

Robin had the most amazing welcoming smile and we immediately started chatting, speaking for a good 10 minutes. I told him I was living in Mauritius and running my pan-African business from the island. I gave him my card and asked him to call me if ever he needed anything or wanted to meet up again before he left. The very next day Robin called me and asked me to join him for lunch at the same place where we had met. I gladly agreed and was excited to have the honour of having lunch with one of the foremost leadership experts on the planet.

Our lunch went on for five hours! That's how good our conversations were. I hadn't even known that Robin had also been born in Uganda of all places. Our friendship grew from that day. Over the years, we have developed a close friendship and I have been an attendee at all of his legendary Titan Summit experiences. Through this network I have been able to forge really great and loving relationships with some amazing human beings, all of them on a mission to make the lives around them better. I was drawn into this world, maybe because of the harshness I was facing on a daily basis with my business in Africa. The Titan Academy has been like a refuge for me; a place to refuel and reenergise. This was the start of my long journey into self-improvement, personal development and looking at life in a completely different way.

The year progressed and there was the continuous daily hustle of orders, payments, productions and all the other things I was working on. The funding side, or lack thereof, was getting to me and we had run out of cash flow to keep financing our operations. I was taking from one hand to pay the other and as a result the fundraising had started to become a priority for me. The immediate challenge we faced was that our sales numbers had dropped. In order to keep getting orders we were being pushed to go lower and lower on our prices, which meant our margins started to get thinner and thinner, yet we were still paying private lenders the high interest rates.

I recall one African PE firm that were very keen on our business. We had arranged Skype calls and shared a lot of information. After receiving our blueprint, they also shut us down with the reason being, "the handset space is not really where they invest".

"Muzzerfuzzer, you could have told me that from the outset before I shared all my confidential info with you!"

This was how it was for us.

We kept giving information on request to people for them to then turn around and say that it wasn't the business sector they wished to get into. Funnily enough, this very same African PE firm then invested in a new handset start-up in Nigeria exactly 12 months later. Again, could it have meant that raising money is cultural?

My wariness of these PE guys was now starting to take

effect. To me they were all highly paid fund managers who never really understood the mind-set of an entrepreneur. Most of them, as individuals, had never built consumer brands. This very same fund I am talking about has had virtually no success with any of its investments. Even the Nigerian start-up ended up being a massive loss-making entity. Yet when I met them they always said things were going great.

"Yes it's 'cos you not playing with your own money!"

Africa was full of these suited bullshitters. Very few of them actually had any of their own skin in the game.

The 50 Cent management team were also continuously on my case and I was under major pressure to come up with some money to secure his services. By February 2013 we had been in talks with his team for a year and had still made no progress. I had searched every part of my brain and my soul to try to find a solution. We were desperately keen to have him on board, but it seemed the original deal was forgotten and now it was a simple case of us paying them money and handing over shares. I had spoken to a few people to help me with raising the funds solely to secure 50 Cent's service fee. None of these channels materialised and when it came to the crunch, I had one final call with our associate and he was clearly frustrated with the situation. He asked me straight.

"Can you come up with a minimum $250,000 now or not?"

As much as I had wanted to say yes, I simply could not tie myself to a commitment that I could not meet. I couldn't give promises and not deliver. My word has always been my bond, so I had to decline the final deal. There was no alternative; we had to walk away from what could have been the biggest game changer for Mi Fone.

This was just one of the many conversations 50 Cent was having with brands and for him it was no big loss, but I had pinned so much hope on getting this deal. We had been given some great promises on the funding as we had been advised by the financial go-betweens, who all seemed confident that Mi Fone + Mi Card + 50 Cent would be a great story worth investing in. Unfortunately, for me it was a battle that I was simply not winning.

By mid-2013 I had the following issues to deal with.

My hopes with 50 Cent had not worked out despite a huge amount of time and effort being spent on the deal; my hopes with Mi Card had stalled as TS had pulled a fast one; and, finally, the company had to file for liquidation. My hopes for additional funding for Mi Fone had not worked out, which had meant more private borrowings to fund our orders. Our overall business had dropped and payments due to us were starting to get increasingly delayed.

I also had a problem at home. I was in London during a fundraising trip and called Rene to see how she was. After some initial chitchat, she went quiet and I asked her what was wrong.

In a very sad voice she replied, "I feel very lonely here. I'm all alone. I don't like it here."

I felt a lump in my throat. Mauritius, the paradise island, could also be a hellhole. It was one of those places where there simply was no social life for us. It was a big change from Dubai. Of course, I was constantly travelling, but Rene was stuck there all the time. Being on an island in the middle of the Indian Ocean and not knowing anyone can take its toll. I immediately knew that if I wanted to save my marriage I had to focus on making sure my wife was comfortable. I had to make a decision. If we continued to stay in Mauritius I would have to curtail my travelling, which would have hindered my progress. We could go back to Dubai (which was pointless) or we could go back to a place where Rene had family and friends.

After just one year in Mauritius (51 weeks too long for my liking) we decided that it would be best for us to move back to South Africa. There were no visa issues, schools were good and there was a family support structure for Rene. I could operate Mi Fone from there and still keep our Mauritius office open.

So back to South Africa we went. Gauteng Province to be precise. The abbreviation they use is 'GP'. In some circles GP is known as 'Gangsters Paradise'.

DON'T JUDGE PEOPLE BY THEIR CLAIMS

The proof is in the pudding.
You are smarter than you think

CHAPTER 15

THE AFRICAN DREAM

Moving back to Johannesburg was bittersweet for me. Bitter in that I had never really enjoyed living there since landing that time from Tokyo. Apart from my pay cheques at Harris and Motorola, I had never made any money in South Africa, despite having tried so many different angles. For me South Africa was, is and will always be a very strange nation. I'm sure many of my foreign friends who live there will agree that it's not the easiest place to do business or to make money. The only foreigner I know who made money there was my French friend Stef who now owns all the top clubs in South Africa, but, then again, his main cash always came from the big-spending Nigerians visiting South Africa. Go figure.

The sweet part in moving back to Johannesburg was that for us it was a simple 'plug and play' move. We had lived there before, we knew the ropes and being South African residents there was no issue over residency visas, medical tests or filling in the numerous forms that we had had to do in Dubai and Mauritius. Sweet also because operating out of Johannesburg was an unknown secret when it came to managing costs. It is a very cost-efficient place to operate from and the infrastructure is great with the best flight connections into sub-Sahara Africa.

I have always said that if the South African government had their heads screwed on right Johannesburg would be the 'Silicon Valley' of Africa. Everything was in place for entrepreneurs to set up, especially those who had pan-African aspirations for their business. South Africa has its fair share of entrepreneurs, but most of them tend to have a local market focus. Maybe the history of the country and the fact that it was closed off for too long made the South African folks very late in coming to the international forum. Even today when you ask an average South African if they have travelled in Africa, most of them would reply,

"Yes, we went to Botswana and Lesotho once."

They see Africa as being very separate from South Africa.

Today a few large companies from South Africa have an Africa-wide presence. There are success stories like Mobile Telecommunications Network Group (MTN), a behemoth MNO headquartered out of South Africa, but with a massive African footprint. MTN, for example, has made most of its money out of Nigeria and not South Africa. Some South African groups have invested in Africa, only to get a major beating because they 'assumed' they knew what they were doing. A classic example here would be Tiger Brands, a consumer goods company that lost a huge amount of money in Nigeria.

Johannesburg has it all, but there is no clear entrepreneur ecosystem in place. The government will proclaim massive investment into small and medium enterprises (SMEs), but in reality, the money does not get to the people that matter. It gets lost in the system somewhere. South Africa is one of the richest countries on the planet (in terms of mineral wealth) and yet there is more than 30% unemployment, most of it being youth aged 18–25. How can this be? How can the government and large corporates fail its people and yet continue to make money from them? I have always felt this pain for the people of South Africa, but they have simply never stood up and fought for their rights. All the big corporates – parastatals, insurance companies, MNOs, banks – just continue to rip off the consumers and no one does shit about it.

Despite the shortcomings of moving back to Johannesburg, ultimately, I wanted my wife and family to be happy. I also needed to cut my costs further. By now, virtually all the UK funders we had met had either gone quiet or declined investing in our business. I was back at square one. The only thing that kept Mi Fone going was the Sinosure credit lines we had from China and the private borrowings we were managing to upkeep. Once we were settled into South Africa, by late 2013 I had decided that we needed a massive marketing push – not only because of orders, but also because we needed to increase our brand awareness in South Africa itself. We had supplied into South Africa back in 2010 via some retail channels and I now felt that we had to give it another shot. I knew it was not going to be an easy ride – I had dealt with the South African MNOs and retail groups before.

Not everyone looked at Mi Fone in a favourable way, especially in South Africa. For the past six years we had been making a lot of noise and because we were brash and rebellious I am sure we had also upset a lot of people along the way. I knew that the South African market was expensive for mobile brands to enter. South Africa is an MNO-controlled environment. There were four major operators; MTN, Vodacom, Cell C and Telkom. In order to get your products into these operators it would entail months of meetings, testing of product samples, getting approvals and having deep pockets for marketing budgets.

None of these MNO guys were willing to stock our products, even though we were the first African device brand distributing in 14 markets. It didn't really make a difference when it came to South Africa. They couldn't give a shit if we were patriotic Africans or not.

As I touched on earlier, the South Africans have always considered themselves separate from the rest of Africa so no matter what successes you might have had in rest of Africa it doesn't really mean anything when trying to convince South African resellers to take on your product. We had always faced difficulties in selling stock to South Africa. It was just a very frustrating place to do business. South African corporates love to have meeting after meeting; you can actually have a meeting simply to plan the next meeting, then nothing gets done and once again aspects of the Double G phenomenon show up here and there. Knowing that we had been stalled in the past and would most likely be stalled again, we had to embark on our own PR mission to gain as much press coverage as we could. This was the only way we could show the market that we had history.

Mi Fone had always been a compelling story. No company had ever done what we had. No company had created a pan-African consumer brand from scratch with no funding and one that was now present in more than 14 countries. The South Africans in particular needed to know about this, so we embarked on a massive PR campaign.

Luckily for us, as much as we'd had objections from the South African MNOs and big retailers – the international press was quite the opposite. They loved our story. We had a genuine feel-good story and we had been going since 2008 with hard numbers to back up our existence. With the help of our PR partners, Mi Fone very quickly became prominently featured on Forbes Africa, CNBC Africa, CNN and in a myriad of radio and print publications. The press articles were then quickly distributed via our own database and social media pages throughout South Africa, Africa and the rest of the world. We used these press articles to obtain more local press in the various countries in Africa. This was to ensure that our current customers in Africa continued selling their Mi Fone stocks at a rapid pace.

Even though 2013 generated another downturn year in terms of revenues, in the last quarter of the year Mi Fone managed to secure some of our biggest orders in history, many of them from new customers. Our manager PN was now travelling Africa-wide and doing a good job when it came to securing the orders. However, in the process of chasing these orders we began to screw ourselves. We thought we could handle these large orders, even though we had several cash flow and funding issues. I negotiated paying the Chinese factories within 60 days of receiving their goods as part of our credit arrangement. We would give 30–45 days credit to our customers. On paper it looked fine, but in practice none of our customers paid on time.

The actual cash flow cycle worked against us. In order to release new stocks from the factories we had to ensure their invoices had been paid. Why would they release new stock to us if they had not been paid for the previous stocks? We never managed to settle all the outstanding payments in one go because we *never* received payments from customers in Africa in one go. Our customers would always either short-pay us or split up their invoices due into smaller payments. The reality of this was that we would receive customer payments almost

90 days from the issuing of our invoices. In practical terms, we were timed out because don't forget we had to pay the factories within 60 days too. Of course, we could not even think about charging the customers extra interest charges on their late payments – they would have taken it as an offence and told us to simply fuck off. Our Mi Fone customers really tested us when it came to our politeness and diplomacy, but I was not going to shout at someone who owed me a lot of money.

Meanwhile, on the China side, the new stocks we had ordered were piling up on the factory warehouse floor because they would not be released due to us delaying our previous payments. In Q4 2013, with an order book of close to 200,000 phone units (our largest sales quarter ever), we simply did not have a large enough working capital line to fund our productions and collections. We were still five people running a multimillion dollar business. Since 2008 we had clocked close to $40 million in revenues. Yes, this is a small figure in the world of mobile phones but not small for us who had started with nothing and had no funding.

I'm not looking for sympathy here and this ain't no story with violins playing in the background. I know what you might be thinking. 'Oh, if you didn't have the funding then it's your fault. You should have arranged it way before.' We had been trying to arrange funding since 2011. The enormous number of times we had approached banks and other funding houses cannot be underestimated. We would even get term sheets from some banks *agreeing* to fund us, but then they would go silent. A classic example is one of Africa's largest export/import banks. They had checked all our financials and via a working paper we were virtually assured a $3m finance facility at interest rates much lower than those we were used to paying. When we tried calling them to tell them we were ready to sign, the muzzerfuzzers simply disappeared into thin air. Whoosh! Like the movie *Gone in 60 Seconds*.

By 2013 the majority of our business had converted itself to open-market supplies to distributors and retailers rather than our traditional supplies to the MNOs. We had deliberately curtailed our MNO activities because we could not take the risk of doing consignment deals with them. It was good to sell to retailers so we could provide more varieties of our phone models. However, each time we ordered a model with our China factories we had to adhere to a minimum order quantity (MOQ). In our MNO orders, we could make the MOQ based on a back-to-back order from them. They ordered 20,000 phones – we made them and shipped 20,000 phones in one go. Deal done.

For our retail market, none of our distributor partners could commit to our minimum order quantities so we had to make our MOQ with the factories of 20,000 units and then hold the stock in our Hong Kong warehouses. This stock would then be broken up into smaller parcels as per our customer's forecasted orders. I say the word 'forecast' because we would always try to get some kind of pre-order feedback from our customers. They would always forecast a high number, but in reality, when it came to ordering, it was always a minimum of 50% or less of their initial requests. This meant we did not sell all our warehoused stock in a quick manner. Our customers would take what they wanted, considering they too were still owing us money for past stocks we had shipped. Our cash would therefore always be tied up either in phone stocks or with customers. At times, I had no choice but to clear phone stocks at ridiculous prices just to get some cash back, pay the factories and start a new order production. A case of rinse and repeat, but for me it was a case of being rinsed repeatedly. This was, after all, the cell phone hustle.

Every few months new, more advanced chipset processors in new phone models were introduced by the Chinese factories. The chipset guys would make massive announcements of new products entering the markets, but the markets of Africa did not respond to product launches as quickly as China came out with them. This was another dilemma we faced.

On average, it took nine months for Mi Fone to build product hype, marketing and sales in Africa, but every few weeks China would be coming out with newer, cheaper models. Some of our customers would see all the press and then tell us they had decided not to take our current stocks, preferring to wait for the new models. This would then fuck up our stock situation even more. Mi Fone was a juggling act of note. In a circus, a magician or a clown would do the juggling; in our African circus, we ended up as the clowns.

By 2013 the mobile phone business itself had also become much more cutthroat. We had started the white label game in 2008, but by 2013 everyone and their mothers were putting their brand names on phones. It had become very easy for someone to hop on a plane and get a Chinese factory to make a phone for them with their name on it. The MNOs also started ordering their own phones directly from China. If they were going to order from us it would have to be on their consignment-deal terms. With them, either way we were screwed.

I had to keep going though. I had no choice. I had put too

much time and money into Mi Fone to let it slide. I knew I had been outspent by the competition that had deeper pockets. I lay awake most nights thinking of how to rescue the situation and how we could get out of this never-ending vicious cycle of cash flow worries.

We hadn't done anything innovative for a while, but when you take away the money the only thing we ever had was our creativity and our innovation. I had to think very hard about what else we could do to enhance our revenues besides just phone sales. My limits were being tested again.

SOMETIMES ONE STEP BACK MEANS TWO STEPS FORWARD
*in business that can be the difference
between survival and extinction!*

CHAPTER 16

OJU

I had a meeting with my design team Eserick and Zelia. They were a South African husband-and-wife team who had a boutique design agency called 1k based in Johannesburg. They had some of the coolest design skills I had ever seen. Eserick and Zelia had been by my side since 2008 when they took the initial Mi logo created by my friend Vanessa Holmes to the next level. This included our whole brand guidelines, box designs, event promotional material and merchandise. My design team was a core part of my belief systems. For me it had always been important to present the brand as a luxurious, but affordable offering. We never did the smack bang cut and paste shit. When we designed it was an intricate process and would involve several rounds going to and fro with the ideas until I was 110% satisfied. At times, I'm sure they were majorly pissed off with me, but not once did we get into an argument – not because I'm not argumentative, but simply because Eserick and Zelia don't have one ounce of aggression in them. I give them credit for keeping up with my demands.

At our meeting, they said they wanted to share something special with me; something exciting, but confidential that could *possibly* lift Mi Fone to new heights. I listened eagerly, thinking it was probably a new box design they wanted to show me. When it came to design I was always open to see what they were thinking about. They then asked me to imagine what we could do with the software of our phones; a software file that was unique to us. 1k had an open glass cabinet that showcased all the phones we had done in the past – a kind of tribute wall of trophies. They brought out one of our latest smartphone models, turned it on and started swiping on the screen. They got to the message icon and opened it.

"Alpesh, this is how we write messages right?" Eserick was pretending to write a message in the text box of the icon.

"We all write hundreds of text messages all the time right?" he continued.

"So, what can we do with the biggest momentum of this time – chat messaging?"

I kept nodding my head.

"Look at the phone software currently. Look at the emoticons."

"OK, so?"

"Well imagine if we, as an African mobile phone brand, took all these yellow emoticons ... *and made them black.*"

At that very moment, whilst Eserick was showing me the phone, his wife Zelia had already switched on her laptop and turned the computer screen around to show me her slide. There she showed me an image they had designed. *Black emoticons.*

I was flabbergasted.

I looked at both of them and stood up. I walked around their studio shouting, not because I was angry or anything, but because this was the missing piece from our business jigsaw puzzle that I had been so desperately looking for. The sheer simplicity of creating our own set of Afro black emoticons could change our path completely. All sorts of thoughts were rushing through my mind. Mi Fone could create its own intellectual property for *only* our phones. This would start making Mi Fone famous in the marketplace. Why would an African not use emoticons similar to themselves instead of the standard yellow smileys? Eserick and Zelia showed me a concept design of a black emoticon. It was far from perfect, but the point was that the idea was revolutionary.

"Imagine what we could do with this? No one else in the world is doing it!" I shouted.

We all smiled collectively. This was it. 1k had worked on ideas for us before, but this was very different. They had created the concept, but it was now up to me to decide what to do with it. They had my immediate buy-in for sure, and they had clearly thought this one out, whether I was going to like the idea or not. I truly believe they were as passionate about Mi Fone as I was. They wanted us to get better and better at what we were doing.

"Please send me the presentation and I'll work on it overnight, then let's meet again tomorrow to see what we can do," I said on a closing note.

That night in December 2013 I couldn't sleep due to the excitement. It was like a breath of fresh air in the midst of all the crap I was going through on multiple fronts with Mi Fone, Mi Card and our overall business. This was exactly what we needed, but I needed to figure out how to convert Eserick's design slide into reality. How could we take this to the market? How could we create a new sub-brand that initially would be exclusive to Mi Fone handsets before eventually opening up into a general offering for *all* Android software devices sold globally? Yes, that's where my thinking was. This idea was too big for Mi Fone alone. It had to be part of a bigger vision.

What a fucking awesome idea!

I had to think of a name for this new concept and

commercialise it as soon as possible. I have always said that ideas are a dime a dozen – what counts is the execution of those ideas into real life and into revenue-generating business models. Our collection of black smileys *had* to have its own identity. I definitely did not want to call them 'the Mi Fone Smileys'. The name had to be catchy, short, easy to remember and *original*. The name also had to reflect a character rather than just an image. This emoticon and its emotional variations needed a life of its own, it had to reflect our African heritage and, ultimately, we needed to address the lack of cultural diversity in the tech world. There are more than three billion people on this planet of colour – from light coffee to dark complexion – and there was nothing in the tech world that represented us. When you look at your WhatsApp emoticons all you see is one Indian guy with a turban, never any black images. Why?

I wanted a cool African name and seeing that my favourite country in Africa has and will always be Nigeria I actually wanted to give it a Nigerian name. For me the Nigerians are probably the most patriotic people on the continent. They love their country and their culture regardless of the immense amount of crap they go through on a daily basis. They are a proud nation that has some of the sharpest minds on the planet. We wanted to use the Nigerian philosophy as a shining example of what it *meant* to be an *African*.

I looked at several names and then it came to me: OJU.

Cool and easy to remember by anyone in the world. It is a name that can be easily pronounced anywhere in Africa, Europe, China and the USA. In the Yoruba language of Nigeria oju means 'face' – some Yorubas later told me it means eyes but I knew I could get away with it. Oju – *the face of Africa*. An African character that would be Africa's first digital character and lifestyle brand. Africa had never had its own Mickey Mouse characters (except maybe some of our leaders).

In our next meeting, just before Christmas 2013, I presented my reviews and counter-proposals to my design team. They would do the design work and I would do all the commercialisation. We agreed there and then that we would both be co-founders of Oju, but we would need to create a separate company with Mi Group holding 65% and Eserick and Zelia holding 35% of the shares respectively. We would set up the company in Mauritius and Mi Fone would pay for the business development of the Oju app that we needed to create as soon as possible.

Our proposed app would be embedded into the Mi Fone software, but would also be immediately available on the Google Play Store. We went to work as soon as the new year of 2014 had started. We enlisted the help of a local app development company in South Africa and we paid them to develop the technical side of the app. By early March the app was done. It wasn't to my liking as it was not part of the keyboard. This in itself was a mission to accomplish. What we did was to create a basic Beta version app that could be used by people when they were messaging. They could then add the Oju emoticons as an attachment to their text. Not ideal and not that user-friendly, but I was of the belief that we simply had to come out with something first and build it from there. I wasn't prepared to invest thousands and thousands of dollars to develop the perfect app and then launch it, and neither did I have the time.

As part of our South Africa market re-entry, besides all the press we were getting, we had also planned an event to showcase Mi Fone again to the South African crowd. I had penned down 15th April 2014 as our event date and we would unveil the Oju offering as a surprise. I wanted to talk about Mi Fone, but also launch Oju to the world.

Perfect timing – or was it?

On 25th March 2014, whilst going through the daily email newsletters from various tech sites, I came across an article in *TechCrunch* (a famous industry daily newsletter). Of all people, the superstar celebrity Miley *fucking* Cyrus had sent an email to Apple to complain about the lack of racially diverse emoticons. The article then mentioned that MTV had also asked Apple on when they would be adding more diverse emoticons to their offerings. I immediately gathered Eserick and our PR agent. Somehow, we had to use this to our advantage. We had our conference call at 9pm on 25th March. After giving them the background of what I had just read, we all agreed that we should immediately issue a global press release to announce the Oju offering. We wanted to claim first mover advantage and ownership of this topic around racially diverse emoticons.

"But what about our surprise for the launch?" said our PR agent.

"Fuck that! We go live *now*," I shouted back.

That very night, a press release went out to all the major media across the world. In that press release we highlighted the *TechCrunch* news article and announced the fact that there was no need for anyone to develop any diverse emoticons because a small African company already had the solution. The press release was our way of making Oju official. We had already, that same night, put the basic Oju app onto Google Play Store so people reading the release could also immediately download the app. We weren't bullshitting in any way. Oju was for real.

That same night I sent an email to Apple to tell them about Oju and I also called the Unicode Consortium in the USA to ask how we could get our emoticons to be part of the consortium. How could Oju be part of every mobile phone keyboard and sit next to the yellow standard emoticons? We were not saying get rid of the yellow smileys, all we were saying was please add more choice to the current offering by having some black smileys as well. Surprisingly, Unicode replied the next day with a note saying it was next to impossible to just add Oju. It was long process that needed to take place and all members of the Unicode Consortium had to approve any additions. Those members included the likes of Microsoft and Apple. I left it at that.

The international press – *oh man* the press. These guys went crazy on our release. It was absolute mayhem over the next few days. Every major press had picked up our release – this was like Mi Obama all over again with the only difference being we were not piggybacking on anything this time. Oju and the black emoticons had simply never been done before. The talk around Oju gave me some much-needed positivity at a tough time. Within seven days of the press release the Oju basic app had been downloaded more than 60,000 times on Google Play. We took these statistics and added Oju to our overall Mi Group business plan. We owned 65% of Oju, but it also needed its own funding and support if it was to ever take off in a big way.

The fervour and excitement of the international press was

very different from the reaction we received from the African press – more so the South African press where the release was first issued from. Not one of them wrote about Oju.

When we did our big launch on 15th April I stood on stage for 45 minutes that night and took the crowd through our Mi Fone journey and some of the successes we'd had – we then darkened the room. An animated video came on (which we had spent the previous two days in a studio getting right) and then BANG ... the Oju image flashed on the screen.

*"Ladies and gentlemen. Today we are proud to announce the launch of Oju, the first black emoticons in the world. Oju is not just an emoticon; this is our way to give the world something from Africa. Our continent is traditionally portrayed with many negative stereotypes, so we wanted to create something positive to show the world that good things can come out of Africa. Oju is our brand that can address more than three billion people in this world who are not currently represented on tech platforms. We have reached out to Apple, Facebook, Skype and many others. No one has replied to us, but it's cool ... we are just happy to have done this **first** and the record proves that we beat Apple to it."*

I then backed up my talk by displaying all the hard press evidence and the statistics from Google Play. There is nothing like being able to talk the talk and walk the walk.

The event was simply awesome. Our two top-dawg DJs, Nickie 'Cartel' Duku and Shaun Harry, were on hand with the finest music. The place was packed with friends, family and some of South Africa's top celebrities. We had even arranged our own Oju photo booth in which our guests could take pictures with the Oju brand on the instant print. A nice memento we thought. It even got to the point at which certain celebrities would stand next to the Oju banner wall and have pictures taken with the Oju character that most reflected them

Our initial range was only 15 Ojus in the standard emoticon styles (smile, cry, laugh, etc.), but by the time we had our event our design team had put together 50 different Oju designs on a big banner that was hung on the wall (some with glasses, different African hairstyles, etc). The whole thing was a double whammy for us. We could use the images for our Mi Fone social media pages and have the secondary story about the Oju launch.

For me, Oju was that breath of fresh air that we had been needing and being a creative self-starter I could not think of anything I wanted to be more fully engrossed in … *but* I was there as Mi Fone. Oju was simply an offshoot we had created, although it could only have been created because of what Mi Fone had done. Mi Fone was still the one paying all our bills.

I was the last one to leave the event that night. I wanted to ensure all our guests had had a good time and, besides, I had to settle the bar bill too! I remember it being around midnight as I drove up to the gates of my apartment complex. Despite all the fanfare, the media, the smiles and the laughter from a night of immense highs, I was now alone with my own thoughts. I was back in reality and needed to follow up on a customer payment. Our customer in the Democratic Republic of Congo (DRC) was due to pay us a large sum of money for goods we had shipped, so I thought it best to get the call done while I was in the car as I was on my own. Unfortunately for me, the customer actually picked up my call. If he hadn't I would have most certainly slept much better that night.

"Mr F, how are you? How's everything going for our payment? I hope you have made arrangements to send it now."

"Alpesh," he replied. Then there was moment of silence … "We have a *big* problem."

INNOVATION
*is all about taking a traditional business model
and flipping the script!*

CHAPTER 17

THE AFRICAN PAIN

By early 2014 we were in a negative cash flow situation as we had not been able to plug the gap with any sort of bridging finance or working capital and now the customers themselves had started to take the piss. Our receivable list was growing larger and larger. I remember the nightmare by the end of Q1 March 2014 when we had approximately $2.5 million in receivables and were owing people on our side.

Had we expanded too fast? Had we taken on too many orders? Had we given out too much open credit without securing ourselves? Yes.

My biggest mistake to date, and one of my biggest failures, was giving open credit to the market. Open credit means open payment terms without securing my debt. This is when, due to relationships, trust and goodwill, you sell goods knowing customers will pay you back. We had always given the MNOs open credit because they were too big to default on their payments. Giving open credit meant I was making it easier for my customers to do business with me. It was my urge to get orders, but ultimately it led me to trouble.

Alpesh we have a problem. These words kept ringing in my head.

We had been dealing with a distributor in the DRC for more than a year. They were a father-and-son team, guys who had made the DRC their home for many years. They commanded a huge amount of respect in the market and when they first approached me in early 2012 they were big Samsung brand dealers who wanted to expand their portfolio and not rely only on their Samsung business. I had met so many Samsung dealers who would not even touch us due to their relationship with Samsung. For them Samsung was a 'cash cow'. Samsung was a popular brand not because they made great phones, but because they spent *so much* on marketing that the products practically flew off the shelves. I even recall employing an ex-Samsung guy for a couple of months thinking he would bring in more business, but I had to fire his ass after a dismal two months of pure bullshitting. I told him straight, "You cannot call yourself a true grass-roots sales person when you sell a Samsung phone. The product moves itself from the shelves. With Samsung, you are merely an *order taker*. You are only a real salesman when you can sell something like Mi Fone."

It was the same for me when I was at Motorola – I thought I was a proper salesman, but the truth is if you can sell something that no one has ever heard of, such as Mi Fone, then you can call yourself a super-salesman.

The phone dealers knew they had a good deal with Samsung; a much better deal than I could have ever given them. Samsung's rules and regulations also made it possible for many of these distributors to play tricks. For example, they would order a certain model at price X, but sell it below cost at price Y, because they would simply rely on Samsung to give them distributor rebates due to achieving volume targets. Of course, it's easier to achieve your volume targets when you are selling below cost price. The manufacturer therefore becomes your paymaster.

The DRC distributors had checked us out for a while before

agreeing to start with us. They told me that they only worked on credit and if I wanted a piece of the massive DRC market I would have to make it easier for them to do business with us. I agreed straight away because their opening order was only a few hundred phones. We started the business and the Mi Fones were selling well in their distribution channels in DRC. They then started offering our phones to the MNOs in the DRC and after several rounds of testing our samples and bouts of price negotiations, we started to get larger orders of between 5,000 and 10,000 units. The guys would send us a purchase order and pay the deposit to get the orders started, then I would ship and collect the balance 30 days later. These were all customised phones.

In the DRC, our business went well over the course of 2012 and into 2013. We shipped close to 50,000 units into that market within a period of one year. I regularly met the owners when they came to Dubai as they would pay me in cash – dollar notes. I was quite used to going to Nasser Square, the hub of the Dubai traders, entering dingy buildings and being led into a room full of people sitting behind desks with mountains of cash and the sound of cash counting machines going off every few seconds. I would simply sign a piece of paper and collect $50,000, $100,000 or $150,000 in cash. This would go into my sports bag and I would walk away, hail the next cab and head straight to the bank to the deposit the money. I had been used to these payment methods ever since my Hong Kong days.

This was how most of the African traders ran their books. It was the Hawala system of money transfer, a system of underground money transfers in and out of Africa without going through official banking channels. Someone in Africa pays their local contact and a few minutes later you pick up the cash in Dubai. I didn't care where the money came from as I had my invoices and proof that we had shipped the goods. Whatever made it easier for my customers to pay me – I accepted. Cash was my lifeline.

Around mid-2013 the DRC guys had negotiated a large volume order with one of the MNOs. The order value was close to $1.25 million. There was no way I could finance the production of the goods, so I contacted the African bank that had given us the previous discounting line and explained to them our predicament. The bank had dealt with this MNO group previously so they promptly agreed to give me an advance of 50% of the purchase order value. This was done via a discounting facility so that I could finance the production of the phones in China.

The deal had to be done in a certain way. The DRC MNO would place the order on Mi Fone, but we had to deliver the goods to their nominated local agent (our distributor, the father-and-son team) who would then ship and clear the goods themselves in their own manner and supply locally to the MNO operator's local warehouse.

DRC was, and is, one of the most challenging markets in Africa to do business with, simply because of the high rates of duties that are charged on virtually all imports. The duties for phones were 40% of the invoice price. There was no way that an MNO could import the goods under their own name simply because they would have to pay official duties and hence would have priced themselves out of the market. They therefore used local distributors to bring in the phones and everyone knew what tricks the local distributors would get up to, although at least no one spoke about it publicly. Distributors would simply bring in goods using their own ways of transportation with the main aim to avoid paying the 40% duties as much as possible. What did I care? I had my purchase order and our paperwork showed that we were to supply on an ex-works Hong Kong basis. This meant that our responsibility ended when we handed over the phones to our customers, Hong Kong-based freight agents. All the forwarding shipments and logistics were to be handled by the distributor in conjunction with the MNO's knowledge.

We had agreed that due to the scale of the order and the logistics challenges, the 50,000-phone order would have to be split into five equal shipments of 10,000 phones at a time. This way it would be easier for all parties to manage the deal. There was price pressure as well, so we had to be competitive. When we negotiated the price with the factory, we received a price for a one-off 10,000 phone shipment, but were offered a much better price if we ordered 50,000 phones with 10,000-unit split shipments every four weeks. We had the purchase order on hand, so we took the price based on the 50,000 order. I obviously wanted to maximise our profitability wherever possible.

We planned that with a fine-tuned system it would take us five months to complete the full 50,000 order. The distributors insisted that they pay a 20% deposit on each 10,000 production/shipment rather than paying me the 20% deposit on the total 50,000-unit order. It was all a cash flow issue. For us, in order to secure the price for 50,000 phones we had to place our order with the Chinese factory for the whole 50,000 phones, but with split shipments of 10,000 phones at a time. The only way the factory could give us the better prices we needed was for them to secure all the component materials that made up the phones way in advance. The cost savings by doing so were then passed on to us in the form of lower unit pricing per phone. Ordering components for each 10,000-unit batch in China over a five-month period could mean receiving a completely different set of components at varying price points. We had already assured the buyers that the product would be uniform for the complete order.

After gaining the approval from the bank, they duly wired to us 50% of the purchase order value, approximately $600,000. We immediately spent $250,000 (20% of the total 50,000-unit order valued at $1.25 million) to pay the factory the deposit to secure the total components and bill of materials required. Also, they had to start the production for the first 10,000 phones. We now had the balance of funds to pay to the factory, which was the difference between the deposit we had paid and what the bank had sent to us. Thank God for this because it meant I didn't have to scratch around looking for money to pay the factory when the goods were ready – that would have completely fucked up my order cycles.

Everything progressed according to plan and we shipped the first 10,000 phones on time. There were some expected delays in shipping and clearing, but after a few weeks we duly received our first payment, some of which we then used to repay the bank. We had instructions to start the second 10,000-phone production as soon as the first batch had been shipped to save time and to ensure we kept to the four-week shipment cycle. The African bank was charging us a cool 20% on our borrowing, so my clock was always ticking.

In early February 2014, we shipped the second batch, which then arrived into DRC by the end of February. We had calculated that by early March we would be paid for that batch and we could immediately ship out the third batch. The factory had the materials in their warehouse, so when they received our instruction it took them literally five days to assemble and pack 10,000 phones. That was the speed at which the Chinese factories worked. In early March, we started calling for our payment for the second batch.

"It's under process," we were told by the distributors. "The MNO is processing the payment and we will then transfer to you." We had their official purchase order signed off by all their management and we had been paid promptly for our first batch, so I didn't really worry about a few days' delay here and there. This was Africa after all; a snail could move faster than some of the people I have met. In mid-April I had a call with our DRC customer after our event launch in South Africa. I called him because the delay in payment was worrying.

"Alpesh, we have a problem. Our accountant has disappeared and has stolen the money from the company."

"What?" I shouted. "That's not my issue I still need my payment!"

Their story was that their accountant had absconded with the company funds and as a result, they needed some time to pay me. I knew from the start that he was lying. A trader never gives his bank account over to anyone, no matter how big his company is. He would have been the only signing power. Of course, I couldn't accuse him of this because I wanted to remain polite to ensure we could get our money. I didn't even think about how to finish the balance of 30,000 phones as there would be no 30,000 phones to ship if we didn't get paid for this previous shipment.

I slept three hours that night. Genuinely worried. A beautiful fun-filled evening had immediately turned into a head-beating nightmare. As soon as I woke up I called China to inform them to stop the production on the third batch until I had "resolved some issues". I dug more into this and started calling the MNO in DRC directly, but the fuckers kept fobbing me off. At that time, no one seemed to speak English. *How convenient.* My suspicions started to grow that someone somewhere had our money, but were not willing to play ball with us.

Now I have no proof and these are my own opinions, but I think I know what happened. The procurement guy at the MNO probably had his own side hustle going on with our distributor and was receiving his own kickbacks for giving us the 50,000-phone order. I believe that the $250,000 due to us was diverted elsewhere to some other account locally and shared between them all at our expense. Most likely this procurement guy was about to leave the job as he may have had previous heat on him and wanted to make his final bit of cash on his way out. I also don't really know about the relationship on the ground between the local distributor and the MNO – had they fallen out over something?

As I write this in 2017 we have still not been paid, despite chasing this debt for more than three years. Later, I found out that the same distributor happened to owe monies to some other guys in Dubai as well. Mi Fone had been clearly defrauded. It was as simple as that. I now had $250,000 owing to us from DRC while I had money tied up in the 30,000 component materials. I called DRC every day at least five times to ask for the money and was given all the assurances that we would be paid. We never were.

Now depending on what kind of business you are in or what kind of numbers you deal with every day, these figures can be big or small, but at the end of the day – for me – money is money and every penny counts.

The pressure of all this started getting to me and by mid-2014 I recall being in Las Vegas for the International Licensing Show (where Oju was exhibiting). I simply lost it that day. I was in the lobby of the Encore Wynn hotel, shouting and swearing at the DRC distributor down the phone. I remember people looking over and security guards asking me to be quiet. I had been angry before, but never had I shouted, screamed and sworn as much as I did on that phone. What upset me the most was the sheer arrogance of this guy – there he was assuring me that we would get paid, but knowing fully that he was fobbing me off. I can never forgive these guys for what they did to Mi Fone, but I know how karma works.

By June 2014 I knew that the chances of us getting our money were getting slimmer by the day. We were introduced to a local DRC lawyer who wanted an upfront payment of $20,000 just to look at our case. There were no guarantees and in a place like DRC how straight were the law courts? You could end up paying a lawyer, who would collect your money and then cut a deal with the other side by charging them to keep you waiting. I knew we had been scammed. There was no other way to put it. We had been played for two years with orders and payments and finally when the big one came we got slapped.

As Mike Tyson says:

Everybody's got a plan
until they get punched in the mouth

That was exactly what happened to me.

We'd had a plan to execute 50,000 orders, but we had been stopped dead in our tracks. It felt as if I had been punched in my mouth, in my stomach and in my balls, all at the same time. What made it worse was that our financial planning was such that, as cash came in, we paid our bills; marketing bills, freight bills and the factories. All of this was solely reliant on the cash we had coming in. Besides the DRC issue, we also faced a potential loss of $250,000 in Nigeria with a similar party who had defrauded us by using irregular bills of exchange, which we then found out had not been authorised by our banks. We complained to the banks, but in the way that banks are, they simply would not admit to their own shortcomings.

To top this off, some of our customers continued paying us late and some continued to short pay us. All of the above would lead you, the reader, to think that Africans are completely corrupt, but let me assure you most of the guys who owed us money were not local Africans. They were of non-African descent. This is not a race issue, but I just want to make it clear that most of our black African customers did not have the same purchasing muscle power when it came to buying phones. Most of them were small-time traders and if they owed us, it was only a few thousand dollars max. The big hits we got came from the outsiders living in Africa.

You will recall in terms of purchase orders we had a fantastic Q4 2013. Well those factory bills were also due in Q1 2014 and not all of them had been paid on time (the DRC second batch being one of them). The pressure had increased on me. I was caught in a spinning cycle of misery. I had to pay the factories as our payment cycles to them were getting lengthier, I had to pay the bank, I had to pay our private lenders whose money we used for our normal retail stocks and I had to cover salaries and overheads.

Before I left for the International Licensing Expo show in Las Vegas early in June 2014, my CFO DS had arranged a coffee meeting with some of his partners in their Pretoria office. He told me they wanted to meet me to learn more about Mi Fone and how they could possibly help us increase our distribution reach.

At that meeting, there were about five guys around the boardroom table and I noticed a quiet gentleman sitting at the end of the table. He was from a large publicly listed South African company and was keen to know more about Mi Fone. He told me that he wanted to take up a Mi Fone distribution for Africa, but he needed to know what markets were open for supply. I replied that he couldn't sell in Kenya because we had an exclusive authorised distributor there already. He couldn't sell in Angola either, because we had an exclusive partner there too, and he couldn't sell in Rwanda or a host of other countries...

"So where can I sell?" he asked.

"Well we will have to map it out," I told him. "It really depends on what markets you are strong in and those we are weak in, then we can match those up."

"Yes, but if we buy your stock we want to warehouse them in Dubai and trade them across Africa."

Suddenly it jumped out of me. It must have been the pent-up frustrations as a result of what I was going through. I really didn't have the energy or the time to discuss how these guys would and should distribute Mi Fone, especially when I was in deep shit all around.

"We are looking for funding for our operations. In fact, we have been looking for funding for nearly three years now. Our growth speaks for itself. Instead of all this pussy-footing around with 'this market and that market', why don't you just invest in us and you can have a slice of the whole pie?"

We left it there. I didn't have much else to say. I thanked everyone for the meeting and walked out. *Just another meeting*.

As soon as the meeting was over, the very next day I left for my USA trip. Before I got to Las Vegas for the licensing show I had to stop off in New York for a few days to make another investment pitch to a well-known firm owned by some heavyweight players. They had created a fund specifically aimed at African investments, all centred on impact investing. Impact investing is investment made by companies, funds and organisations to generate a measurable social impact and a financial return.

This New York based PE firm had been around for a couple of years and I knew they had funded a new, unproven vehicle brand start-up in Kenya. One of their associates, WN, and I had met in late 2013 at the African Leadership Network conference in Mauritius. We started to chat more frequently and he was genuinely interested in getting his company to invest in us. His job was to find credible investment opportunities for his firm on the continent of Africa. We had a proven track record, we had bootstrapped our operation for six years and we were well-known on the continent.

Mi Fone was also ideally placed for impact investing as we were empowering millions of Africans to be connected for the first time via a low-cost smartphone. If that was not digital inclusion then what is? Add initiatives like Mi Card and Oju and our case became even more compelling. With Mi Card, we could impact the consumers by achieving financial inclusion with very little costs and with Oju we could take something from Africa and make it globally available on all tech platforms.

Thanks to some good coordination on the part of WN, I managed to secure a time slot to present to his management and team. When I got to their office in New York the whole team met me. They had an MD for this fund and if she liked the deal, she could take it to her bosses for further consideration.

I had presented many times in boardrooms, so I basically got on with putting our case and explaining why we needed investment. At no point did I show desperation, even though I was urgently in need of a $5 million capital injection. From my perspective, initially the meeting went very well, but it was when I introduced Oju that the whole table erupted in awe-filled laughter. I could tell they were impressed. WN told me after the meeting that the firm seemed convinced and he was hopeful about getting us a deal. I had been disappointed so many times before, so I didn't set any high expectations.

A couple of weeks later WN called me and told me that his firm would not be going through with the investment into Mi Group. No reasons mentioned. Again, everyone loved our story, but no one was willing to commit to being part of it.

Rejection had always bothered me. I hated it. A few times was fine, but this was becoming a joke.

Why?

Why were people rejecting our business?

What was I not doing right?

Maybe these investors thought as we had carried ourselves for so long, why would we really need their financial support if we had been able to finance ourselves up to now? Maybe they decided it was too much of a commoditised business – but then, so are many other sectors in the world. Commoditisation is not peculiar to phones only.

Or was it because we were in Africa?

By being African, was our value discounted from the onset?

Was it all role-play for investors to say that Africa was going to be the next big thing, but in reality, nobody actually gave a shit about Africa?

Or did it all come down to trust?

Were we too slick?

Were we too cocky?

Were we too vocal?

I also questioned why an unproven African vehicle start-up would receive funding when Mi Fone, a proven seven-year business could not?

The car market in Africa is extremely competitive with cheap Japanese imports coming in every day. What made the investors think that a 26-year-old non-African guy could grow the business to a multimillion-dollar valuation?

So, there I was, scratching my head with all these questions and comments.

And there we were, a multimillion-dollar business offering

our shares at very favourable terms and yet we were getting shut down constantly. This did not only happen to Mi Fone. I have seen lots of African entrepreneurs be rejected and then all of a sudden see some Western company with similar ideas getting funded for the same market – *Africa*!

I never heard from the New York firm again. I'm sure they are still operating, but I don't know how many of their African investments have worked out. WN left the company pretty soon afterwards as well.

In Las Vegas, Oju won the "One to Watch" newcomer brand award, which was a nice moment of celebration. Our small African company had made some major noise at the licensing expo.

After Vegas, I made my way back to South Africa to carry on with business as usual. It had been a whirlwind trip and we had to inform everyone that Oju had won a major award. It was critical for Oju to raise its own funds to assist in its roll out. We had masses of feedback from the 60,000 Google downloads indicating that Oju needed to be a proper messaging app. We knew we had launched a simple basic beta version of an app, but to create our own world-class messaging app would have cost us close to $50,000. I didn't have that kind of money lying around.

Mi Fone's cash flows had been funding the entire Oju rollout, but now Mi Fone had its own problems to fix. As soon as I got back I checked all my unread emails in my inbox. I noticed an email from the gentleman I had met a few weeks before at DS friend's office.

Dear Alpesh. Further to our meeting a few weeks ago, we would like to discuss more about the Mi Fone distribution opportunities in Africa. Please let us know when you can be available to meet our CEO for a face-to-face meeting.'

I had nothing to lose. I was back in South Africa and didn't see any harm going to meet a CEO of a well-known public listed company. He wanted to know more about Mi Fone. They had money and could be a potential distributor for us. At least our bloody payments would be secured. At that meeting, I was warmly welcomed at the reception by the gentleman called MO with whom I had met previously.

"How was your US trip?" He politely asked me.

"Great. Absolutely great. Oju won a nice award and we made some noise."

I had already explained to him at our previous meeting about how Oju and Mi Card fitted into our overall Mi Group business. I was then led into the CEO's office. I figured out that this CEO was the boss of MO. The CEO was a big South African with Afrikaner roots – you could see he was a hard man. He meant business for sure, but, oh, was he ever so polite and courteous. Funnily enough some of the most pleasant and courteous people I have ever met have been the Afrikaners.

"Please tell me more about Mi Fone,' the CEO started. "Besides the usual info on products and pricing, I'm more interested in knowing when you started this and how you managed to achieve so much in the past few years. I understand that your operation is completely bootstrapped?"

I explained the history of Mi Fone. I had my laptop open to showcase some of the great things we had done like Mi

Obama, Western Union, the countries we were shipping to, an indication of our orders and so on. I talked for a while with my normal intense passion. I had made the same presentation 100 times before. I knew my words inside out. Whilst MO was looking at the screen, the CEO kept on looking at me, nodding his head now and then. I was getting an uneasy feeling. It was clear that this guy didn't give a fuck about how many megapixels our phones had or what different colours or types of customisations we could do. Then, abruptly, he stopped me.

"Alpesh we like what we see. We understand you are looking for funding. We would be very keen to become your partner. We would be very keen to take a stake in Mi Fone."

That was the last thing I had expected.

Yes, I had mentioned it at our previous meeting, but I never suspected that this guy MO had taken my comments seriously, let alone had gone to tell his CEO everything he had found out about Mi Fone.

"Your business is very interesting and we have been looking for the past two years on how to get into the mobile space in Africa. You could be a good fit for our overall 2020 vision," said the CEO.

He asked me if we would be keen to talk further. I said yes immediately.

I didn't exactly have a dinner plate full of choices.

"We would like to see some numbers first," he finished.

I left that meeting and immediately called DS from the car.

"DS, these guys are not keen to distribute Mi Fone. They want to be *part* of Mi Fone! We will now need to do the whole set of numbers for them."

Luckily for us, we had our investor pack ready at all times

as we had presented and given our documentation to so many people before.

"Let's just give them our financials. We don't have anything to lose. If they reject us – what's new, right?" I said to DS.

He agreed and within a few days we sent off a preliminary set of numbers with our business plan. By late July 2014 we had received a positive reply from the company and we met them again at their offices, this time with a much bigger team from their side.

"We like what we see so far," they said. "We hope to send you a deal memo in the next week or so, but we need to go through some Q&A and how we plan to structure a deal with Mi Fone."

After all this time, having travelled all over the world several times, had I found a serious potential funder from a local South African company not even 20 minutes' drive from where I was living? I just couldn't believe it.

In August 2014, I travelled to Cape Town as the guest of the prestigious consulting firm Frost & Sullivan as they wanted to award us with Entrepreneurial Company of the Year 2014. I did a keynote speech there and recall meeting my friend WN from the New York investment firm in the evening. He just kept shaking his head.

"I don't know what to say, bro, but it was very hard for me to convince my guys in New York to invest in you. They just didn't get it."

"I already knew that," I replied.

I was disappointed in the way we had been treated by the investor community. We would be asked for all our info, our strategies and our financials, only to then get shut down. I don't know why they couldn't tell us no from the start. Why waste each other's time?

I was now quietly positive about our potential funding from the publicly listed company because they were not a PE firm, a VC firm or a bank; they were a trade buyer, a conglomerate with a $5 billion market cap and they had expressed their interest in writing to me. Could they be my saviour? This group was a giant of a company with close to 50,000 employees. They knew how to build businesses, unlike the PE/VC guys who only looked at squeezing the life out of a company to get their return on capital or to make an exit to some other punter on the next round.

The year 2014 was filled with awards, but, of course, awards didn't pay our bills, unfortunately. They were a nice to have and winning increased the amount of times we were mentioned in the press, but that was about it. The Frost & Sullivan award was followed by a very surprising win at the prestigious Loeries South Africa awards. Oju won the Grand Prix Prize in the digital category. The Loeries are the premier awards in the South Africa advertising and marketing industry. It seems Eserick had filled out our application without even telling me. What a shock it was to receive a call from him, telling me that somehow Oju had won the top Grand Prix honour. This was unheard of in the industry – a small six-month-old African start-up winning the top prize, killing off all the industry heavyweights.

The main judge of the Loeries was Mr GP Perreira, an industry heavyweight from New York. He made a small video about why they had chosen Oju. He said as soon as he and the other judges saw Oju, it was game over for the rest. He said that the Oju emoticons brought tears to their eyes through the sheer simplicity of creating black smileys. It was that simplicity they loved. What an honour it is every time I look at that video. Not surprisingly, the South African press did not even mention us winning this award. It was so strange that our home-grown press was not embracing a home-grown brand. I wonder at times what the outcome would have been had we set up Oju in the USA. Even from our Google statistics, only 10% of the 60,000 downloads were from Africa. The most downloads came from the USA.

Our window dressing was superb. Appropriately so, I was also one of the winners of the GQ South Africa award for Best Dressed Man. The perception about the success of Mi Fone, Oju and Alpesh kept growing. To the market we were hot, but I knew this was all bullshit. I pretended to be happy, but inside I was dying from the pain of knowing that my business had dug a hole for itself that might prove impossible to get out of. Not only were people not paying us, we had no luck with any fundraising and were exhausted from running around putting together investor proposals. The awards were nice to have, but none of them translated into better paying customers and investors didn't exactly come flocking to our door. Everyone cheered, but when it came time to 'show me the money' they all went silent.

Except ...

A South African publicly listed company was to issue a deal sheet imminently. In late September 2014, we received the term sheet from the company outlining all the points we had discussed and agreed to. It was a legal document that stated that they would purchase 51% of Mi Fone and an option to purchase some shares in Oju. The deal involved a large upfront payment, a lump sum capital investment into Mi Fone – the main operating business – and an eventual earn-out for me based on the business hitting certain targets. MO came over to my apartment building, where we sat in the lobby and signed the paperwork. There was only one caveat – the deal was subject to an in-depth and thorough due diligence process.

I fully respected the fact that every investor had the right to conduct a thorough check on our business, especially a publicly listed company which had to disclose all findings to the board for final approvals. They had every right to check us out; from our customers to the factories and to the legalities of our brand. In order to sail through this process, I knew that I had to put all other matters aside and focus on this 110% so that the deal could be finalised and we could get the money to keep going. I had to hold their hands at every stage. Only if we passed the due diligence phase (DD) would the deal actually be activated. There was no way I was leaving them to talk to my staff – it had to be me. That was a priority.

So, now I had the burden of showing an investor our full business, which had been mine for the past seven years. Luckily for me, I knew our ducks were in a row. I had nothing to hide. Yes, we had created a complicated structure, but at least all our documentation was up-to-date and legit. I explained to my team that everything for us hinged on this deal going through, hence it needed all of my attention. The team had to carry the burden of managing the daily business operations. To the disappointment of Eserick, we also had to put Oju to the side for a while as nothing could move until we got the investment.

By late 2014, we still had not collected any money from

DRC. Our receivables were taking longer and longer to be paid and I found myself getting increasingly frustrated and angrier as each day passed. Mi Fone had slowed down. Our numbers for 2014 were even worse than our 2013 results. The orders we had were taking longer to produce and deliver as we were always waiting for cash from receivables in order to pay the factories for these orders. Our cash was not being collected on time and every day the whole team would do nothing other than call customers to find out about our payments. It was like talking to brick walls. Naturally it was hard to maintain the morale in the company and our operational side of things also started to deteriorate. There was a general air of frustration and I guess me being the leader of the company had a lot to do with that. My team immediately felt my anger. I had trusted them to continue with the Mi Fone daily operations whilst I focused on the bigger picture, but I kept being dragged back into the daily stuff as they simply could not handle certain things. The team had also started making silly mistakes, such as not reading customer purchase orders properly, ordering the wrong stocks from the factories and ordering more stock than we actually needed. As I was not on point 100%, I had left certain decisions to my team. Yes, I know I should have looked at all the paperwork myself, but I was simply all over the place and exhausted. I have always been a pretty good multitasker, but not on this occasion.

I was close to burning out.

Once I had signed the term sheet with the investors, it meant that I was committed to doing this deal, and I would duly oblige to all their requests. I told my team that we were slowly running out of money and that they (the investors) would most likely be our only hope in moving forward. We had to keep our business going, but we had to go into fifth gear to collect all our receivables and clear whatever stocks we had left in our Hong Kong warehouse just to get some cash back. When the investor's funds came in, we would then resume with a complete new production cycle and a much more disciplined way of managing our business. That was the plan.

We handed all the internal documents over to the investor's due diligence team. Their job was to check all our documents to ensure there were no anomalies or deviations in what we had stated. All of this should have been pretty straightforward as we had all the documents they had requested for. Yes, complicated as it was, we had documents from Hong Kong, China, South Africa, Dubai and Mauritius; we everything on hand. The general agreement was that it would take two months to complete their review. This meant that by the beginning of December 2014 the deal would be done; there would be money in our account and a fantastic 2015 to look forward to...

Really?

IN THE MOMENT OF CRISIS
the wise build bridges
and the foolish build dams

Nigerian proverb

CHAPTER 18

DUE DILIGENCE

We signed the term sheet. In summary, the new investors would buy 51% of Mi Fone and take over the control of the company. An upfront payment would be made to Mi Fone. In addition, the investors would pump in a few million dollars as a working capital line and, based on a five-year forward performance, there would be a massive earn-out for all the shareholders. Putting this term sheet together was not easy. Naturally the investors wanted to pay the lowest price while I wanted the highest price. My plan was hopefully to meet in the middle somewhere. I knew I was dealing with much smarter people than me because the investors bought and sold companies all the time, but I asked myself several times, 'Do I really have a strong negotiating position?'

Knowing my internal desperation to get the company funded, I knew I had to make concessions in many areas, mainly in the valuation of our business. One thing for sure is that the investors did not value the company as high as the value I had placed on it. Call this ego, call this pride, call it whatever – I simply could not, in my mind, discount the value we had created since 2008. To achieve what we had, any outside company would have paid millions in setting up and expanding. The difficulties we had been through made me value Mi Fone even more highly. Not many companies could or would have done what we did.

Our African struggle *was* our value.

In order to save money wherever possible I didn't even

bother hiring outside financial advisors, because those guys would have asked me for a large upfront fee payment and a monthly retainer. By now I had been through my fair share of financial advisors with their retainers and none of them had performed to my liking, but at least I had DS on my side.

I didn't want to tell anyone about this deal. If I had opened my mouth I'm sure I would have jinxed myself somewhere. By the time we had signed the term sheet, all the points had already been negotiated with most of them being in favour of the new investor. I mean, what choice did I really have? I knew they had the money and I knew that they were a very credible and proven company. I hadn't heard from any of the other companies that we had pitched to, so if we wanted to remain in business then we had to go with this investor's proposal.

As mentioned previously, this included an in-depth analysis on us, otherwise known as due diligence. Now, due diligence in the investor community means a comprehensive assessment of a company by a potential buyer to establish its assets and liabilities and calculate its marketable capability. It is natural to assume that before anyone parts with their money they have to check the terrain fully so there are no surprises or skeletons in the closet. The deal sheet was a deal in principle subject to satisfactory due diligence.

Basically, Mi Fone had to pass their tests.

We were an offshore entity with structures in Mauritius, Hong Kong and various parts of Africa. We were fully prepared for some of the items they had requested:

- Mi Fone audited accounts since inception 2008 – tick
- Mi Fone brand registrations – tick
- Mi Fone bank statements since 2008 – tick

- Full list of Mi Fone creditors and Mi Fone debtors –tick
- All copies of purchase orders, shipping documents and certifications since Mi Fone started in 2008 – tick
- Mi Fone full staff headcount – tick
- All Mi Fone list of suppliers – tick
- All Mi Fone IT and web information – tick.

Everything on the investor's list, we had on file. We had always had it on file. A piece of cake, we thought. Mr MO was the nominated person to carry out the due diligence exercise on behalf of the investor. He was the guy who had introduced us to the investor in the first place and now it was his deal. He was the head of their taskforce to dig deep into the Mi Fone history.

MO had instigated the whole deal process, so I knew he was keen to do the deal, but his attitude was more like a forensic detective than anything else. This guy was like a cop. If he had been bald, he could have been Kojak Part 2.

Even though we had all the documentation in place, his task was to look for any red flags during the due diligence process. I had no issues; this was how they should be. They were going to part with a lot of money, so they had to do their own homework. All I had to do was to provide all the information when requested, let them go through it and answer any questions they would surely have. My team and I were ready for them.

The investor's first point of call was to visit our key customers in Africa, but I was not going to allow them to travel to see any of our customers without me next to them. It was the same issue on the China side – they wanted to meet Alex and the HK/China team and visit the factories. As a listed company, one major issue for them was to check the status of our supplier factories. They had to ensure all factories had a strict code of conduct in place and that none of them used illegally sourced materials to make our products or conducted irregular practices such as child labour. Fair point.

Between September and December 2014, we made trips to Hong Kong, China, Kenya and Zambia. On our first China trip it was just me and MO from the investor side. He inspected our main factories and he drilled all our HK and China staff. I think he was very surprised with what he found. We had been self-funded from day one and Alex was responsible for all our HK and China operations. We paid him a fee per handset made, but how he spent that was up to him. Alex was a very prudent guy and his setup was certainly not a fancy one. For starters, our China office was a three-bedroom apartment converted into an office. For me, as long as we got 100% good-quality products on time with the right software and support, I couldn't have given a shit if Alex had been operating from the back of a chop suey house. We never burnt cash on fancy offices. Even our front-end offices in Dubai, Mauritius and Johannesburg were all small premises with a few desks.

Within a few weeks of signing the deal sheet, we had delivered all the documents to the investor and, based on their availability, we had taken the trips to China and Africa to show what we had on the ground. In Kenya, they wanted to see Mi Fone in action. Again, we did not have anything fancy, so all we could do was take them to our retailer partner stores where they could clearly see the Mi Fone range on sale. During the due diligence phase, every trip, costs and expenses had to be covered by each separate party. I wasn't happy about all of these costs, but I had no choice.

By mid-December 2014, I started to get nervous. We had submitted all our documents as per the due diligence checklist, but still I had not heard anything back from the investors. What made it worse was that the South African annual summer holiday had set in. Everything shuts down then and everyone switches off. There was fuck all I could do about it.

The year was dismal for our numbers and once again, we dropped our revenue performance from the previous year. DH, the young lady who had been with me from day one, also left the company in early 2014 because she was getting married. She had been the backbone of my administration and, to me, she was the most important part of my back-end structure; an amazing multitasker and a genuinely smart young lady. For the first few years it had been just me and her running the company and whenever I travelled, she would hold the fort back at base, ensuring all the payments were coming in, orders were placed and all the books were in order. If it hadn't been for her, I don't think we would have had all the paperwork in place that we had – which would have meant no due diligence, because we did need to have all our paperwork in order.

Luckily for us, we had never taken any shortcuts when it came to paperwork for our business. I'm so glad we kept every record, every order, every payment and every bank statement on hand. When she left in early 2014, I immediately felt the pressure, which added to all the other pressures that had built up around me. With her gone, it was as if I had lost my right arm, but we had to make the most of it and I took on three new full-time staff to see if the gaps could be filled. PN then became our chief operating officer (COO). I knew this was not the right title for him as he was not seasoned enough to handle the role of a formal COO, but we had bullshitted our way up to now so who was anyone to question us?

We also employed an interim junior finance manager because DS was taking on other roles elsewhere and we had a new admin lady – someone I had worked with at Harris. She was a great girl who I knew had my back in terms of loyalty, but now, of course, it was a different environment as back in the Harris days we'd had the comfort and support of being part of a large organisation. I agreed to take her on because I didn't wish to use the services of an HR company and pay massive fees. I also wanted someone whom I could trust and she had been bugging me for a job for months, so I decided to let her come on board.

We had a service manager based in Mauritius handling all our after-sales and support and we had employed a couple of people in Kenya. All in all, by late 2014, we had about eight full-time staff and a further 10 working in our Hong Kong and China offices.

We had a multimillion-dollar business with a bare minimum staff count. I am proud of the fact that we built the business to this extent with very few people, but in hindsight we killed ourselves for having too many unseasoned staff doing things they were not able to handle or doing things they need not have been doing in the first place. I never had a set leadership style and even though I have always been a people person, I admit my people management skills are terrible. The team and I would laugh and joke, but over the course of 2013 and 2014 the strains had started to show. The disappointing results of 2014, coupled with the fact that our receivables had grown and grown, showed me that something was not right with my choice of team members.

Something was not right with me and the choices I had been making.

At our peak in 2011 we had been very successful with much fewer people. Now we had more people, but our numbers had dropped in a major way. Our performance in general had dropped. How could this be? I had sold the merits of my team to the investor – they had met with a few of them because, of course, no investor is going to buy a one man-show. They were buying Mi Fone, the brand and its team.

"Once we get this investor on board all of you will be smiling as you will all have jobs with proper payrolls and peace of mind." I had to constantly remind my team what was at stake.

The severe cash flow issues and late payments from customers meant that I was also late in paying salaries. That was the most painful part. Every fucking end of the month my heart would start beating. I had to pay people as they had their own bills to pay. Alex too had to be paid as he needed to pay his teams there. The cash flow cycle was a nightmare.

Imagine this as a scenario – and please stick with me on this one example so you can get the real drift of what we had to go through. Customer XYX orders $100,000 worth of phones and three months later only pays $70,000, thus leaving us with a shortfall. We owe the factory $90,000 for the cost of those phones. On paper, we have made $10,000 profit but from the $70,000 received we have to pay the factory something like $50,000 to keep them happy. We then have to pay $10,000 to Alex in China so he can pay some of his urgent bills. This leaves us with a balance of only $10,000 to cover our salaries and other overheads. Customer XYZ still owes us the balance payment of $30,000, but conveniently decides to deduct $5,000 for local marketing expenses so now we only receive $25,000. Ideally all of that needs to be sent to the factory, but we still owe them another $15,000. So now we have no choice, but to wait for a payment from another customer to settle with the factory for an order that was shipped more than four months earlier.

This was the vicious, relentless cycle that Mi Fone was caught up in. I had to short pay my staff, not to mention covering other overheads. I was always left with nothing at the end of each month and we would move into the new month chasing payments again. With whatever cash we received, I thought it was best to keep everyone happy by paying them all a little bit rather than just one or two parties and having others wait. The fact that DRC and Nigeria owed us close to $500,000 had really fucked me up big time. Had they paid this balance, it would have allowed me to breathe.

When we resumed in the beginning of 2015, the pressure had grown even more. Now all the factories and Alex would call me several times a day asking for payments. My internal stress and anger with the way things had worked out grew and kept getting more intense until one day in the office, I just snapped. I shouted at our admin lady, but not just a normal shout. It was a tirade of expletives one after another. She had not done something to my liking. On a normal day, it would have been overlooked, but here I was looking for something/someone to vent my anger at. Anything. She completely broke down in tears. She told me this was all too much for her to handle and immediately packed her stuff and told me she was leaving Mi Fone. I looked around at the other staff and everyone was in shock. I knew I had fucked up. I could have handled it in a much more professional manner. It was never my intention to make anyone cry, especially a woman. I still feel it today.

That was not the only time I lost it. The more I looked into my team's work, the more mistakes I found. This made me even more angry. Mi Fone was putting food on their table, but they were not showing respect to the company by making all these mistakes. Costly mistakes.

Besides the expertise of DS and the now departed DH, none of my team was fully capable of handling their work. I had taken on people without checking them out and I had let them run with things. Yes, I had read all the books about allowing your team to manage themselves and make their own mistakes, but how the fuck could I allow these continuous mistakes that ultimately damaged the company? HR advice was not something I relied on at the time. My team were fucking up and, more so, I was fucking up all over the place.

Ultimately, whatever happened, the buck stopped with me. The anger and frustrations also stemmed from the fact that the investors were taking their time to get back to me. We had estimated the deal would have been done by December and that we would start the new year from a better position.

I picked up the phone to call the investor party because I knew they had resumed work. They managed to find an open timeslot for me to come and see the CEO – the Afrikaner guy. We quickly sat down and he came out with his documents.

"Alpesh we have good news and bad news. We have done

the due diligence and the good news is that everything seems to be in order, but the bad news is there is no way we can buy the company in its current state of affairs."

This was the last thing I was expecting. I had submitted everything according to their wishes.

"You have got to be kidding me!" I replied. "After all the trips and all our submitted documents? What was wrong with our submission?"

"There was nothing wrong with what you had submitted, but as a public company we simply cannot entertain this in its current format. You have so many corporate structures everywhere and everything leads back to the offshore entity Mi Fone BVI. Our auditors will be hard-pressed to justify us buying into an offshore BVI company. You also have a hell of a lot of money owing to you – how on earth are you going to be able to collect all this money? We have also noted that you are late in paying your factories, how will you keep them on your side if you always owe them money? If we were to buy Mi Fone you will spend the next six months signing warranty documents and we simply cannot be part of a structure that is that complicated. Your business may have all the right documentation, but you are in a mess

"I know why you did things the way you did them, Alpesh. We are not saying you did anything wrong, as you did what you had to do to make sure your business was continuous and we applaud you for that, but as a publicly listed company we simply cannot buy Mi Fone in its current form."

Another punch in the stomach and a slap in the face.

After all the work, to receive this news; I felt sick. We sat in silence for a good few minutes. He got up to get some water and walked to his private office balcony to light up a cigarette. He started checking his phone. It was as if he had given me the bad news and he had done his bit of talking.

"There must be a way, though?' You mean to tell me you don't want to be in the mobile space all of a sudden?" I pleaded.

"Of course, we like the business. It makes a lot of sense for us to get into the mobile space and we would rather partner with an existing brand with an existing footprint than try to do it ourselves," he replied, puffing on his cigarette. A few minutes of silence passed by, then he looked at me.

"Look, there is another option we can explore. In order to avoid the hassle that will come with signing warranties and having offshore entities, plus all the receivables you have, maybe it's best that you simply set up a new company, say in Dubai, and transfer all the brand rights to that entity, together with your management and team. Once this is done, we can then buy 51% of this new entity. We simply wish to avoid all the legacy issues. We don't want to get involved in any of your current creditors or debtors. You must fix your problems yourself. This would be the only way to do the deal."

I thought about it for a minute. He was right. He was actually doing me a favour with the suggestion of setting up a new company. I agreed in principle. I fully understood where he was coming from.

"To set up a new company in Dubai will take a couple of months," I said, really trying to say to him that we simply didn't have the time.

"Yes, so be it," he replied. "You have to set it up from now and we will buy into that. But you have to pay for all the set-up costs for Dubai. We cannot be seen to be part of the set up. For us it has to be a fresh investment in a fresh new entity."

Fuck!

Now I had to spend even more money at a time when I didn't have any. To make things worse, I had to deal with the whole Dubai company set up nonsense all over again knowing how tedious, time-consuming and expensive the process was. I had to also pay to transfer all our brand trademarks over to the Dubai company once it was set up. I was also to close down all the Mi Fone entities everywhere so that there was no conflict of interest. During this time, I was to also continue as is with our business as usual.

FAKKKKKKKKKKKKKK!!!!

I was losing my mind.

The CEO then said, "We have to sign a new term sheet similar to the old one, but to say that instead of buying Mi Fone, we will now buy into a new company. I also want to go to China and Hong Kong myself to see your set up."

This was another surprise. Just two months ago, I had taken his manager MO to China and Hong Kong and now, all of a sudden, this guy wanted to go himself. I wasn't in the mood to go anywhere at that moment, as that meant leaving my team again to fend for themselves, together with spending more money on travelling to hold someone's hand, money I did not have. This guy wanted to see Hong Kong and China – that meant hanging out with him not only during the day and at night too.

Gosh!

I had to agree to all of his demands. I had been cornered by his new suggestion. He could walk away from the deal, I couldn't. We shook hands and he promised me that he would have a new deal sheet done within seven days. He stood by that because within seven days of our meeting we did have a new deal sheet in place, now with the added *caveats* of the Dubai set up. The deal was still alive, but this was yet another fucking hurdle that I had to go through.

The next day I broke the bad news and the good news to my team. The bad news was that the company did not want to invest in the current Mi Fone, but the good news was that we had passed the due diligence phase and they simply wanted to structure the deal in a different way. In short, they *still wanted* to buy the brand. There was a five-minute sigh of relief and temporary smiles all around, but we all knew that our mission was going to get tougher. We had expected the deal to be done in December 2014 so that we could start 2015 on a bang, but now it seemed the deal would only get done sometime in March 2015 because we had to rearrange structures and start moving things around. At this stage Mi Fone had come to a complete standstill. Our last shipment was in November 2014. We had no more stock in the warehouse and our new orders had dropped because the same customers who wanted to order still had to pay older invoices. We also dropped a number of the new customers we had built during 2013–14 because we were no longer in a position to offer any of them any sort of credit terms.

With no credit terms our new customers also shied away from dealing with us. Mi Fone had been a free bank to all of them. We had been way too generous and it had come back to bite us in the ass. Now if they wanted to buy from us, they would need to pay us cash in advance. Not many of them agreed to that and that made me question their loyalty to us as a brand. They had all made great money on Mi Fone and were getting interest-free credit terms from us, but actually there was no loyalty. How stupid of me to think that the world was a great honest place. Throughout my life I had put too much faith in other people and now I was paying the price for it. This was something I had kept doing over and over again and not learning from it.

What made me love people so much in that I would do anything to please them?

"So, what do we do between now and when the deal is done then?" one of my team asked.

"We continue as is,' I replied. "We collect whatever money is owed to us and we try starting with new production cycles for new stock. If we have to hit the road, we have to hit the road. I'm going to have to hold these guys' hands again for the next couple of months and now I need to open the Dubai company and get all that shit sorted out," I said.

Again, I left my team on their own and agreed that PN, our COO, should continue travelling to collect money, but to push our still available customers to order from the new production so we could kind of pre-sell it.

Mi Fone was not broke; we simply had a cash issue. Our receivables were larger than the sums we owed, so we were very solvent. On paper Mi Fone was still pretty profitable. If we could get this right for the next few months, we could hold steady until the new investor came aboard. Regardless of how much I had screamed and shouted at my team, I do now realise how much loyalty I had from them. Yes, they were naive and made mistakes all the time, but their faith and loyalty in Mi Fone – and more so in me – could never be questioned. In their eyes, why worry? Alpesh would always make a plan.

In February 2015, I flew with the investor CEO and MO to Hong Kong and China for a four-day visit. They wanted to go through the whole exercise of checking everything out. Over those four days we got to know each other better over a few dinners and drinks.

One thing that stuck in my mind was a comment made by the CEO. "We are planning to invest in Mi Fone, but more so Alpesh – we are investing in *you*."

They knew that I was Mi Fone and that Mi Fone was me. Without me nothing worked, so in a way they were getting a brand and my skillset on board.

"The only thing is, we don't take any risks. You have taken too much risk, we are baffled as to how you are still surviving with the kind of risks you have taken."

Little did they know that I had been taking risks ever since I was a teenager.

After a gruelling few days, it seemed as if they were satisfied, even though I could see their disdain with the way Alex had set up our China operations. Upon their return to South Africa they then had to submit a formal report to their board with their latest findings. Again, we had to play the waiting game, but by early March I had received the good news that the deal would go ahead. Now began the process of scouring through all the heavy legal documentation. The investors had nominated their lawyers in Dubai to send us all the agreements, including the sale and purchase agreement, the shareholder's agreement and my own executive management contract. I was going to be a corporate employee again. The last time I had seen that kind of contract was back in 2003 when I joined Motorola.

By mid-April 2015, we had received all the legal documentation and it was now for me to reply with our lawyers in tow. The only problem was I had spent so much already on the whole Dubai set up that I didn't actually have much left for any lawyers. I could only rely on the ad hoc payments we were receiving from our customers. I immediately read all the documents. The amount of never-ending fancy clauses just made me take deep breaths now and then. How the hell was I, a non-legal guy, meant to decipher all of this? I would have to get a lawyer on board as I didn't want to make any sloppy moves with a deal of this magnitude. I then approached my good friend AS in Dubai who headed up a top local law firm.

The deal was to be done in Dubai under our new Dubai entity. It made no sense for me to stay in South Africa. I had to be close to my own action, so I made a conscious decision to go to Dubai. I left South Africa with a firm mission. I told my wife and daughters that I wouldn't be seeing them until the deal was done – it could be a few weeks or it could take a few months depending on how things progressed. Fortunately for me, I have always had the support of my family to do whatever has needed to be done. I left with their blessings.

I was dreading my unknown prolonged stay in Dubai. I really did not wish to stay in a hotel due to the costs, so I looked around for a serviced apartment. Luckily for me, my good friend WN from the New York PE investment firm was based out of Dubai at the time and he kindly invited me to stay with him. I decided to take him up on his invitation.

My first point of call in Dubai was to see my lawyer friend AS. I explained my situation and he agreed to help me just so I could get the deal done; however, his firm was not cheap.

He instructed one of his partners to handle my case. From the deal sheet, they could see that the investors would be paying me an upfront fee and that this fee would have to be paid into my lawyer's escrow account first. So, the deal I made with AS was when they received the money, they would then simply deduct their legal fees from that amount. I asked my lawyers how much this would all cost me. I had budgeted $30,000 as fees, but after they saw the mountains of documents sent by the investor's lawyers they called me back and told me that they had revised the quote to $200,000 just for their legal work.

FAKKKKK! How could I pay $200,000 just for legal fees?

I politely declined, but knowing that I still needed them. The lawyers then suggested that the only way to cut the bill down was for me to act as my own legal intermediary. In order to save costs, I would not have the lawyers talking to each other. This would have taken much more time and would have cost me a hell of a lot more as I had to pay per hour regardless. This meant I had to educate myself on the legal terminology and liaise with the investor's manager MO, who would then liaise with their own lawyers.

After the first read of the legal documents I was given a list of questions and comments from my lawyers that needed addressing by the other side. My first days, therefore, were spent at my lawyer's offices getting their feedback on each clause, understanding what each clause meant, taking notes and then deciding what outcomes I wanted from the other side. I would then go back to WN's apartment and prepare my notes and questions per clause and then send them to MO via email, who would then send them on to their lawyers for their response.

Day by day I would get an answer to each clause from the other side and transfer those back to my lawyers for their further review and comments. On the flipside, the investor's lawyers also had clarifications to ask and, hence, it was a two-way street of legal jargon that I had to handle. I understood why these lawyers used all the fancy terminology – that's how they justified being paid such big sums. It's a time game. The more complex the clauses, the more time it takes for clarifications and the more the bill meter starts adding up. As desperate as I was to get the deal done, I was not prepared to simply sign away.

Between negotiating the clauses, I was also making frequent trips to my company agent to get the Dubai company set up, but Dubai works in a funny way. Setting up a company or getting visas in Dubai is a bit like playing Monopoly. You roll the dice and at every stop you need to pay something. You may think you have all the correct documents, but when you get to a government office, they tell you something is missing and you need more paperwork completed. Some needed board resolutions signed and stamped by authorities in Mauritius as that was our legal HQ for Mi Group.

We had to also open a company bank account in Dubai as part of the rules of the overall company set up. We needed to show inward capital infusion to the banks, who then would confirm to the licensing authorities that we had been capitalised. I had to, therefore, be in touch with my office every day for them to keep chasing customers for payments. The quicker I made this bank capital injection, the more days I would save in this long, drawn-out process.

During my first two weeks in Dubai I didn't even bother socialising. I would spend the whole day running around in taxis from my law firm to one government department or another. By the time I got back to the apartment, regardless of how exhausted I was, I would have to prepare all my notes and send them off to the investor. I would follow this up with a phone call to push, but MO would simply tell me, "We will send to the lawyers and see what they say."

Unlike me acting as a legal intermediary, the investors passed each and everything by their lawyers. They were simply doing their bit and as much as I tried to rush them, I couldn't. Early May 2015 came and luckily for me I hadn't pissed off WN to the extent that he wanted to kick me out. Three weeks staying with someone as an adult is not a joke. We were grown men and needed our space.

Finally, after two and a half weeks, we seemed to have all the clauses discussed, negotiated and agreed to by both sides. Both sets of lawyers seemed to be happy with the conclusions. The documents were ready for sign off. Now I had to push the investor for the final nod. It was Wednesday afternoon of 12th May 2015 when I received a phone call from MO.

He gave me some bad news and informed me that his CEO, the Afrikaner guy, had suddenly *resigned*.

"Resigned?" I screamed on the phone. "So, what now?"

In my mind, it was the CEO who had loved Mi Fone and had wanted to do the deal. He was the one who had sold us to his board.

"Well let's wait and see what happens," MO replied.

"Wait? You know I can't wait!" I shouted back. "I need to speak to the CEO!"

I knew that MO did not want me to call the CEO, but he had no choice as I had no choice. I was in the cab driving back to the apartment. I called the CEO. There was no need for formalities at this stage as I was so pissed off with what I had just heard.

"What going on?" I asked.

"Yes, Alpesh, sorry to let you know, but I just handed it in my resignation to the board.

"So, what about Mi Fone? What about all this work we have done?"

"The Mi Fone deal is still on, but as none of the board is familiar with you they will need you to come to South Africa and make a presentation to them again. I have resigned now so the matter is now between you and my board to sort."

"You've got to be fucking kidding me!" I shouted back.

"I have spent six months making sure you guys are happy with everything. We have signed the term sheet and I took you guys all over the place. I have spent money I don't have on doing things the way you wanted them done and now I have lawyers on the clock charging me!"

"Hey calm down," he told me. "We are going to try work it out, but this is a publicly listed company, so unfortunately things don't happen as fast as we would like them to."

"Yes, you can say that as you have the luxury of time. Now you have resigned, but we have not finished our deal. I *cannot* go back to South Africa without finishing this deal otherwise it's all over for me."

He could sense the desperate plea in my voice. He knew that they had pushed me to my limits as everything they had wanted I had done. I had stuck with my side of the bargain. He told me he would be in touch and put the phone down on me, not in a bad way, but in a way that meant that he had nothing more to say to me.

As I walked into the cool, quiet air-conditioned apartment I drank some water and went to my room. WN had travelled to the USA, but he had told me to stay as long as I needed, so the apartment for now was all mine.

I remember sitting on the bed in shock. I had just had a phone conversation that I was simply not expecting. Not now. I held my head in my hands and I couldn't control the tears that started coming out of my eyes. I was in real pain. I looked up at the ceiling and shouted out.

"God please *help me*! *Please.* Why is this happening to me? What have I ever done so that every day I am facing one issue after another. Please tell me or show me where I have gone wrong. I have done everything to get this far and now this?"

For the rest of the evening I could not eat or sleep. I saw that WN had a nice collection of drinks, but I didn't want to turn to alcohol. That was not the solution to numb the pain I was going through. It was just too much for me to fathom – I was so near, but yet so far. The future of Mi Fone and my own destiny was tied up in the hands of some guys I didn't even know far, far away.

That night I honestly felt all alone, mentally, physically and spiritually. I couldn't bear to tell the news to my family as it wouldn't have been fair on them to give them my stress. I did not know who to turn to as I knew no one out there had a viable solution for me.

I went to sleep that night with a prayer. I needed some kind of divine intervention from somewhere as the next day was a Thursday – the last working day of the week in Dubai.

The next morning, I called MO and explained that I had spoken with the CEO and that it did not sound promising at all.

"You must be able to do something?" I asked. "Surely, everyone in your company is aware of this deal; it cannot be down to one person only? It's much bigger than just one person. Please can you call someone to sort this out?"

He knew that they were now taking the piss and he assured me he would do whatever he could to get things back on track. Thursday afternoon came – nothing. Thursday evening came and still nothing. I was well and truly screwed! Everything in Dubai was closed on Fridays as that is their official weekend, but I knew South Africa was working, so I called MO again. It was his day off, but fuck it, I needed some answers!

"Any news?" I asked.

"Yes, Alpesh. I managed to get hold of one of the board heads last night and I explained the situation we are in. They were reluctant to move forward until hearing more, even though in principle the deal has been approved at board level. I have advised them that all the paperwork has been finalised and we are good to go on this side, but they need one more document to be signed off by you and if you can get it done today and email it to me I can try to get it in before the close of the business day in Johannesburg."

I was all ears.

Within 30 minutes of the call, MO had sent me a one-page document that the board of the publicly listed company needed. It was a slight amendment with regards to the brand rights to Mi Fone. It seemed pretty straightforward to me. I knew Dubai was closed, but I knew the city well enough to know where to get the documents printed and scanned. I immediately saved the file on my USB, showered and jumped into a cab to take me to the nearest print centre. Once there, I printed it, had a good read, signed it, scanned it and then saved it back onto the USB stick. I got back into the waiting taxi and returned to the apartment. I connected my computer to the Wi-Fi and sent the document. I waited about 30 minutes and called MO. He confirmed receipt and then told me to wait for his call.

Noon on Friday came – nothing.

Friday afternoon came and again no news.

At 6pm I *had* to call MO.

"Did you get any answer from South Africa?"

"I just did, Alpesh. We got the sign off. We are good to go for Sunday. I will instruct the lawyers now to print everything out and have it ready for us to sign at 1pm on Sunday. Are you OK with that?"

"Listen, mate, I am happy to sign right now, later tonight and tomorrow, but I know no one works at the weekend, so if it's Sunday then so be it – as long as there are no other changes or surprises."

"No, I think we are there. See you on Sunday," said MO.

With that in mind, I dropped the phone and breathed a huge sigh of relief, even though I know it was still not a done deal. I had to get through the next couple of days. One would have thought I could have relaxed, had a few drinks with some old friends, hit a club or something – but none of that crossed my mind. I didn't want to go out drinking and pretend to celebrate. I simply did not feel like taking any sort of risk. I decided that weekend to not do anything but hit the gym and swim. Despite having told my wife, my team and my two best friends Doron and Deji, this deal had always been a big secret. I had told everyone to keep their mouths shut until it was done. For nearly a year we had kept our silence to the outside world.

The day arrived. Sunday is the first working day of the Dubai week. I got up early and called my lawyers to tell them that all was set for signing.

"We are happy to accompany you, Alpesh," they said.

I politely declined.

There was not much they could do as all the points had been agreed to and, besides, the last thing I wanted was to have to pay lawyers again just to stand next to me. At 1pm I met MO at their lawyer's offices in the Dubai International Financial Centre (DIFC). I wish to make it clear that there was no 'us' and 'them' situation here. They had a job to do and we had come to sign. The air of politeness and courtesy was *par excellence*. There was no tension in the air. They led me into their boardroom and before me lay a 20-foot expensive-looking boardroom table with piles and piles and piles of documents.

"Are you ready for this?" They looked at me.

"I have been waiting for this moment for a long time," I replied.

"So, you see here we have seven different sets of documents as per the seven agreements we had sent and agreed to. Each agreement is in four original copies. All you have to do is initial each page and sign where it is marked X. Then our client and their representative MO will co-initial each page and sign as the authorised signatory and buyer. When that's done, we, as the lawyers, have to initial each page, sign off and put our stamp to it.

"How many cups of coffee would you like?" he joked.

That morning, knowing that I was to sign, I had already booked my air ticket to go straight to Hong Kong from Dubai. I had to be at the airport by 5pm to catch the early evening flight out. It was now 1.30pm; I had to get through all the signatures, go back to the apartment through the Dubai traffic, then pack and get to the airport. I started signing and as I was doing so I remembered to give my phone to the lawyer's assistant who was overseeing the whole thing.

"I would really appreciate it if you could take pictures of this signing ceremony. Just click and click away as you please." She happily complied. I wanted this moment to be recorded.

We signed and signed and signed – one document after another, one pile after another. When I had done my bit, I had to sit back and hand it all over to MO to sign his bit. I saw the clock. It was now 2pm – it had taken me just 30 minutes to sign all the documents because I had moved fast – now I had to get this guy to sign in the same way and he wasn't having any of it; he was leisurely flicking through the documents. 'Muzzerfuzzer will you please hurry the fuck up?' was all that was going through my mind then. It was as if he was teasing me. By 3pm all the documents were signed. We all smiled, shook hands and congratulated each other. I hurriedly tried to excuse myself.

"Well done, Alpesh. Congratulations," said MO.

Now, this guy MO was just an employee of the investor firm, but at all times he had always treated me with respect – yes, he was a hard nut to crack, but I think he had also finally accepted the fact that we had nothing to hide and that at the end of the day they were buying a genuine readymade seven-year-old business.

"Thank you so much," I said to him. "I appreciate all your help and support in order to get this all done. I know you didn't have to go out of your way, but you did and for that I'm really thankful."

"You have a new partner now," he said.

"Yes, but please ensure you send me my upfront payment as soon as possible because I have things to sort out."

He nodded as though I had just made a stupid comment. The investor was bound to make the initial payment to our lawyers Escrow within 48 hours and that would then be transferred to me. I needed that money.

I rushed back to the apartment and packed my bags. I was feeling excited, happy and over the moon, but I had to get to the airport. I arrived at the airport late at 6pm with an hour left to catch my flight. I had planned a couple of weeks earlier to make sure the first thing I did after the actual deal was signed was go to Hong Kong and break the news to my team there and see the factories that I owed money to face to face. As I sank into my seat, the stewardess served me some champagne. I looked out of the window as the plane taxied along the runway.

'You muzzerfuzzer, Pesh. You did it. You fucking did it,' I said to myself.

I said a small prayer to God and gave my thanks. I then said cheers to myself and started drinking the champagne. After seven hard years, having done things nobody would have imagined, I had finally raised money for Mi Fone and had exited selling 51% of my African brand to a $5 billion-dollar publicly listed company.

Now, that, ladies and gentlemen, is what you call being *SERIOUSLY TESTED*!

SOMETIMES CHANGING THE GAME IS THE ONLY WAY YOU CAN PLAY

so make sure the new game is one you want to play!

CHAPTER 19

THE BLUES

I still couldn't fathom that such a large prestigious and credible company had just bought us. Mi Fone, one of Africa's first tech hardware start-ups, had gone all the way to exit to a public company. This was not a PE or a VC transaction. This was also not a dodgy deal in which someone pulls undeclared money out from under their mattress. This was an outright sale of the business. This was clear validation that one could start a self-funded pan-African business and actually exit to a large group. Every entrepreneur's dream, they say.

After my Hong Kong trip, I went back to South Africa and the first thing I did was give my family the biggest hugs of their lives. I hadn't seen them for nearly four weeks.

"We did it." I smiled as I spoke to my wife. I could see she was in awe and I knew she was extremely proud, especially as she had followed the struggle from day one.

I broke the news to my team in person, but at the back of my mind I knew there were some changes coming. From June 2015 onwards, things happened pretty quickly. As part of our deal I had to go and meet my new owners. They still wanted to know what Mi Fone was all about. I knew that I had a new mission ahead of me. The hustle had now changed. It was no longer about Alpesh and Mi Fone; it was about taking the company to the next level knowing that there were funds in place to do so.

My thoughts at that time were also on the missed opportunities, not so much for me because I had missed many opportunities in my lifetime, but for those same PE, VC and family fund offices that we had pitched to a few years back. What if they had accepted in 2011–2012 to invest in Mi Fone? With their money, we could have created much more value and by 2015 we could have exited to a trade buyer like this publicly listed company at a much higher valuation.

At the end of the day, I was proud to be able to exit, then look back at all those guys who had rejected us and stick my middle finger up at them. They had torn me apart. My message to those guys is very clear: next time you get an entrepreneur who has put his own skin in the game and generated revenues from day one, please take note, he is *committed* to his business. He needs help to grow, so don't think that we are here to steal your money; we are here to better ourselves and *make you money* in the process.

I also wonder what would have happened if 50 Cent had come on board? Maybe he also missed out big time on the Mi Fone opportunity, because, with him on board, we would have become a global brand in emerging markets and would have expanded out of Africa. Who knows what would have happened? Maybe with his star power, we could have exited to an even larger firm at an even larger valuation. Who will ever know?

Mi Fone now belonged to someone else. We owned a 49% minority stake. Besides the upfront payment we received and the inward working capital invested, I still had another cheque to collect in the form of a future earn out. In essence, we had to restart business as soon as we could. We needed to start getting the numbers again and get closer to our profit targets, so I could get my earn out payment. Having looked at the past seven years and the challenges we had overcome, our problem had always been a lack of sufficient funding. Now we had the money but wait … I couldn't spend it as I had planned to. I was now an employee of this firm and I had to abide by a new way of doing things. I had to accept that I had now lost control of Mi Fone. This was understandable. When an entrepreneur decides to sell a majority stake to a buyer, you have to follow their rules.

The first thing the new investors wanted to do was to officialise the business. The way I had been running it with all those structures and freelance consultants everywhere was not going to cut it with them. They wanted everything to be official. I could not use whoever I wanted to use to provide services to us as everything had to be presented as a business case and approved. I was a co-signatory to the bank account, but I could not touch that money as they had the final sign-off.

Our new financial year was to be 1st July 2015, so there were a few grace weeks between this date and when we had signed the deal back in May 2015. I used this opportunity to start cleaning the house and the first thing was our staff. Our investors did not want all of them to go into the new entity; therefore, I had the unenviable task of telling some of my team that their time was up. It was not an easy exercise for me as a few months previously I had told them that everyone would have secure jobs. There were a few tears, but the parting team members also understood my situation. Mi Fone was no longer mine and, hence, I was no longer the one calling the shots.

It was decided by the new owners that Dubai would be our HQ and we would need to set up our African HQ in Nairobi, Kenya. I didn't agree with my investors on this as I was all about making sure we spent the money in the right way to drive orders. The last thing I wanted to do was to set up an office again, but this was their corporate policy. I spoke to PN and told him that he would need to consider moving to Kenya with his family. He wasn't too happy as up until then he had been in South Africa under our local Mi Fone South Africa Pty Ltd work permit. Part of my obligation to the investor was that every previous entity we had would need to be closed down, so we had to close down Mi Fone South Africa and, hence, all our team would either be made redundant or have to move out of the country. PN had no choice, either he went to Kenya or he left the company.

I was in two minds about the role of PN within the whole new organisational structure. I had sold my team's qualities to the investors in the first place, so the investor had also concluded that PN would be a key part of the team, but by mid-2015, there had been too many fuck-ups for me not to be mad with him every day. I had let him drive Mi Fone over the past 18 months while I was focused elsewhere. Since he had been driving Mi Fone daily operations, our numbers had dropped and the business was much messier than when he had started. He showed promise here and there and his loyalty and belief in the brand could never be doubted, but, overall, I had been on a losing streak ever since he had come on board back in 2012. As much as I had personally wanted PN to leave Mi Fone altogether, in front of the investors it would have been very strange of me to suddenly let him go. The last thing I needed was them questioning why I sold them a dream team and now wanted to let our COO go.

PN reluctantly agreed to move to Kenya. The investors did not want to underpay anyone, so they took into account the whole package PN needed to operate efficiently out of Kenya. I didn't agree with how the investors were allocating the finances they had invested into Mi Fone. They wanted to dictate how it was spent, but the agreements we signed made me, the founder, and the CEO accountable for all the spend. It didn't seem right to me for some reason.

The investors also wanted to change the way we did our procurement via Alex in Hong Kong and China. They were not too happy with the fact that Alex was operating out of a three-bedroom apartment converted into an office and did not see why we had to go through Alex when we could deal with the factories directly. I had explained to them that for the past seven years we had done everything in China through Alex and our operation had been running very smoothly, other than the cash flow crisis. In terms of their performance, the Hong Kong and China team had been superb over the many years we had worked together.

The investors were having none of that. They wanted to start everything from scratch. Each and every factory had to sign long-term supplier contracts. Each contract was the size of a mini telephone directory. We had never done this before. For us, the factory commercial documents, such as invoices and purchase orders, were sufficient. For seven years we had operated like that and whenever we'd had a problem, the factories always fixed their mess. The factories were already pissed off with me for making them wait for payments due and now I had to get them to sign long-term 150-page contracts in English when none of them really understood written English. These guys worked on next-to-nothing margins and wouldn't be hiring any lawyers on their side to translate the legal documents into Chinese.

I broke the news to Alex.

All our factories now had to sign in-depth supplier contracts and he had the task of convincing them to do so. There was nothing wrong with this, but it took up time that we simply did not have. With the new investor, we lost considerable momentum just because of paperwork, some of which was unnecessary.

I had planned for a great opening Q1 (July–September 2015) to get the new company rolling, but, alas, by the end of September we had only just managed to pay the deposits for new productions as the factories themselves had taken so long to sign off on our lengthy contracts. We finally received our first official new Mi Fone stocks in late October, meaning our first quarter was a complete write-off. I wasn't too concerned, because at least we now had money to pay expenses and salaries. The biggest relief for me was that after seven years, at the end of every month, I no longer had to sit on my computer paying salaries and bills. There was now someone else doing all of that. The investors had bought 51% of my headaches!

By October 2015, Mi Fone had been out of the market for more than a year. You will recall that we stopped trading in late 2014. We were cocksure that the investment deal would be done by December 2014, but it wasn't completed until May 2015, five months behind schedule. With the further bureaucratic delays, we only actually started real trading again in the October of 2015. In practical terms, we had lost *one* year of sales and brand awareness. In the mobile phone business one year is a fucking decade. A lot can happen in one year. I was meant to be on a high but the post-acquisition blues had started sinking in.

They say the grass is greener on the other side.
Yes, probably because it's been fertilised with bullshit

We now faced hurdle after hurdle in our dealings. Our payment requests took ages to be approved and I was also very eager to restart Mi Card and Oju. As part of our investment, the investors also retained the rights to Mi Card and Oju, but a few weeks into the deal it was like talking to a brick wall. We needed to get back on our feet with Mi Fone sales and the opening up of new revenue streams.

The biggest issue was the new payment terms that all our customers had to adhere to. The new Mi Fone was simply not entertaining any open account credit terms with anyone – it was their money on the line now. Fair enough. Giving credit openly was what had got me into trouble in the first place, so I was very much opposed to repeating this exercise with my new investors.

We agreed that the only way we could give credit was to insure our risk. This had to be done via one of the large trade insurance risk companies that could insure our receivables. The annual fees for insuring risk were not low and we had to allocate a budget toward this cost. We had one in mind that was of French origin, but their Dubai office seemed to be the laziest bunch of folks on the planet. I had worked with all the large trade insurance companies before and no one was as slow in replying as these guys. They took two to three weeks to get back to us on credit applications and then simply refused with no immediate explanation unless we went back to them and pushed them for their justifications. Their answers would take another few weeks to come through and when they did eventually reply, they would state the political and individual country risk of our target African markets. As a large global trade insurer, surely they had enough reports and IT in place to tell us this in a matter of hours rather than weeks and we all would have saved so much time? If I'd had my way I would have called them myself and given them a piece of my mind, especially as we were paying them for a service, but with the investors in charge of all the administration I had to bite my tongue.

The opening six months were not good. We had new phone models, but now we could only sell for cash or an acceptable payment instrument. It had also taken us quite a few months to set up all our previous customers under new distribution agreements – again the size of mini phone directories. Most, if not all, customers simply could not be bothered to go through 100-page documents. These were hardcore traders. Some of them didn't even check their emails.

Angola was the trickiest market to deal with. We had a great partner there – DM – with whom I had built a solid relationship over the past few years. Here was someone whose first order with Mi Fone in 2013 was just 100 units and our last shipments to him had grown to 20,000 phones per month. At one point, he owed us $750,000 on an open account. He could have run away … but he didn't.

DM had paid every single cent back; yes, he made us sweat and he took his time, but in the end, he paid back every penny. I know he would have paid us sooner, but the Angolan Central Bank regulations on acquiring foreign exchange dollars were not the easiest to deal with. I only wished that Africa had more people like DM; people who understood the meaning of credit, goodwill and how to keep the cycle going. It would have been a much nicer place to do business. Under the new Mi Fone, we had projected the business forecast with 50% of our target numbers to be delivered out of Angola. However, for Angola the investors simply would not budge, even when DM promised them advance deposits of local kwanza, the Angolan currency, into our accounts in Angola. For the investors, all orders from Angola had to be in cash in US dollars.

The shit then hit the fan in Angola towards late 2015. The drop in global oil prices had immediately affected all the African oil-producing nations of which Angola was a major contributor. This drop in oil prices meant that there was very little availability of US dollars as foreign exchange for people to pay for their imports. DM could simply not get money out of the system to pay us on time. Even though he was always late in paying, I knew he was a stand-up guy. Unfortunately, that was the past. The investors were not prepared to wait as long as I had waited in the past and my hands were tied. We, therefore, slowly started losing our market share in Angola. This was our highest profit market and the only way to rescue it was to get business from elsewhere – Kenya being the main market.

PN moved to Kenya and his title was changed from COO to regional manager. He was tasked with building the business in the region by establishing Mi Fone Kenya Ltd and taking on new staff all under long-term employment contracts. Considering that his salary was higher than most seasoned bank and corporate CEOs in Kenya, he had to step up to the mark. It was the least he could do.

For some reason, though, PN's performance dwindled

even further. Maybe it was the move to Kenya, maybe it was the family pressure for setting up a new home again or maybe it was a new *laissez faire* attitude with the very comfortable expat package he was receiving. PN had never managed to create his own relationships with our local partners, who were also shareholders in Mi Group. They had simply seen him as an inexperienced kid. They would only deal with me and I was cool with that. I handled this part and advised to PN and our investor team that with the amount of money we were spending on our Kenya set up we *really* had to be able to get new business from other customers in the East African region so that we were not only relying on our traditional retail partner's orders.

Somehow the momentum never accelerated and by December 2015 we were way behind on our numbers. Our overheads had sky-rocketed because we had to spend more on set up costs, rents, salaries, and taxes. A saviour for us was Nigeria. Or so we thought.

My old friend PB from the Hong Kong days had moved to Nigeria to assist his family's trading business. He called me out of the blue seeking my support for a potentially massive order with one of the main Nigerian e-commerce companies. They wanted to have an exclusive customised phone made with us. Nigeria had not really figured in our new forecasts as I still had that burning problem of having a bad debt from that market. We had supplied there before, but since our old customer still owed us close to $250,000 we hadn't bothered going back into the market in a big way. I welcomed the enquiry from my friend PB, as they were talking about a massive 50,000-smartphone order with an order value of $5 million. How could we say no to this – especially now that we had the funding in place?

The Nigeria deal had to be explored in more detail. I needed a replacement for the standstill in the orders coming from Angola. There were no credit issues with Nigeria because they agreed they would pay us via a guaranteed bank letter of credit. It was the perfect deal. After weeks of negotiation, we finally received the purchase order – and, boy, was it needed. MO from the investor's side had also now become a director of Mi Fone. Little did I know, but he was promising his board that somehow Mi Fone was going to come up with some good news. He needed us to show something so the board could start justifying their investment into Mi Fone.

The Nigerian order was a pretty straightforward order, except that the phones we had to make were the most expensive products we had ever customised. The e-commerce customer was extremely demanding. They wanted everything their way; the phone in a certain colour, the box with a certain look, the phone software with a certain user interface and so on. The production itself was to be split into shipments of 10,000 units to assist in everyone's cash flow. We weren't going to make the mistake we had made before with our old DRC order, so we just bought materials to handle the first order. We planned to ship the first completed phones by January 2016 with the aim that, by April 2016, we would have completed the whole 50,000 phone order – just in time for our last quarter to finalise our first year in business.

The Nigeria order turned out to be a big slap in our faces. The drop in global oil prices had an immediate downward impact on the Nigerian economy. In 2016 the country fell into a major recession. Nigeria was the biggest economy in Africa with an official population of more than 160 million people, but everything for domestic consumption was imported. With low oil prices, the government's main source of revenue in dollars also dropped. This led to an immediate shortage of available US foreign exchange. The Central Bank of Nigeria had stopped issuing dollars out to the market and this cutback directly affected us – the official rate was 200 naira to the dollar, but nobody could get dollars at that price – the only dollars available were at a black-market rate of 350 naira to the dollar. This meant our phone prices in US dollars were now much more expensive when converted into local currency.

My friend PB, who was now our customer buying on behalf of the e-commerce giant, could not get the dollar allocation from his banks for all the stocks. They did manage to pay us some cash and against that we shipped some phones, but the majority of phones had now piled up in our Hong Kong warehouse awaiting some kind of payment out of Nigeria. The e-commerce end buyer was buying the phones from PB locally in Nigeria at a pre-agreed local naira price. PB, however, could not do the deal anymore because he could not get the dollars at the appropriate rate without making a massive loss. We had pleaded with the e-commerce company to help us out because we had made the product specifically for them, but they seemed to want to wash their hands of the deal. It was a problem that belonged to our local partner PB and ultimately Mi Fone that was now stuck holding stocks that we'd had made as part of our commitments.

When you do business with some of the African companies, you have to also anticipate doing business with some massive egos in the room. I had explained several times to PB that it was a mistake for the e-commerce company to make specialised customised phones and that they were better off buying generic Mi Fone products so that they could sell the phones into other channels as well. We, too, could have had an easier time because we would have been able to sell the generic phones into other markets. Now, due to the dire macro-economic conditions in Nigeria, we had these stocks that we could not liquidate elsewhere. The e-commerce company and PB were not able to respect their own commitments as the buyers. I felt badly let down. Again, why did I have to say yes to all their requests just to get an order?

The investors were fully aware of the situation in Nigeria, but with these corporate guys we must always remember that they don't actually give a shit – the only thing that counts is the numbers. I had to make a plan, but I had exhausted plans A, B, C, D and E.

I was now at plan F … like what the *fuck* do I do next?

Re-emerging into the market after one year of silence proved to be more difficult than we had anticipated. This was not due to the demand, because we have always had decent demand for our product, but it was due to us internally making it very difficult for people to do business with us. Africa has always been a challenging place to do anything. I always saw its problems as potential opportunities to fix. Even in a down cycle there is a way up. A down cycle is a great situation for repositioning yourself back into the marketplace because you can do certain things that no one else would. Mi Fone had this opportunity with the likes of Angola by simply adjusting our pricing and terms of trade in such a way as to enable local sales of our products in local currencies. To restart in other markets, we needed to work on bare-minimum margins in order to remain competitive and get the brand awareness going again.

Kenya, for example, was the base of our African HQ. It had been our market for many years, but somehow our growth there was also not going to plan. There were no currency issues in Kenya. Our failures in Kenya came down to me and my team on the ground. We now had 10 full-time staff who had been hired by PN. We had fancy offices and we were showing a stronger local presence, but still we could not crack through to new high-volume shipments. I had to visit Kenya a couple of times to meet with customers and to see for myself what needed to be done to get more orders. I would negotiate new deals with our customers, but the minute I left, the situation would go back to normal. This is what happens when an entrepreneurial company changes its methods drastically. We lost our deal-making capabilities.

We were also spending way too much on team salaries in Kenya in terms of what was being delivered. It clearly showed me that our team had become very comfortable to the point of being downright lazy. They knew at the end of the month they would get their pay cheque. One thing I could never stand was sheer laziness in people, especially when they were paid to perform a service. My frustrations had started to show and arguments had started with my investors about the poor performance of the staff. They couldn't give a shit as the fingers were pointed at me.

"Your shit, you sort it out," they kept saying.

"OK, so let's get rid of some of the staff and cut back on those expenses, so we can invest more of the saved money on actual brand marketing. That way we will get more sell through of our phones and consequently more repeat orders."

"No, we cannot do that. We have proper employment contracts with all of them. We need to give them formal notice and Kenya is the only place where we have a team. We must give them more time."

In my mind, I was fuming. 'Give who what time?'

The team in Kenya were six months into the new game and they'd had more than enough time to prove themselves. The employees were all laughing. They knew they would not be held accountable for their lack of performance, yet come month end there would be a nice salary deposited into their bank account. It always frustrated me how some employees simply did not respect the hands that fed them.

What had made things worse was that in October 2015 a multibillion-dollar Chinese company by the name of Xiaomi had decided that they, too, would now enter the African market.

SOMETIMES TOO MUCH CHANGE IS NOT A GOOD THING

The key is knowing what to keep and what to let go, beware of those who accept change without question

CHAPTER 20

XIAOMI

Xiaomi was established in China in 2010 and by 2015 had become one of the top 10 smartphone brands globally. At that time, they had a valuation of around $45 billion. They were the number one smartphone brand in China and had started expanding across Asia and India. They had now signed a deal with an African distributor to introduce their range of Mi handsets to the market. Yes, you read it correctly. Xiaomi also used the same 'Mi' name on their phones. This was a big problem for me. I had to protect what we had been building since 2008.

Besides the non-payers, the risk of doing business in Africa and the daily case of dealing with the Double Gs, the Xiaomi episode really showed me the ugly side of doing business in Africa.

We had setup Mi Fone as the first African device back in 2008, two years before Xiaomi was born. From day one, I had ensured that our brand was duly registered in most African countries. Xiaomi and their distributor entered Africa with not a care in the world. They had the money and very quickly put out press releases that Xiaomi and its Mi range of smartphones would now empower the continent with low-cost phones.

Excuse me?

Having another phone brand in our markets with the same name was going to cause a lot of confusion. We had already received emails from people either congratulating us or asking for clarity about where they could fix their Mi phones.

Some of the products were ours but some were Xiaomi's that individuals had purchased whilst outside of Africa. One guy in South Africa even sent us an email complaining about the racist attitude he had received when he attended the Xiaomi launch in Durban, South Africa. He said he was treated unfairly due to the colour of his skin and that he would never buy a Mi Fone. He thought it was us he dealt with, but we hadn't had any promotions in Durban on that day. To add to the confusion, the Xiaomi phones were not as cheap as ours. Their price points were around $150. It would have killed our business, as everyone would have assumed that we – the real Mi Fone – were now too expensive to purchase.

We now had the money to take on Xiaomi legally in all three of our major markets – Nigeria, South Africa and Kenya. The investors and I debated on the best approach to take. In Nigeria, I quickly instructed a lawyer friend of mine to see what they could do to put a stop to Xiaomi trying to start sales in Nigeria. I got away with this because I had started the process without asking anyone's permission. In Kenya, we went with lawyers recommended to us via our local office and in South Africa I was eager to use the same lawyers we had used for so many years to set up our brand registrations, but our investors were thinking different. They wanted to use their set of corporate lawyers. I had nothing against this, but from the first day I met with these lawyers in their Sandton offices, I could see trouble brewing. They may have been a reputable firm, but to me they were not qualified to give legal advice on trademark law. I had questioned this with my investors, but they insisted that we use their own law firm.

I was in China having dinner with Alex when my Nigerian

lawyers called and gave us the good news that we had received a court injunction in our favour in Nigeria. We had won an interim injunction against Xiaomi. They were not allowed to sell any products in Nigeria because we already had the Mi trademark registered and had previously used it there. This was a major win for us and we promptly announced it in the press as well.

Being a passionate African, I would also widely state our case.

"Why should we even think about allowing a foreign company with the same brand name as ours to come into Africa just as they please? We have our trademarks established everywhere and our Mi brand is in many countries. All they had to do was some research to find out that there is already a Mi brand in the same mobile device category in Africa. So what if we are not that big or well-known internationally? The fact is we were here *first* and we have a proven history."

The Nigerian courts seemed to get it, but unfortunately for me the biggest headache was coming out of South Africa. I had instructed the South African lawyers (who were charging us an arm and a leg) to ensure we go for the jugular. We had to get an immediate court injunction similar to the one we had in Nigeria, but I could see that the lawyers themselves did not believe we had a case in South Africa.

"You have never been strong in South Africa, so it's very hard to defend your case. We must show valid proof that you had prior existence in South Africa and that you are now re-entering the market since your acquisition."

Then the onslaught of legal response work laid into me. Every day I had to go through old records to dig up evidence, such as sales records and shipment documents, that had existed in South Africa ever since 2010. I even showed them the various press clippings, including my CNBC Africa interview from late 2013. Xiaomi and their distributors simply claimed that CNBC could not be recognised as a *bona fide* media house. It was comments like these that would lead to more frustration as our South African lawyers would then lay into me like bulldozers every time they got a response from the other side. They wanted me to *yet again* prove that we had existed. At one point, Xiaomi and their African distributor also alleged that I had committed some kind of fraud by providing fake or irregular airway bill documents to back up my claim that we had shipped Mi Fone products to South Africa a few years back. The onus was one me to prove everything.

In one of our legal meetings we had to address the issue of this so-called fraud and alleged fabrication on my part of the shipping documents. I knew our documents were genuine, but I had to physically call and instruct Emirates airlines to send me all the old historical airway bills and confirm that the goods had indeed landed in South Africa. It was all clearly verified. There was no wrongdoing on our part.

Our lawyers were also very clear with their instructions to me.

"Alpesh, get the evidence and we will then go for closure."

This never happened because our lawyers simply did not know *how* to go for Xiaomi's jugular vein. They had made me run around for six months for nothing. In no uncertain terms, we had paid the lawyers in order to educate them on our kind of case.

The Mi Fone brand had been promoted across the whole of

the African continent in the cheapest manner possible. Mi Fone was known by so many people across Africa and now I had our own lawyers and the other side somehow putting forward the notion that we had never had a business, even after all the proof we had provided. Can you imagine how that feels?

The episode with Xiaomi and the experience with the lawyers in South Africa clearly proved to me that in Africa there are no rules. You can register your trademarks, have huge amounts of industry recognition and you can build a business, but the onus is always on you to prove it, especially if you are not a famous brand.

I am thankful to the Nigerian courts and their rule of law for acknowledging the fact that we existed, but in South Africa – it was a case of us the real Mi Fone being guilty until proven innocent. Our lawyer's attitude and the grumpy behaviour from our investors confirmed that even they thought I was not telling them something. I actually felt as though they were treating me with no respect. We had done so much business in Africa and, yet, because we were not big and powerful in South Africa, they felt our case was weak. Just because our lawyers or any of the old judges had themselves not seen any Mi Fone billboards on their way to work meant they thought we had no existence. What they forgot was that our market was not the fancy Sandton upper-class white crowd – it was the township folk, the urban black youth. There had never been a need for us to put up billboards or embark on a costly advertising campaign. We conducted guerrilla marketing exercises. That's who we were. Mi Fone had done what it had always done; we kept our marketing to the streets with events and activations. The lawyers had never lived or experienced the urban black world; hence they had discounted our contribution from day one. Even with all the stuff we had done in Africa, this was not good enough for our South African lawyers when it came to helping further in backing up our case. In addition, not one ounce of support for us as an African brand was received from any government departments, business organisations or networking groups.

Let us turn the tables for a moment and consider if we, as Mi Fone, had decided to enter the Chinese market. What would the Chinese government have done? Countries like China make it very difficult for foreign brands to enter their market. They prefer to promote their own home-grown brands. So why should African governments make it easy for foreign brands to enter Africa, especially those with the same Mi name as ours? Where was our protection in all of this?

The whole point for us when registering our brands from day one was because someone else might come in or copy the name. Now we had someone else coming in with the same name and we could do nothing about it. What was the point of spending money on legally registering our brands, only to find some foreign brands coming in with not a care in the world? As for the Xiaomi distributor – what the fuck were they thinking?

They knew there was a Mi brand already in Africa. I had met the owner three years earlier at a Wharton Africa conference in Kenya where we had drinks together. Why would African companies not partner with each other and assist in building each other – why get a distributorship for a Chinese phone? That is not exactly going to solve the problems of Africa. I am sure many Africans reading this will agree with me. We need to create, develop and protect our own local brands. We need to give ourselves a chance to flourish, just as much as China gives its home brands the chance to flourish. If we don't build and maintain our own brands, then foreign brands will always have a way to come and eat our lunch.

You will remember the famous movie *Alien* with its infamous tag line, 'in space no one can hear you scream'. Africa was similar to space – NO ONE can hear you scream!

The Xiaomi fight was, and still continues to be, a long, drawn-out battle. They had the money to stretch this out, but funnily enough, even though they are selling a few phones here and there, they too have been on the receiving end of some nice African slaps for thinking they could simply come and take over the continent. Africa has not been a walk in the park for them either.

Personally, the case had winded me. It had been just another burden to bear while we had been trying to resurrect the Mi Fone business. We had the money now, but it seemed so much more difficult an environment to operate within. The past seven years had been tough, but somehow in some way, we had managed to scrape through. Now I found myself sitting looking at an abyss of problems and pressures. I asked myself, 'What did I give up?'

THERE ARE SOME FIGHTS YOU JUST CAN'T WIN

especially when the real enemy is the enemy within
(your own organisation)

CHAPTER 21

POST-ACQUISITION

To get acquired and have an exit is every entrepreneur's dream come true. You give up control and in return you get some money. You receive further funding into your business, but now you have to toe the line. When a corporate giant buys an entrepreneurial brand like Mi Fone there is an inherent shock to the system with the immediate change in processes. The actual transition can take many years. In our case, what the investors forgot to ask themselves was why they bought us in the first place. They bought an entrepreneurial company. They tried to fix something that was not broken. Yes, we were beaten and bloodied, but we were not broken.

This is the challenge that every entrepreneur will face in his lifetime. Change is inevitable, but at all costs try to remain as entrepreneurial as you possibly can. The minute I signed those papers I gave up the very thing that entrepreneurs stand for – freedom. Taking money from anyone comes at a cost – and our acquisition had come at a big cost to me. I lost my drive and I lost my passion. It seemed that everything we were doing was like swimming against the tide. When you have an established business and you get a cash injection you are meant to take it into fifth gear and accelerate your growth. It didn't happen for me.

Since the day I signed the deal in Dubai in May 2015, my experience with the new Mi Fone has been nothing short of heart-breaking. We simply could not do the things we wanted to do. Our plans for Mi Card and Oju were shelved; our own investors were risk-averse; there were no sparks igniting any sort of innovation; and my entrepreneurial spirit was trapped. I became a caged animal that once used to sprint, hunt its prey, catch it and devour it like a beast.

I lost that spirit with the new Mi Fone. The highs of exiting and putting something in our pockets will never justify the fact that we lost something in the brand we had built. The same creativity and innovation that had kept us going for so long had now been cut off at the knees. At times our investors did not want to even acknowledge the fact that we were a 'black' brand. They had bought into a world they simply did not understand.

By early 2016, with the decrease in our growth of sales, I could see things were not working out with our investor. We were just so misaligned in our thinking, in our way of doing things and in our approach to the market. I felt that every ounce of the passion I had once had for building an African brand had dwindled away. My own team had let me down and our efforts in the marketplace were simply not working out.

In a way, I had let myself down.

I started turning more inward. I began questioning everything. What was my purpose here? How could I continue in this manner, waking up every day with a heavy heart? It had taken a year to do our deal. In all the waiting and waiting, had the investor and I both missed the boat and the opportunity altogether because we were so caught up in our own bullshit? Should I have seen the long list of requests and the consequent delays from their side as warning signs telling me to simply walk away from the deal? This is the dilemma every entrepreneur will face – do you go all in or do you simply say no?

The whole experience has been a real eye opener for me.

I began to spend more time alone with my thoughts. I had hustled for years and years and had finally built a successful brand that had validated its existence and its credibility by exiting to a publicly listed company. What did this all mean for me? We had built something not many people could have done, but to honour the brand we needed to take a new direction. I had to sit down with our investors to discuss all the options on the table. For them it was all about their share price. They didn't care that Nigeria had fucked us due to the dollar situation. They couldn't care about the issues going on in Angola and they couldn't give two shits about our poor performance overall. They simply looked at me as being the one who had fucked up

I admit it. I had fucked up!

I had fucked up because I had let others take over the management of my business. Control is one thing, but running the show is another. I had let them do what they wanted, thinking that they knew better than me. They didn't. It was the same as the time when I dealt with TS and Mi Card. I had assumed they would know more than me, but they didn't. None of them had ever built their own brands before. They were all highly paid employees. Our costs had exploded since they had come in, because they thought we had now become a corporate entity all of a sudden. To burden the company with unnecessary structures and processes killed our vibe. It killed our flexibility and our nimbleness.

We all met to discuss what we would be doing for our next financial year. We had already burned a major portion of the initial cash injection. The leftover stocks from Nigeria, our Kenya setup costs and the legal costs of taking on Xiaomi had taken a nice chunk of our working capital. We had to discuss new budgets and I had to submit a request for additional funding to carry us through. I could see in their eyes that it was just too much to comprehend after their first 12 months' experience of being in the mobile phone business. The budgets were not approved when I asked for the major spend to go on an Africa-wide marketing campaign. My plans were not embraced with fervour. It was clear that they did not want Mi Fone to be known any more as a rebellious urban brand aimed at the black youth of Africa. As a public company, they felt our messaging had to be toned down. In a way, they were trying to change the very thing that had excited them in the first place.

Unfortunately for me, at the meeting they had decided they could not invest more money into Mi Fone for the time being due to having to sort out of the mess they had in Africa. Their other businesses had also felt the pain of the recession in Africa. It would be hard for them to invest when they had to cut back on costs as per board directives. They asked me what I wanted to do and I asked the same question back to them.

"Well what do you want to do?"

They all looked at each other – it was clear they didn't want to say it, but I could read between the lines.

There I was sitting in front of seasoned Corporate guys and they didn't have a clue on what to do.In their world they could make moves but they did not know how to play in the entrepreneurs world. We had a 5 year agreement supported by several sub agreements that had caused excruciating pain to decipher. Now here they were not knowing what do to next. They were panicking without taking into account the fundamentals. No one makes a return on investment in just one year of doing business. You simply cannot expect miracles from a place like Africa.It showed me how naïve people are even though they are very smart and seasoned .It also showed me the true but sad nature of how a lot of Corporations don't stick to their commitments.

We had spent one year in doing the Mi Fone deal and then lost momentum in restarting the business due to delays in restructuring ,implementation and general execution. Instead, of panicking a true partnership would have come together to embrace the 'pivot'. In business terms, a 'pivot' simply means that a company should make efforts to take the business in a new direction. One cannot keep doing the same thing and expect a different set of results and that's what the issue was. The investors were simply not built to pivot.

So,whether we are entrepreneurs or corporations, whether we are individuals or groups, there is always a price to pay in everything we do. We can all dream as much as we want, but when it comes to executing our dreams into reality we have to be prepared to pay the costs.

As they say, 'the dream is free, but the hustle is sold separately'.

AT SOME POINT YOUR JOURNEY MUST END
even if it is sooner than you would like.
Then it's time to start a new journey

WHEN YOU CLIMB AND REACH THE SUMMIT
you will be surprised to see how many other peaks
still need to be conquered

EPILOGUE

They say an entrepreneur is someone who jumps off a cliff and decides to build a plane on the way down. I was used to jumping off cliffs. I simply had no fear. I had jumped so many times in order to do what I wanted to do and not once did I ever give a shit about the status quo. My last jump with Mi Fone was the longest jump of my life. In the past, I had done things that had lasted a few weeks or a couple of years, but besides my corporate hustle, Mi Fone was the one thing that really taught me about life in general.

I thought I was slick at the age of 40, I thought life could only get better. I was at the top of my game at Motorola and, when I left, the momentum was there to join another firm, do another corporate hustle and simply collect a pay cheque. I know I would have been able to enjoy life more and who knows what today could have been for me? Would it have been better or would it have been worse? One will never know because at that crossroads in my life I made a decision that I was simply not prepared to run around building someone else's dream.

Ask me if I would do it all over again.

Not the way I did it and not where I did it from. Building a brand in Africa has been an eight-year education lesson. I remember back at Hull University I was being paid to be educated and now 30 years later I have had to pay my share of school fees to get educated in the art of hardcore entrepreneurship. I have learnt through trial and error how *not* to do things. For me, there was simply no manual to follow; there was no blueprint to follow. We were the pioneers. We were literally in the jungle with no weapons to protect ourselves. We had to make it up as we went along and tons of mistakes were made in the process.

I tell people all the time, "If there was town called Mistake City ... I would be the gaddam mayor!" They say it's all about being in the right place at the right time. With Mi Fone, my deepest shade of hustle, we had the right product, but neither the place nor the time seemed to be right. The market we were chasing was way behind our time. All the things we did at Mi Fone were done way before others had even caught on. We paid the price for being the *first*. My learnings from all these experiences are something that I will always be grateful for.

I now know why I had to suffer. It was to really understand myself. I had to test my limits and constantly go beyond them. I have been pushed to the edge and back several times and each time I have learnt a little bit more. It's like when you fully stretch a rubber band, you will notice it never goes back to its original size.

The sad part is that I was never in a position to take Mi Fone to the heights that it deserved. I accept my own shortcomings for the way I managed things. I may have been foolish to start this venture, but I always had the hope that something big would happen for us. We were, after all, operating in the last emerging market – Africa.

I can now look back with hindsight and think about how I *would* have, *could* have and *should* have done things, but one of my biggest regrets was that we did not position Mi Fone in a proper manner. For example, I know that after the first couple of years, I should have brought in a seasoned CEO/COO to help me. Yes, I was the founder and chief strategist, but when it came to running the show, I simply did not have the skills required at the time. Another example is if we had set up in the USA or UK as a mobile brand aimed at *all* emerging markets and not just Africa, we may have had better support from the international community. Had we been based in Silicon Valley from 2008 at least our eggs would have been spread out and we would have had access to an ecosystem that actually nurtures innovation and risk; a place that embraces entrepreneurs with open arms, unlike Africa where entrepreneurs can be seen to be pests; a place where the big boys continue to buy from the big boys and if you are a small guy, get to the back of the queue unless you can pay your way to the front.

Africa – my dear Africa, with the structures in place, the red tape, the corruption, the bureaucracy, the frustrations of waiting, the pain that goes with getting paid and the challenge of always having to prove yourself. All these conditions make it very hard for anyone to start or build their business in an efficient and respectable manner. The love that I have for the people of Africa can never be taken away, but the love I once had for my continent has waned. Africa has not done a good job of building its reputation. It is its own worst enemy. This is a continent that still needs to awaken from its drowsy state of affairs. The narrative by some so-called 'experts' on Africa has been layered with too much sugar. It's a sweet story to tell, but in reality it is very challenging. Africa will never be able to build a strong future if it doesn't fix the shaky foundations it has today.

Today I see many more entrepreneurs in Africa. The start-ups, incubators, accelerators and the whole ecosystem are slowly falling into place, but at a snail's pace. The continent is still controlled by people with their heads in the clouds and most of them have sold their souls to outsiders. My heart goes out to young entrepreneurs who are just starting up. I don't wish my journey on any of them, but my two cents worth of advice would be for them to really understand the realities of the game and not get carried away. Yes, we all want to be the next Mark Zuckerberg, but we will end up being Mark *Suckerbergs* if we do not think out our plans in a realistic manner and consider that, above all, access to funding is not as easy as everyone likes to make out. As the rap group Public Enemy says, "Don't believe the hype."

I tell entrepreneurs and intrapreneurs today to build businesses that are bigger than the confines of our borders and, more so, build businesses that are bigger than the confines of our own minds. We in Africa must train our minds to think globally. Our mind-sets have been programmed to think small. Why should we be satisfied with being big fish in a small pond when we can be big fish in a big pond? We have a scarcity mind-set rather than a mind-set of abundance. All of us are competing, chasing the same dollar, when what we should be doing is creating value.

It's everyone's dream to build their own business, but there is a dark side to entrepreneurship that not many people talk about. 'True' entrepreneurs all over the world face psychological issues because it's a tough game. The term 'entrepreneur' has been glamourised to a large extent. The truth is that entrepreneurship is not for the faint-hearted. I always say to folks that if you have a highly paid job, you sleep well at night and you have time to hug your kids, think very hard whether or not you are willing to give up all of that just to follow your passion. You will see all these folks talking about passion but, trust me, following your passion does not always mean profits. I was extremely passionate when I set up Mi Fone and for many years we grew our business year on year. We received many accolades, tons of high fives and tons of pats on the shoulder for a job well done, but at the same time we also took beating after beating. That is the reality of running your own show. Some days you will win, but most days you will lose.

In Africa, had the leaders, governments and large corporates embraced entrepreneurs with open arms, today we would have been a much more industrialised area and would have created many more jobs. Instead, everyone got caught up in the hype of Africa. The over-exaggeration of the lucrative opportunities that exist in Africa without checking the fundamentals. This is clearly reflected in that today, in 2017, most African countries are in recession with dwindling currencies and massive unemployment. Here, we have the richest continent on the planet and yet it remains the poorest. How can that be?

I believe it's the short-term mind-set without long-term thinking. In Africa, there is a mind-set of wanting to win today, but fuck tomorrow. Get what you can today as tomorrow is not promised. Rather than investing in our economies to build long-term, sustainable wealth, our countries have short-changed the people for short-term gains. Leaders duck and dive and promise investment into industries, creating jobs and empowering entrepreneurs, but in reality, nothing ever gets done. The failure of our economies to function well has directly impacted many companies across the continent. I am not saying there is no promise in Africa or there are no opportunities; what I am saying is that for anyone trying to get into the continent, *please* be fully prepared to take on the challenges. Yes, you want the African rose, but don't forget how many thorns you need to go through to pick that rose.

Very few true entrepreneur stories come out of Africa, although there are many successful businesses on the continent – one-man shows, family businesses and businesses that were built and acquired. Many companies have gained immense wealth, but at what cost? Did they by-pass certain regulations? Did they make certain pay-offs? Did they participate in irregular tenders? Did they cosy up to certain vested interests? Or do they just want to keep quiet in order not to attract any jealousy?

Why are we so fearful of telling our own stories? Why do we allow outsiders to write our stories for us? That's why I wanted to write this book as I have no issue whatsoever in telling my story. I have nothing to hide nor do I have anyone to protect. I tell it how it is with zero fucks given. My story is a harsh, raw and non-sugar-coated tale of an entrepreneur's experience.

My consulting and business counselling work today allows me the freedom to network with others who have written about the realities of building a business in emerging markets and compare war stories. Yes there is much more to say about my entrepreneur experience but I will leave that for my next book. I will be writing a hard-knocks business book aimed at assisting new entrepreneurs. They won't hear any of that soppy bullshit that you see nowadays on the bookshelf. I hope some of the hard lessons I have learnt can at least help them better prepare for what's ahead. They will have to understand they cannot rely on anyone, because in the darkness, even their own shadow *will* leave them. They will have to anticipate the immense frustrations that will come when dealing with the status quo.

Some of the topics that I will be writing about include the importance of starting lean, the quality of the product or service, the user experience, the funding game, valuations, trust, focus, taking advantage of mistakes and failures and the pitfalls to look out for. Above all, what are you actually building? What problems are you solving? What values are you creating that can make someone's life a little bit better?

I now believe that, after 40 years of hard hustle, God has not put me where I wanted to be, rather he has put me where I *needed* to be. I needed to go through all these trials. I needed to be fully *tested* in order to be fully prepared to handle the even bigger challenges that are coming my way. As they say, opportunity wastes no time for the unprepared.

It is also said that when you find your purpose, you will know, because things just become easy and you are in a state of flow. In no way from any of my experiences did I ever find my true purpose, but then maybe there is no Holy Grail purpose lying out there for me. Maybe my purpose has been my journey. Maybe God had it planned that my soul would experience the highest of highs and lowest of lows in life – an abundance of riches, an abundance of suffering, an abundance of beauty and an abundance of man's ugly nature.

Looking back at the journey, you also realise that no matter how hard you fight there are some battles you simply cannot win. No matter how much you try and control outcomes, there are external forces at work that you simply can't fuck with. You have to know your space. You have to stay in your own lane. The battle is not with others, the battle is with oneself. The only person I am competing with today is me. We have to do whatever it takes to be better people tomorrow than we are today. It's the only way we can keep progressing. We have to accept where we are in our lives from a position of *gratitude*. Let things unfold in their own way and, by this acceptance, we will learn to live in the moment. We will be calmer, more focused and more grateful. I have come to be like this.

Today, I see a whole new set of possibilities out there. I see a world where anything is possible. I feel more prepared to take on new challenges and accomplish them *well*.

We all have our tests laid out for us regardless of our backgrounds and what professions we follow. It is up to us to make the most of them and make them our life lessons. We all need to have compassion for ourselves with all the decisions we have made and to know that when we made those decisions at those specific times, we felt we were making the right choices. Obviously, some choices won't work out, but let's not beat ourselves to death about it. We must have compassion and forgiveness for ourselves in order to move forward.

At the end of the day, I know that everyone out there, including you and me, is simply doing their best. Just accept the fact that we are gonna get *tested* every day.

Eventually it all comes down to how prepared we are to handle these tests.

I am now ...

Are you?

I FIND THAT FAILURE STRIPS US OF ALL THAT IS SUPERFLUOUS
intimately acquainting us with our own nakedness.
Only then are we ready to dance

Okey Onyegbule

ABOUT THE AUTHOR

Alpesh H Patel is an award-winning global entrepreneur and has been featured in more than 50 media outlets including CNN, CNBC, *Forbes*, *GQ*, *The Times*, the BBC and *Huffington Post*.

Alpesh runs Peshmode, an international advisory, business and counselling consultancy specialising in go-to market strategies, entrepreneurship, intrapreneurship and results-orientated sales solutions. He has been dubbed as one of the first tech innovators to come out of Africa and has worked with industry giants such as Visa, Vodafone, Western Union and Uber.

Alpesh is an author and a business counsellor. He is a highly sought-after keynote speaker and has appeared on several panels such as The Titan Academy, The GSMA, The African Leadership Network and The Wharton Africa Conference.

www.peshmode.com

Twitter@Mialpesh

Instagram@iampeshmode

For Press, Business counselling and Speaker bookings, please email **alpesh@peshmode.com**

Join the *TESTED* family to check out the *TESTED* Book Photo Album and win a chance to go on a *TESTED* TOUR.

- Register your email on www.peshmode.com.
- Post reviews on Amazon and iBooks
- Post video reviews on Facebook https://www.facebook.com/iampeshmode/

THANK YOU

Made in the USA
Middletown, DE
11 July 2017